LANGUAGE ACQUISITION
AND HISTORICAL CHANGE

NORTH-HOLLAND
LINGUISTIC SERIES

36

Edited by S.C. DIK *and* J.G. KOOIJ

LANGUAGE ACQUISITION
AND
HISTORICAL CHANGE

NAOMI S. BARON

Brown University
Providence, Rhode Island

1977

NORTH-HOLLAND PUBLISHING COMPANY
AMSTERDAM · NEW YORK · OXFORD

North-Holland ISBN for the series: 0 7204 6180 4
North-Holland ISBN for this volume: 0 444 85077 5

Published by:

North-Holland Publishing Company – Amsterdam • New York • Oxford

Distributors for the U.S.A. and Canada:

Elsevier North-Holland Inc.
52 Vanderbilt Avenue
New York, N.Y. 10017

Library of Congress Cataloging in Publication Data ˙

Baron, Naomi S
   Language acquistion and historical change.

   (North-Holland linguistic series ; no. 36)
   An earlier version constituted part of the author's
thesis, Stanford.
   Bibliography: p.
   Includes index.
   1. Children--Language. 2. Linguistic change.
I. Title.
P118.B28   401'.9   77-13613
ISBN 0-444-85077-5

Printed in The Netherlands

Preface

This book attempts to make sense out of the linguistic truism that normal first language acquisition is the source of much linguistic change. When the study was begun in early 1971, an increasing number of transformational grammarians were turning to historical linguistics, and finding that the types of changes they were hypothesizing bore striking resemblance to the kinds of learning strategies being discussed by students of child language acquisition. Attempts to invoke first language acquisition as an explanatory force in linguistic change have rapidly multiplied during the 1970's. While these discussions have made strong claims about how children must be acquiring -- or have acquired -- the constructions which are of historical interest, they have generally failed to offer any empirical evidence from actual children. The major purpose of this study is to show how such empirical data can in fact be gathered and interpreted.

An earlier version of this book constituted part of my doctoral dissertation submitted to the Committee on Linguistics at Stanford University. I am indebted to Elizabeth C. Traugott, Eve V. Clark, and Charles A. Ferguson for their extensive comments on my dissertation at its various stages of completion, and to Robert W. Ackerman under whose direction I initiated an historical analysis of English periphrastic causatives, which was the embryo from which this study grew. I am, of course, responsible for all the places in this book which suffer from my not having heeded their advice.

There has been a delay of almost five years between the completion of the original study and its publication as a book. During that time, a number of works have appeared which treat some of the issues I raise here. While it has not been possible to revise the entire manuscript to incorporate the most recent literature, I do not believe that current research invalidates or replicates any of my own theoretical or empirical findings. Were I to have updated my discussions of the relevant literature, I would have mentioned the work of Dan Slobin on theoretical relationships between ontogeny and diachrony, of Melissa Bowermann and Lois Hood on children's acquisition of causative verbs, of Lois Bloom and Katherine Nelson on individual language differences between children, and of a number of researchers (some of whose papers are

edited by Charles Ferguson and Catherine Snow) on the
speech of adults to children. Growing research interest in pidginization and creolization (and the relationship between both of these and language acquisition) is now laying the groundwork for an expanded
ontogenetic/phylogenetic comparison of the sort I hint
at in Chapters 1 and 7. The work of Gillian Sankoff
and Derek Bickerton is particularly suggestive here.

Many other people are directly responsible for
making particular portions of my research possible.
Robert Smith and Patrick Suppes of the Stanford
Institute for Mathematical Studies in the Social
Sciences made available to me the Adam I, Nina, and
Erica longitudinal corpora (the latter two under a
project supported by NSF Grant GJ443x), and Robert
Smith wrote and executed all programs based upon these
data. W. Nelson Francis and Gerry Rubin of Brown Uni-
versity provided relevant portions of the Brown Uni-
versity Standard Corpus of Present-Day Edited American
English. Additional sources of data were Susan Ervin-
Tripp at the University of California, Berkeley, Roger
Brown at Harvard, and John Limber at the University of
New Hampshire (via Rhoda Goodwin and Judy Kornfeld at
M.I.T.). Isabel Traugott functioned as an ideal
"native informant" on language acquisition, somehow
managing to utter precisely the kinds of constructions
I sought to illustrate.

Edith Dowley, Director of Bing Nursery School at
Stanford, not only made arrangements for testing, but
also offered personal encouragement. My indebtedness
extends to the entire staff of the nursery school and
to all the children, even those who repeatedly insist-
ed that it would be much more fun for me to play in
the sandbox with them than for them to come to the
"surprise room" to play a language game with me. My
illustrator, Vicky Shu, is responsible for producing
pictures which delighted the children (and adults as
well). While the majority of illustrations were
created by Vicky Shu, Alice Gordon contributed some
illustrations used in her own research. Herbert H.
Clark of Stanford advised me on statistical procedures.

For assistance in translating articles and quotations from Czech, Dutch, Russian and French, I am
grateful to Vera Henzel, Robert Sayre, Bob Kamiker,
and Reinhard Kuhn. Kathy Darwin checked some of my
modern German examples and identified and translated
citations from Middle High German. The Hertzen
Pedagogical Institute in Leningrad kindly provided a
copy of the article by Gzhanyants, which was not
available in the United States.

The staff of the Stanford Libraries was of
immeasurable help in locating sources and in providing
an extremely pleasant atmosphere in which to work.
Edith Moravcsik offered not only stimulating discussion but also a peaceful and spacious "sanctuary"
in which most of the actual writing was done. The
moral support of Jean Beeson and Elizabeth Traugott
was invaluable in helping me through the rougher
moments.
     Stanford University generously supported my years
of graduate study, first in the form of an NDEA Title
IV Fellowship, and then through a University Fellowship. In addition, some expenses from my experimental
work were defrayed by NSF Grant No. GS-30040 to Eve V.
Clark.
     I am grateful to Vicky Shu and Gisela Belton for
typing successive drafts of the manuscript with
precision and patience. Thanks to them I managed to
meet my deadlines. Leslie Kurtz saved me from much
potential embarrassment by assisting in proofreading
the final draft. All remaining errors are, of course,
my own.

August, 1977
Providence

For L.M.I. and L.W.K.

Table of Contents

Tables

Chapter 1

INTRODUCTION

For over a century, linguists have remarked on
certain parallels between the child's acquisition of
his mother tongue and historical developments or
changes in different languages. The immediate aim of
this study is to evaluate the hypothesis that ontogenetic and diachronic processes are related through
an examination of some aspects of the relationship
that has been posited. This study will also consider
the role that such a relationship might play in the
construction of theories of diachronic change and of
language acquisition. The validity of such a hypothesis is important for the eventual formulation of a
single framework within which to define linguistic
variation and linguistic change in general, that is,
not only data from language acquisition and historical
change, but also data from newly emerging languages
such as pidgins and creoles.

1.1 Variation and Change

As even the casual observer may recognize, language constantly varies with respect to such aspects
as pronunciation, speed of articulation, nominal and
verbal inflections, forms of address chosen for
different individuals under varying social circum-
stances, etc. Recently, sociolinguists such as Labov
(1966, 1969, 1971) and Sankoff (1972) have begun to
study some of the social, economic, and cultural
factors that appear to condition the use of one
linguistic form over another. Such research has been
characterized as the study of <u>linguistic variability</u>
(cf. Labov 1971; Bailey 1970). In the present
context, any variation in linguistic form will be
referred to simply as <u>linguistic variation</u>. Variations may be socially conditioned and thus appear
within the speech of a single speaker of the language
in different contexts, e.g. speaking to peers versus
speaking to social inferiors or superiors. Variation
may occur through time, such that one form is gradually replaced by another, either within a short span of
time or over a period of centuries. The speakers of
the language may or may not be conscious of varying
forms in phonology, morphology, syntax, and semantics.
When, after a period of time, one variant is adopted
over all others, the result is typically referred to

as a *linguistic change*. In general, linguists have
reserved the term linguistic change for situations in
which two variants are drawn from temporally distinct
periods in the history of a single language. Both
variants were presumably based on adult usage. There
is no a priori reason, though, why such variants
cannot also refer to stages in the child's linguistic
development. We may, therefore, consider all linguistic variation from a single chronological perspective. Once this is done, it is possible to
examine the chronological effects of idiolectal and
dialectal variation within different segments of the
linguistic community by tracing (a) changes within a
given mature speaker or a speech community over time
(including so-called historical change, acquisition
of a second language, or acquisition (or development)
of a (non-native) pidgin); and (b) changes in the
forms used by children (including both acquisition of
an (established) native language and development of
a pidgin into a creole).[1] More generally, each of
these types of change may be examined with respect to
conditioning sociolinguistic factors (cf. Sankoff and
Laberge 1971; Hymes 1971).

1.2 Parameters of Linguistic Evolution

The term *linguistic evolution* may be used to
encompass all linguistic change within the individual
or the speech community. In discussing linguistic
evolution, it is helpful to distinguish three general
parameters:

    (a) *child/adult*
    (b) *initiation/promulgation*
    (c) *comparative description/path of actuation*

These three parameters necessarily overlap to some
extent, but they are listed separately to stress their
importance.

The first of these parameters refers to the
relative contributions to language evolution of
speakers of different ages or degrees of linguistic
sophistication. The hypothesis that first language
acquisition may be an important force in linguistic
change obviously does not imply that all or even most
variation and subsequent change necessarily originates with young children. Eventually, we will need
a theory of *age gradations* which examines the
spectrum of speakers from infancy to old age, and
asks which segment of the population might have initiated or spread particular types of change in

phonology, syntax, and semantics. However, until such
a theory is worked out, we will refer only to the
dichotomy between the immature speaker (*child*) and the
mature speaker (*adult*).

The second parameter is concerned with the
appearance of new variations (*initiation*) and with
their subsequent maintenance and spread to other users
of the language (*promulgation*). For example, the
current expression "No way!" meaning 'there are no
conditions under which that can be accomplished' or
'you'll never get me to do that' probably originated
among a small group of high school or college age
speakers. Through the infusion of the youth culture
into both older and younger groups, the expression has
now, for many speakers, become part of the colloquial
standard.[2]

The third parameter is concerned with the relation between the *comparative description* of separate
states in the language and the *path of actuation*
whereby the later of two states was derived from an
earlier form. The crucial question here is whether
descriptions of initial and final stages are directly
relevant for understanding the developmental process
or whether they even allow plausible inferences about
the path of actuation. For example, in comparing Old
English and modern English gender systems, the basic
difference between the two is most simply described
as the replacement of a dual grammatical/natural
gender system by only natural gender. This change,
however, was not accomplished in a single step.
Rather, Late Old and Early Middle English data suggest
a progression of several stages before the transition
was complete (see Baron 1971). Without data on the
intervening states or the probable processes involved
in change, little may be said about the path of actuation in spite of the existence of detailed comparative
descriptions. The process involved may be difficult
to evaluate from historical data, but, as I shall
argue, a valuable source of information about
processes is available: the repertoire of processes
that the child brings to language acquisition. These
processes may be used not only to make new hypotheses
about historical paths of actuation but also to
evaluate paths of actuation which have previously been
proposed on the sole basis of historical evidence.

1.3 Ontogenetic/Diachronic Parallels and Dependencies

There are basically three kinds of questions we
might ask about the relevance of ontogenetic studies
to the history of language: (a) do children's early
stages of language acquisition illuminate the
ultimate origins of human language? (b) do children
learning some aspect of their native tongue pass
through the same developmental stages as did the language itself decades or centuries ago when the
construction initially appeared? (c) in what sense
does the normal acquisition of language by children
effect linguistic change, i.e. the eventual introduction of a new adult standard? The first two questions
deal with parallels; the third with responsibility.

During the late 19th and early 20th centuries,
many linguists (e.g. Taine 1876; Paul 1880; Whitney
1889, 1895; Müller 1890; Grammont 1902; Cohen 1925,
1927, 1933; Meillet 1921, 1926, 1951) pursued one or
more of these questions. Scholars generally agreed
that in many cases, children do, in fact, either
recapitulate or influence the historical development
of language. However, most of the research concen-
trated on the simplifications that were made, primarily because they considered little beyond phonology
and morphology. And within the Indo-European inflectional paradigms, it is, in fact, true that the
paradigms have generally simplified over the recorded
period of Indo-European development. However, this
limited perspective fails to consider that the
analytic forms that developed concomitantly might
actually constitute elaboration.

Interest in ontogenetic/phylogenetic parallels
and causal relationships died out in the 1930's and
1940's, especially in the United States. This was
probably because a new idea of what science was in
general, and of what linguistic science was in
particular, had taken over. Logical positivism, with
its distaste for metaphysics and teleology, came to
dominate American philosophy and science, and questions
of ultimate origin or cause became unfashionable. As
linguists, we should not forget that Bloomfield's
"Linguistic Aspects of Science" (1939) appeared as
part of the positivists' version of the Novum Organum,
namely The Encyclopedia of Unified Science. But there
was also a second factor, which involved the particular
focus linguistics came to assume. Nineteenth century
concerns with diachrony were overpowered by the
structuralists' interest in synchrony, a trend which
permeated American linguistics in the first half of

the 20th century. Moreover, with the notable exception of a few diarists such as Leopold (1939-1949) and
Velten (1943), and theoreticians such as Jakobson
(e.g. 1941), structural linguistics displayed comparatively little interest in child language acquisition. The late 19th and early 20th century fervor,
represented by the work of investigators such as
Darwin (1877), Chamberlain (1907), and the Sterns
(1907) never penetrated American structuralism, and
child language acquisition study was largely relegated
to psychologists and educators who counted sentence
length and vocabulary items.

During the past decade, renewed interest in
ontogeny and diachrony has appeared within the framework of generative transformational grammar (e.g.
Menyuk 1964; McNeill 1966; Klima 1964; Kiparsky 1965).
At the same time there has been increasing interest in
how first language acquisition might illuminate
diachronic processes. The early comparative work
within transformational grammar (e.g. Halle 1962;
Kiparsky 1965; King 1969) was reminiscent of late 19th
and early 20th century studies in its preoccupation
with simplification. More recent work by Traugott
(1969, 1972b), Stampe (1969), Darden (1970, 1971), and
Sankoff and Laberge (1971), however, has recognized
that children may initiate elaboration in language.

Most of the studies mentioned thus far pertain to
the question of whether children actually do initiate
or spread change in language. If we tentatively
accept the answer "yes", the next question is, of
course, "how?". In the 20th century, Manly (1930),
Hockett (1950), Weinreich, Labov, and Herzog (1968),
and Andersen (1973), have independently produced
similar models of how change introduced by young
children or teenagers may spread to other parts of the
linguistic community. However, the hypothesis remains
to be more precisely articulated and empirically tested with a wide range of phonological, syntactic, and
semantic data.

1.4 Methodology for Ontogenetic/Diachronic Comparison

Lack of empirical data is the major current
stumbling block in comparing ontogenetic and
diachronic processes. Without imposing rigid dis-
covery procedures, I will outline a general framework
for collecting data and testing hypotheses. I do not
claim that this methodology is the only or the best
approach to constructing a general theory. Furthermore, in my own work, I have only applied the schema

to comparisons of ontogenetic and diachronic change in
the area of morphology and syntax. The same approach
should also be applicable without major revisions to
the description of phonological and semantic change.
Since no other explicit programs have been defined
which add substance to diachronists' comparative
theories of sources and methods of linguistic restructuring, I think it is useful to explain my approach as
clearly as possible.

(a) <u>Choose a construction</u>

        Select a linguistic construction whose diachronic
and ontogenetic development can be traced, e.g.
through examination of historical documents and
through study of children's language acquisition.
Diachronically, it is simplest to choose a construction which evolved within the recorded history of the
particular language being investigated. Ontogenetically, the choice is constrained by whether suitable
and adequate research methods are available to study
the acquisition of a particular construction in
children of the age at which the construction is
thought to develop.

(b) <u>Describe its grammatical properties</u>

        This description may be phrased within a
particular theoretical framework (e.g. transformational grammar, generative semantics) or in a non-
theoretical format felt to be more amenable to ontogenetic and diachronic comparison. Depending upon
one's theoretical interest or persuasions, the initial
analyses may be language specific or may attempt to
consider universal properties.
        While the primary goal is to evaluate diachronic
hypotheses with respect to ontogenetic data, onto-
genetic/diachronic results may also be compared with
independent synchronic analyses. Admittedly, most
work in theoretical linguistics has no immediate
requirements that its constructs must be directly
compatible with results from child language study (or,
for that matter, with diachrony). Yet at the same
time, linguists are becoming increasingly committed
to understanding what speakers must know in order to
use language. Children, in addition to being <u>bona
fide</u> language users, provide one of our most useful
laboratories for observing the construction and opera-
tion of the basic units and processes of the underlying linguistic system.

(c) <u>Tentatively sketch the history of the construction</u>

From the available source materials, attempt to
trace the relevant synchronic stages through which the
construction has passed, hypothesizing how the change
is best described (*comparative description*) and how
the change was accomplished (*path of actuation*). This
diachronic analysis will only be tentative. Historical linguistic records are extremely crude approxima-
tions of normal spoken style (see section 4.1). Even
if preserved documentation were in some sense
representative of adult speech, it is unlikely that
texts and grammars will make explicit which particular
linguistic features were relevant for change. Here we
can only make conjectures. However, within the
proposed framework, ontogenetic data may be used to
help evaluate some diachronic hypotheses.

(d) <u>Hypothesize how the construction develops
ontogenetically</u>

On the bases of synchronic and diachronic descriptions ((b) and (c) above), determine what kinds
of knowledge the child must acquire in order to use
the modern construction with the same facility as
adults now do. Having isolated the grammatical
properties that the child must learn, draw upon the
growing body of child language studies to predict the
order in which the child will acquire these properties
and the fundamental learning strategies he may
employ.

(e) <u>Gather data on child language acquisition
relevant to this construction</u>

These data may assume a number of forms. One
traditional source is diary studies on individual
children. During the past century, a number of
excellent diaries have been published on the acquisition of a variety of languages (see Slobin 1972). A
second source is longitudinal corpora which have been
.tape recorded and analyzed. Within the past decade,
at least a dozen extensive corpora have been collected
on English alone.[3] Finally, experimental procedures
can be used to help determine what <u>modi operandi</u>
children use in elicited imitation, comprehension, and
production of the specific construction under
investigation.

(f) Analyze child language acquisition data

     Attempt to describe the acquisition process
itself, including the chronological emergence of each
aspect of the construction as well as the kinds of
hypotheses or strategies the child may be using to
gain adult mastery. If both longitudinal and
experimental data are available, observe whether both
sources of data yield the same descriptive schema.

(g) Evaluate diachronic and ontogenetic data

     On the basis of the analysis of ontogenetic data
(f), ask whether the historical description in (c)
bears any relation to the process by which children
acquire the construction in question. For example, do
the stages through which the child progresses in
acquiring native competence parallel those through
which the language evolved (with respect to a
particular construction)? How is ontogenetic 'recapitulation' restricted by historical mergers, which
leave no synchronic clues about how a particular
construction developed diachronically? How does a
child (or a language) resolve conflicting natural
tendencies (see Stampe 1969; Traugott 1972c)? How
does a child come to formulate rules which are not
present in his immediate model, and how do some of
these rules get incorporated into the language of the
larger community?
     If the initial diachronic analysis provided only
a comparative description, then knowledge of ontogenetic development may suggest a means of diachronic
actuation which could then be tested through re-
examination of the historical data. Alternatively,
ontogenetic data may suggest that certain hypothesized
paths of actuation do not constitute plausible representations of "natural" linguistic changes (i.e.
changes not imposed by prescriptivism). One example
is the use of ontogenetic data to evaluate theories of
the evolution of English gender. I have shown elsewhere (see Baron 1971) that acquisition studies argue
against the traditional hypothesis that inflections
indicating grammatical gender merely "dropped off"
gradually until English was left with only a basically
natural gender system. In this study, I will show
that ontogenetic analyses of the·verbs have and get
militate against some traditional actuation hypotheses
(see Chapters 4 and 5).

1.5   Scope of Present Study

The construction to be analyzed within this
comparative framework is a set of English periphrastic
causatives. Periphrastic causatives were selected for
several reasons. First, since many periphrastic
causatives developed within the recorded history of
English, it is possible to trace their evolution and
to speculate about the mechanisms directing their
development. Second, although there would seem to be
several ways of studying the acquisition of causatives, there is almost no discussion of this topic in
the literature to date. Third, much current linguistic theory (e.g. Lakoff 1965; McCawley 1968, 1970,
1971; Fillmore 1971; Schank 1971; Halliday 1968;
Anderson 1971) includes causation as a basic notion in
syntactic and semantic analysis. If we grant that one
goal of the study of linguistic evolution is to compare diachronic and ontogenetic results with
synchrony, then ontogenetic and/or diachronic data
may also help in evaluating between alternative
synchronic analyses. Finally, causation may be
expressed by a wide variety of surface morphological
and syntactic means in various of the world's languages, thereby making causation an interesting topic
for language typology and universals. One curious
phenomenon is that the particular formal devices used
to express causation frequently change over time. In
English, for example, overt morphological expressions
of causation (e.g. to fell a tree) largely died out in
favor of other modes such as syntactic periphrastics
(e.g. to make a girl laugh). Yet even within the
realm of periphrastics, the set of causatives
available in Old English and modern English is quite
different While cross-linguistic analysis is beyond
the scope of this book, it is possible that the
kinds of change mechanisms suggested for the historical evolution of English periphrastic causatives are
also applicable to the evolution of formal causative
markers in other languages.
        Causation is a relationship between states of
affairs and intervening forces. If we look at related
events or states of affairs X and X' at time T_1 and
T_2, respectively, and observe a difference between the
events or states, we may hypothesize that this
difference (or change) can be explained by the existence of some intervening agent, force, or state of
affairs Z. In ordinary language, we say that this
external agent, force, or state affairs caused the

change from state of affairs X to state of affairs X'.
The intervening Z is identified as the <u>cause</u>. State
of affairs X' at T_2 is called an <u>effect</u> (or <u>result</u>).
For example, consider the sentence

>   (1) Cornelius Van Baerle grew the world's first
>   black tulip.

At time T_1 the state of affairs X was such that no
black tulips existed. Van Baerle intervened by
developing a bulb and then planting and caring for it.
Through his intervention, state of affairs X (at time
T_1) was replaced by state of affairs X' (at time T_2),
during which a black tulip flowered.

English has a number of formal mechanisms for
expressing causation. For example, causative verbs
may be morphologically derived from non-causative
counterparts, e.g.

>   <u>sit/set</u>
>   (2) non-causative: The package is <u>sitting</u> on
>   the floor.
>   (3) causative: Please <u>set</u> the package on the
>   floor.

Other causatives constitute suppletive replacements of
non-causative forms, e.g.

>   <u>die/kill</u>
>   (4) non-causative: A python <u>died</u> in the
>   jungle.
>   (5) causative: The hunter <u>killed</u> a·python in
>   the jungle.

In a third type of construction, the same lexical form
is used in either non-causative or causative syntactic
frames, e.g.

>   <u>grow/grow</u>
>   (6) non-causative: The tulip <u>grew</u>.
>   (7) causative: Van Baerle <u>grew</u> the tulip.

Periphrastic causatives are two-part constructions expressing causation. The first part is a verb
(e.g. <u>cause</u>, <u>have</u>, <u>make</u>, <u>get</u>, <u>let</u>), which, for
convenience, I will refer to as a <u>periphrastic causa-
tive verb</u> (or simply <u>periphrastic causative</u> or
<u>periphrastic</u>). The second part is a complement, which
has the underlying structure of a sentence. Modern
English allows a wide range of complements, although
there are restrictions in terms of the verbs with
which they may occur. For example, periphrastic
causative <u>get</u> appears with infinitival, adjectival,
past participial and locative complements (n.b. in

general, I shall use the term <u>locative</u> to refer to
both position and direction):

    (8) infinitive: The therapist <u>got</u> his patient
        <u>to relax</u>.

    (9) <u>adjective</u>: The therapist <u>got</u> his patient
        <u>quiet</u>.

  (10) past participle: The therapist <u>got</u> his
        patient <u>relaxed</u>.

  (11) locative: The therapist <u>got</u> his patient
        <u>into the chair</u>.

However, <u>make</u>, while forming causative constructions
with infinitival, adjectival, and past participial
complements, does not appear with locatives in
standard adult English, cf.

  (12) *The therapist <u>made</u> his patient <u>into the
        chair</u>.

There are a number of other restrictions as well. One
of these applies to whether or not the infinitive
takes a <u>to</u>-complementizer. With <u>get</u>, the complementizer is obligatory, while with <u>have</u> and <u>make</u>, it
is ungrammatical, cf.

  (13) <u>get</u> The therapist got his patient
      ⎧*relax   ⎫
      ⎨to relax⎬ .
      ⎩   ⎭

  (14) <u>have</u> The doctor had his patient
      ⎧breathe deeply   ⎫
      ⎨*to breathe deeply⎬ .
      ⎩   ⎭

  (15) <u>make</u> The dentist made his patient
      ⎧flinch   ⎫
      ⎨*to flinch⎬ .
      ⎩   ⎭

In many cases, periphrastic causatives may be
<u>roughly</u> paraphrased by morphological causatives. For
example,

  (16) The tiger made the monkey frightened.

is approximately equivalent to

  (17) The tiger frightened the monkey.

(although

  (18) I made the baby smile.

is not paralleled by

  (19) *I smiled the baby.)

There are also semantic differences between the
periphrastic causatives themselves. For example,

while

    (20) The doctor made the patient flinch.

suggests the patient reacted involuntarily,

    (21) The doctor had the patient flinch.

could only mean that the patient is consciously
flinching under order. Another interesting distinction is between causation and result. For example,

    (22) I got the baby quiet (by rocking its
          cradle).

focuses upon the causative act of quieting the infant,
while

    (23) I had the baby quiet (in ten minutes).

focuses on the result of the action, cf.

    (24) *I had the baby quiet by rocking its
          cradle.

A third difference is concerned with whether the surface subject of the sentence is the immediate cause
of the change in the state of affairs. Consider the
following examples with past participial complements:

    (25) Mommy is having the carrots chopped.

    (26) Mommy is getting the carrots chopped.

In (25), someone other than Mommy (such as Daddy) must
be doing the chopping, while (26) is ambiguous as to
who is wielding the knife.

    In the research to be reported in this study I
compared the ontogenetic and diachronic development of
three periphrastic causative verbs, have, make, and
get, and their related complements. The data derive
from three sources: (a) the tracing of the historical
development of each of the three periphrastic causatives, (b) the analysis of longitudinal corpora on the
speech of several two-year-olds, and (c) the running
of a number of experiments with two-and-a-half to
five-and-a-half-year-old children, with an adult
control group.

    The basic questions I wished to explore were:

    (a) when and how a particular verb first
        acquires causative function (initiation)

(b) how the causative use of a verb spreads to other complements (promulgation)

(c) whether the comparison of the historical and ontogenetic data provides any evidence that children may be responsible for initiating or spreading periphrastic causatives in English (child/adult)

(d) whether the ontogenetic data suggest the path via which the verbs may have acquired causative functions; if so, whether these analyses contradict traditional historical hypotheses (comparative description/path of actuation)

In addition, I wanted to find out what relation the three periphrastics (i.e. have, make, and get) bear to one another in emerging ontogenetic systems. I investigated (a) whether there is a markedness hierarchy, with make being the least marked; get, more marked; and have, most marked; and (b) whether in the earliest stages of development, children are sensitive to syntactic restrictions upon which complement types can occur with which periphrastics (e.g. that make cannot occur with locatives, that certain infinitival complements require a to-complementizer). The non-observance of such restrictions would constitute evidence for what I shall call a periphrastic causative paradigm, that is, a matrix in which all periphrastic causative verbs may appear with all complement types (see section 3.2).

Chapter 2 traces in detail linguistic interest in ontogenetic/diachronic comparison, examining major contributions to the comparative study of ontogeny and diachrony in terms of the three parameters of linguistic evolution which I have proposed. Chapter 3 looks in somewhat greater depth at the structure of English periphrastic causatives. Chapter 4 traces the historical development of have, make, and get in periphrastic constructions. Chapters 5 and 6 describe ontogenetic data which derive from some longitudinal analyses (Chapter 5) and some experimental work (Chapter 6). Chapter 7 summarizes and attempts to evaluate ontogenetic, diachronic, and synchronic findings of the present study on periphrastic causatives, and suggests possible directions for future research.

Footnotes

[1]See Kay and Sankoff 1972:

> It is our belief that the study of contact
> vernaculars can shed light on theories of lan-
> guage competence in ways similar to other study
> areas dealing with non-native or incomplete
> competence of various kinds. These include
> child language acquisition, second language
> acquisition, bilingualism, the study of non-
> human communication, aphasia, etc. The general
> framework is one of language universals and
> language evolution.

[2]In observing the speech of nursery school children, I
even heard the phrase from several four and five-year-
olds.

[3]E.g. Roger Brown's data on Adam, Eve, and Sarah
(Brown 1973); Wick Miller and Susan Ervin-Tripp's
study of Christie, Susan, and Harlan (Miller and Ervin
1964); Martin Braine's analysis of Gregory, Andrew,
and Steven (Braine 1963); Lois Bloom's collections
from Kathryn, Eric, and Gia (Bloom 1970); Patrick
Suppes and Robert Smith's project on Nina and Erica
(Smith 1972).

Chapter 2

ONTOGENY AND DIACHRONY

For more than a century, linguists have looked at
the ontogenetic development of language in the child
as a means of explaining diachronic change within the
larger language system (phylogeny). Since the present
study continues this line of inquiry, it is instructive to see what types of questions have been posed in
the past, to examine what sorts of solutions were
offered, and to ask how recent developments in
grammatical theory and child language acquisition
enable us to consider these issues from new perspectives. Specifically, we shall see that the strong
evolutionary hypothesis that ontogeny recapitulates
phylogeny, i.e. that language acquisition mirrors the
development of language within the species or within
a community of speakers, needs to be reversed to state
that diachrony often reflects ontogeny.

2.1 The Recapitulation Hypothesis

What interconnections or parallels exist between
historical developments in human language and a
child's acquisition of his mother tongue? This question, which has received considerable attention during
the past decade of linguistic research, basically
descends from the 19th century. To understand this
earlier interest in ontogenetic and diachronic relations, it is necessary to reconstruct the intellectual
climate of the mid and late 1800's.
Biology in the 1850's and 1860's was undergoing
major theoretical shifts. Darwin's Origin of Species
was published in 1859. Haeckel's treatises on evolution began to appear in the 1860's and 1870's. It is
Haeckel who, in 1866, explicitly formulated the
hypothesis of ontogenetic recapitulation:

> The History of the Evolution of Organisms
> consists of two kindred and closely connected
> parts: Ontogeny, which is the history of
> individual organisms, and Phylogeny, which is
> the history of the evolution of organic tribes.
> Ontogeny is a brief and rapid recapitulation of
> Phylogeny, dependent on the physiological
> functions of Heredity (reproduction) and
> Adaptation (nutrition). The individual
> organism reproduces in rapid and short course
> of its own evolution the most important of the

changes in form through which its ancestors,
according to the laws of Heredity and Adapta-
tion, have passed in the slow and long course
of their palaeontological evolution.[1]

How does the biological dichotomy between ontogeny and phylogeny apply to language? Is "the history
of the evolution of organic tribes" comparable to the
evolution of human language in general, or to the
development of a particular language in a particular
language family? If the answer is the latter, what
point represents the "beginning" of the language? In
writings of the late 19th century, there was often no
explicit differentiation made between the genesis of
human language in general and the growth of individual
languages. In fact, Paul (1888: 17-18) explicitly
states that the history of Language and of languages
forms a single continuum:

> How was the origin of language possible?
> This question can only be satisfactorily
> answered if we succeed in deducing the origin
> of language exclusively from the activity of
> those factors which we still see in activity in
> the further development of language. Besides,
> no tenable contrast can be drawn between
> original creation of language and its mere
> further development. As soon as the first has
> been made, we have language and its further
> development. There exist merely graduated
> differences between the first origins of lan-
> guage and later epochs.

In practice, however, discussion of ultimate and language-specific phylogeny could easily be kept distinct. The former discussion (ultimate origins)
centered not upon such questions as whether Hebrew was
or was not the Ursprache, but (a) what the primitive
forms of the language looked like, (b) whether these
forms resembled the speech of so-called primitive
(i.e. uncivilized) people, (c) whether children
acquiring their native language "recapitulated" the
"original" primitive forms of language, and (d)
whether child speech paralleled the speech of present-
day primitive tribes. The latter discussion (i.e.
language-specific developments) largely took shape
during the first half of the 20th century, when linguists generally abandoned philosophical concerns in
favor of tracing the actual form of particular languages or language families.

In retrospect, there are three perspectives from

which we can view responses within the linguistic
community to Haeckel's ontogenetic/phylogenetic
hypothesis. First, there is the general recognition
of parallels in the development of children and of
mankind. The Sterns (1907), for example, hypothesize
that "the development of child speech...is based on an
immanent tendency of mental growth, and this is also
likely to be the case in the linguistic development of
mankind" (Révész 1956:46). Whitney (1889:442) takes a
similar position:

> Learning to speak is the first step in each
> child's education, the necessary preparation
> for receiving higher instruction of every kind.
> So was it also with the human race; the
> acquisition of speech constituted the first
> stage in the progressive development of its
> capacities.

Or compare Guillaume (1927a):

> The facts that we cannot examine in the
> history of language are available to us in the
> child. It is true that imitation of a language
> already formed is the principle of acquisition,
> but such assimilation cannot be entirely pas-
> sive; it probably goes through a number of
> stages essential to the acquisition of any
> complex language. The same psychological
> mechanisms (for instance the one which under-
> lies analogical formations) probably play a
> part in languages being maintained and in their
> being acquired by individuals.

Guillaume, however, carefully observes in another
paper (1927b) that recapitulation, when it occurs,
reflects logical similarities in development rather
than structural necessity:

> It is not necessary to believe in some
> mysterious internal necessity which causes the
> individual learning language to go via the
> tortuous routes of history. The only similar-
> ity lies in the degree to which the route is
> constrained by certain logical and psychologi-
> cal necessities for assimilation in a complex
> organism. The ontogenetic 'interpretation' is
> not history: repetition is rather a selection
> of models offered by the language in its actual
> state which includes still-living witnesses of
> a primitive age as well as acquisitions due to
> superior forms of culture.

The second ontogenetic/phylogenetic perspective
attempts to <u>observe the evolutionary process</u> *in vivo*
by observing <u>speakers of so-called primitive lan-
guages</u>, i.e. uncivilized peoples and children.
Representative of this position is Taine (1877:259):

> Speaking generally, the child presents in a
> passing state the mental characteristics that
> are found in a fixed state in primitive
> civilisations, very much as the human embryo
> presents in a passing state the physical
> characteristics that are found in a fixed state
> in the classes of inferior animals.

However, as late 19th century field work in anthropol-
ogy revealed (cf. Lévy-Bruhl 1926), the analogy
between the language of so-called primitive peoples
and that of children is not precise. While the language of children is less complex than that of the
adult standard,

> we find that the languages spoken by peoples
> who are the least developed of any we know --
> Australian aborigines, Abipones, Andaman
> Islanders, Fuegians, etc. -- exhibit a good
> deal of complexity. They are far less "simple"
> than English, though much more "primitive"
> (Lévy-Bruhl 1926:22).

Scholars explained this apparent discrepancy between
a high degree of grammatical complexity (and lexical
diversity) and low level of mental development by saying that primitive languages typically lacked
abstract, general terms:

> The nearer the mentality of a given social
> group approaches the prelogical, the more do
> these image-concepts predominate. The language
> bears witness to this, for there is an almost
> total absence of generic terms to correspond
> with general ideas, and at the same time an
> extraordinary abundance of specific terms,
> those denoting persons and things of whom or
> which a clear or precise image occurs to the
> mind (Lévy-Bruhl 1926:170).

Similarly, early ontogenetic studies maintained that
the language of children is largely restricted to
concrete terms.[2]
    Third, the recapitulation hypothesis may be seen
as a framework for examining the <u>development of
individual constructions in individual languages</u>,
asking (a) how children, in learning the construction,

recapitulate the diachronic process and (b) what
either the recapitulation or even general developmental properties or learning strategies of children
have to do with the diachronic process itself. This
third perspective, i.e. interest in explicit parallels
and in responsibility, is one of the main sources of
ontogenetic/diachronic theory-building to be found in
current linguistics.

Having outlined three perspectives on Haeckel's
ontogenetic/phylogenetic hypothesis, I will discuss
early work on the link between ontogeny and diachrony
under two headings: (a) hypotheses or examples of
children serving as initiators of change, and (b)
theories or data suggesting children are promulgators
of change.

(a) Initiation
One of the most explicit statements of the
hypothesis that children function as sources of linguistic change is found in Paul's Prinzipien der
Sprachgeschichte.[3] Paul (1960:34) hypothesized that
language change in general is caused by variations of
idiolects which are then adopted by other speakers in
the community. Idiolects change during the process of
learning language:

> the processes of language learning are of
> supreme importance for the explanation of
> changes in Language Custom...they represent
> the most important cause of these changes
> [emphasis appears in the original German].[4]

While learning continues throughout one's life, most
of it occurs during childhood. Thus, children are
seen as the principal force of change in language.

What shape do children's idiolectal variations
assume? Paul is not explicit, but he appears to consider only cases of incomplete learning of adult
paradigms which result in an overall simplification of
the grammar. In general, discussions of language
change during this period tended to focus on change
strictly as a means of decreasing what is now referred
to as "surface" phonological or morphological
complexity, operating chiefly on analogical principles.

Paul's failure to define the types of idiolectal
difference between children and older members of the
speech community is partially rectified by such
writers as Sweet, Sully, Müller, and Grammont. Sweet
(1888:15) states in its general form the 19th century
hypothesis that phonological change results from
imperfect learning by children:

Natural speech is incessantly changing,
both as regards its phonetic and its logical
structure. The child learns the sounds of its
vernacular language by a process of slow and
laborious imitation. This imitation is always
defective...even under the most favourable
conditions there is some divergence, for it is
impossible for the child to reproduce by mere
imitation the exact organic movements of its
teachers. Even when the individual has settled
down to a definite sound-system of his own, he
is still liable to modify his sounds from lazi-
ness and carelessness. Even if the changes
thus produced in the transmission of a language
from one generation to another were impercept-
ible to the ear, their repetition would be
enough to account for the most violent changes,
if we only allow time enough.

Sully (1896:152-153) extends this hypothesis with some
examples from Indo-European:

We know...that...changes are due to imperfect
imitation by succeeding generations of
learners. Hence we need not be surprised to
find now and again analogies between these
nursery transformations and those of words in
the development of languages. In reproducing
the sounds which he hears a child often
illustrates a law of adult phonetic change.
Thus changes within the same class of sounds,
as the frequent alternation of 'this' into
'dis,' clearly correspond with those modifications recognised in Grimm's Law.... Nobody
again can note the transformation of n into m
before f in the form 'hamfish' for 'handker-
chief' without thinking of the Greek change of
συν into συμ before β, and like changes.

Müller (1890:75) offers the general hypothesis
that children tend to simplify inflectional paradigms:

The attempts of single grammarians and
purists to improve language are perfectly boot-
less; and we shall probably hear no more of
schemes to prune languages of their irregulari-
ties. It is likely, however, that the gradual
disappearance of irregular declensions and
conjugations is due, in literary as well as in
illiterate languages, to the dialect of
children. The language of children is more

regular than our own.

He proceeds to cite some examples, implying that such overgeneralizations by children affect the shape of future adult linguistic systems:

> I have heard children say badder and baddest, instead of worse and worst.... [T]he auxiliary in Latin was very irregular. If sumus is we are, and sunt, they are, the second person, you are, ought to have been, at least according to the strict logic of children, sutis. This, no doubt, sounds very barbarous to a classical ear accustomed to estis. And we see how French, for instance, has strictly preserved the Latin forms in nous sommes, vous êtes, ils sont. But in Spanish we find somos, sois, son; and this sois stands for sutis.

Grammont (1902:61) turns to careful observation of language acquisition as a means of studying historical change, unequivocally stating that

> [t]outes les modifications fonétiques, morfologiques ou sintaxiques qui caractérisent la vie des langues apparaissent dans le parler des enfants.

> [a]ll the phonetic, morphological, or syntactical modifications that characterize the life of languages appear in the speech of children.

Grammont does not make explicit the implied relationship between ontogeny and phylogeny whereby children initiate a restructuring of their input, such that these formulations subsequently come to be accepted as the new norm. He does, however, attempt to explain the actual mechanisms children employ in effecting this restructuring, and proposes that this set of mechanisms is responsible for diachronic shifts (1902:61):

> En réunissant les particularités de langage d'un très grand nombre d'enfants, on pourrait constituer une sorte de grammaire de toutes les transformations qui se sont produites et peuvent se produire dans toutes les langues umaines.

> By bringing together all the peculiarities of the language of a very large number of children, one could constitute a sort of grammar of all the transformations which have been produced

and which can be produced in all the human
languages.

The three mechanisms which Grammont discusses and
illustrates in detail are dissimilation, assimilation,
and metathesis. Relying primarily upon data collected
from a small boy named Robert between the age of one
and three, Grammont notes how the kinds of processes
used by the child are paralleled in various languages.
For example, Robert dissimilates i-i sequences to é-i:

child	standard French
néni	nini
bébi	bibi
méni	fini

The same dissimilation appears historically in the
Romance family, where Latin finire ("to finish")
became fenir in Old French, and Latin diuinu ("sooth-
sayer") became devin in modern French and Provençal.
Assimilation is clearly illustrated in the realm of
nasality. Among Grammont's examples are

child	standard French
na-ni	la nuit
menèt	fenêtre
maname namon	madame Grammont

Again, there are historical parallels. For example,
Latin glomere ("to form into a ball") appears as
ñemaru in the Lecce dialect of Italy. One type of
metathesis is the exchange of c-p for p-c, as in

child	standard French
capet	paquet
cópou	beaucoup
coupé	bouquet

Grammont observes that the same metathesis
distinguishes Lithuanian kepù from Old Slavic pekạ,
Greek πέσσω.

(b) Promulgation

In addition to various forms of the hypothesis
that children initiate change, various early 20th
century linguists assigned to children the role of
promulgation. Typical of this approach is the work
of Cohen and Manly. Cohen was very much aware that
children may introduce linguistic innovation, typically in the form of a simplification.[5] However, he also
cared about how a particular change, once initiated
by whatever source, actually became incorporated into
the standard language. Focusing upon morphological

and lexical usages which persist in deviating from the
adult norm until fairly late in child language, Cohen
(1933:393) compared these spots of child "resistence"
against the standard language to non-standard
dialectal usage:

> on peut dire que la langue des auteurs
> classiques est pour les enfants même de
> milieux cultivés une source de quiproquos
> comme le langage cultivé est un réservoir de
> coq à l'âne pour les gens peu lettrés.

> it could be said that the language of classi-
> cal authors is a source of quid pro quos for
> children even from cultivated backgrounds,
> while cultivated language is a reservoir of
> misunderstandings for people of little educa-
> tion.

We might represent this ratio as[6]

$$\frac{\text{(spoken) child language}}{\text{classical (written) standard}} = \frac{\text{(spoken) non-standard adult dialect}}{\text{(spoken) cultivated adult standard}}$$

Cohen seems to suggest that change in the standard
language is effected indirectly through growing
support for the non-standard dialect. In principle,
children raised in "cultivated" milieux eventually
abandon the last vestiges of child-like usage, "sans
influer sur le langage adulte, par conséquent sur
l'évolution de la langue" (p. 399). However, in
actuality, the late persistence of child forms reinforces the use of parallel forms already occurring
in non-standard dialects, bringing the child/non-
standard dialectal forms closer and closer to possible
adoption as the cultivated adult standard.

Cohen offered a number of examples of this "re-
inforcement" process in French. Consider the third
person plural pronouns ils, eux and elles. In the
popular French of a region near Paris, Cohen (1933:
391) observed the use of ils and eux in place of
elles. This same substitution occurred in the speech
of his two daughters, e.g.

> Laurence, age 7:   Les dames croyaient qu'ils
> étaient à l'ombre; mais ils
> étaient tout à fait au
> soleil.

> The ladies thought that they
> (masculine) were in the

> shadows; but they (mascu-
> line) were completely
> exposed to the sun.

Similarly, both children and popular dialects tend to
collapse the formal distinction between the
interrogative adjective quel and the interrogative
pronoun lequel.

Cohen does not explain the source of the popular
forms of these constructions. While they may
originate in non-standard adult speech, it is also
conceivable that the non-standard adult forms represent a promulgation of children's late stages of
acquisition. If the latter hypothesis is correct,
then it is not, as Cohen hypothesizes, that children
support the non-standard forms, but rather the other
way around.

The real-life situation of promulgation is
addressed by Manly (1930). Manly focused his argument
on phonological change. While interested in sources
of change, Manly's purpose was to explain

> the reason, or one of the reasons, why when
> a tendency to phonetic change in a certain
> direction has been established in a speech-
> group the tendency persists (1930:288).

What is the reason? Quite simply, it is (according
to Manly) the fact that children in the continuous
stream of generations offer to their younger peers a
model containing the reanalyzed form. Since children
are, in general, more strongly influenced by their
(slightly older) peers than by adults, the peer model
remains dominant and the change is perpetuated. As we
shall see, Manly's recognition that (a) generations
are not discrete, and (b) peers are a more significant
source of input to children than are adults, was
largely ignored during much of the heyday of American
structuralism and transformational grammar. For this
reason, I quote Manly's argument at length:

> each and every child, during the formative
> period of its speech habits, is more closely
> and intimately associated with children slight-
> ly older than itself than with adults, and is
> psychologically more receptive of influences
> from these children than from adults.
>   If then the speech habits of the younger
> members of a group or community represent -- as
> they do -- the more advanced status and
> tendencies, the learning child will have set

before him for imitation, not the composite
model furnished by a combination of the habits
of the whole community taken in proportion to
the actual numbers of adults and children --
which is the speech status of the community at
any given moment -- but a model in which the
more advanced speech habits characteristic of
the children predominate in direct proportion
to the predominance of the associations of the
learning child with other children and to its
greater receptivity to these juvenile
influences. Any tendency, therefore, that, by
any cause, physical or psychological, has once
been propagated in the speech-group will be
continued, and in the same direction, by the
continuous stream of children (1930:289).

In summary, how does this initial phase of onto-
genetic/diachronic inquiry mesh with the three
definitional parameters outlined in Chapter 1, i.e.
child/adult, initiation/promulgation, comparative
description/path of actuation? Grammont appears to
claim that all phonetic, morphological, and syntactic
change appears (if not originates) in early child language. This sweeping generalization overlooks innovations which, for example, teenagers or adults may
introduce. Several scholars (e.g. Cohen) seem to
distinguish between the origin (initiation) and "re-
inforcement" (promulgation) of a given construction,
but there is no systematic attempt to differentiate
between the two or to make explicit the role of
children in either. Finally, while Müller, Grammont,
and others speak of the processes of analogy and overgeneralization, there is little discussion of the
step-by-step manner in which such processes effect
change. Even in such comparatively transparent
changes as assimilation or dissimilation, linguistic
or social factors may condition the actual stages by
which a change comes about (cf. Labov 1971). Furthermore, with the exception of Manly, no one in the late
19th and early 20th centuries explored the actual
sociolinguistic mechanisms by which a specific change,
once initiated, actually spreads to other language
users.

2.2   The Rebirth of Ontogenetic/Diachronic Inquiry in
      Generative Transformational Grammar

Transformational grammar developed as an explicit
attempt to analyze phonology and syntax from a syn-

chronic point of view. Allusions to diachrony or even
to dialectal or idiolectal variation did not emerge
until the early 1960's. These initial writings in the
60's, however, used dialect variation and diachrony to
illustrate the power of formal transformational rules
rather than to address the problem of linguistic
variation itself. None of this work suggested that
analysis of change should influence the construction
of synchronic descriptions. The most important of
these early papers is Halle (1962).[7] Other examples
include Keyser (1963), who illustrated the power of
rule ordering in describing dialect differences, and
Saporta (1965), who applied rule ordering to both
dialectal and historical variance.

　　During the mid and late 1960's, linguists
interested in ontogeny or diachrony rather than just
in synchrony began to apply transformational
techniques to language acquisition data and to
historical problems. Assuming the basic correctness
of transformational theory, these investigations
attempt to show how such notions as phrase structure,
rules, and ordering might explain the process of
change itself. Menyuk's early papers (e.g. 1964)
exemplify literal application of transformational
grammar to ontogenetic data, while McNeill (1966) uses
selected parts of the synchronic theory as the founda-
tion of a model for language acquisition. In
diachrony, Klima (1964) and Kiparsky (1965) illustrate
the use of transformational grammar in structuring
historical data. The Klima/Kiparsky approach gradually gained momentum, as illustrated by Kiparsky (1968)
and Postal (1968). The trend reaches a plateau with
King's survey (1969), which is, as its subtitle
implies, "A comprehensive picture of historical linguistics in the perspective of the theory of
generative grammar".

　　With this renewed interest in diachrony among
transformationalists, the question of whether the
shape of synchronic analysis might influence diachronic description and explanation, and vice versa,
was open for discussion. There was no consensus of
opinion. Stockwell (1964) and later Kiparsky (1968)
argued that employment of a particular rule or usefulness of a given notation in describing an historical change might constitute evidence for the prefer-
ence for, or even psychological reality of, the rule
or notation in synchronic analyses. Others such as
Chomsky and Halle (1968) have denied that diachrony
is an appropriate evaluative measure for synchronic
analysis, yet the Chomsky/Halle discussion of the

English vowel system suggests that the authors find it
natural to introduce diachronic data in a discussion
of synchronic base forms and rules. More recently,
Givón (1971:394) has proposed that the interaction
between synchronic and diachronic formulations should
be bidirectional:

> in order to understand current morphologies
> and morphotactics of a language, one must
> construct specific hypotheses about the syn-
> tactic order and transformational structure of
> the language at some earlier stage of its
> historical development. Further...the syn-
> chronic syntax of a language must constrain the
> range of alternative courses through which its
> affixal morphology evolves.

Givón's generalized attempt to make descriptions at
one level of grammar (i.e. synchronic or diachronic)
dependent upon another approaches, in principle, my
thesis that language acquisition data may be used to
evaluate alternative diachronic (or even synchronic)
hypotheses.

   Concomitant with their growing awareness of
possible uses for transformational grammar in describing diachrony, linguists also began to discuss the
function language acquisition might play in linguistic
change. The seminal article is again Halle (1962).
Halle acknowledges that both children and adults
figure in linguistic change, and attempts to define
sharply the roles of each: children restructure
grammars by constructing "optimal (simplest) grammars
on the basis of a restricted corpus of examples";
adults are restricted to "the addition of a few rules
in the grammar" (1962:344). King (1969:81) further
defines and partially relaxes this strict dichotomy:

> it was argued that adult grammar change was
> confined to rule addition. Rule loss and re-
> ordering, simplification, and restructuring
> originate in the child. This is the purist
> picture. It may well be that adults are
> capable of participating in certain minor
> grammatical changes other than rule addition,
> e.g. loss or simplification of certain low-
> level rules. Adults may even be capable of
> minor restructuring though we assume subject to
> disconfirmation that major change in underlying
> representations is beyond the adult's ability
> [emphasis my own].

While this division of labor is very tidy, it is almost void of empirical content. What would constitute
disconfirmation of the hypothesis? King's examples
from child language acquisition data, used to
illustrate the child's potential contributions to linguistic change, are restricted to the most elementary
acquisition processes, e.g. overgeneralization of the
regular plural morpheme -s (e.g. foots). Of course,
overgeneralizations of inflectional paradigms, and
grammars having the pivot-open look[8] constitute
simplifications of the adult model.[9] But what about
more complex syntactic constructions in which it is
not immediately obvious what relation the child's
acquisition strategies have to diachronic or synchronic models? Does it even make sense to say that
the child is constructing the optimal, simplest
grammar possible? Turning to King's comments on
adults, how do we know that adults can add rules, and
perhaps do a bit of simplification and minor restructuring, but cannot undertake major restructuring?
While I grant King's schema is intuitively appealing,
it is an empty hypothesis until we actually examine
what kinds of changes adults do introduce into the
language, and then ask what status our grammatical
theory assigns to these innovations. There has been
very little systematic study of adult innovation,
though socio-linguistic research is now beginning to
take up this problem.[10]

    Switching now from the child/adult dichotomy to
questions of initiation and promulgation, we find that
within Halle's framework, the initiation/promulgation
dichotomy makes little sense. While obviously aware
that the grammar of a single child does not effect a
change in the entire language, Halle does not discuss
promulgation in the sense of spreading the innovation
from speaker to speaker. I submit that the framework
of language transmission which Halle adopts prevents
him, in principle, from doing so.

    Halle assumes that (a) children basically learn
language from their parents and (b) the spectrum from
infancy to adulthood is divisible into two generations. Rereading Halle's footnotes, however, we discover an argument by authority based upon Meillet.
Because the questions of sources and generations have
become so critical in discussions of ontogeny and
diachrony, I quote in full the passage from Meillet
(1926:235-236) from which Halle has taken excerpts,
underlining those portions which Halle cites:

Il faut tenir compte tout d'abord du caractère essentiellement discontinu de la transmission du langage: l'enfant qui apprend à parler ne reçoit pas la langue toute faite: il doit la recréer tout entière à son usage d'après ce qu'il entend autour de lui, et c'est un fait d'expérience courante que les petits enfants commencent par donner aux mots des sens très différents de ceux qu'ont ces mêmes mots chez les adultes dont ils les ont appris. Dès lors, si l'une des causes qui vont être envisagées vient à agir d'une manière permanente, et si, par suite, un mot est souvent employé d'une manière particulière dans la langue des adultes, c'est ce sens usuel qui s'impose à l'attention de l'enfant, et le vieux sens du mot, lequel domine encore dans l'esprit des adultes, s'efface dans la génération nouvelle; soit, par exemple, le mot saoul dont le sens ancien est « rassasié »; on en est venu à appliquer ce mot aux gens ivres, qui sont « rassasiés de boisson »; les premiers qui ont ainsi employé le mot saoul s'exprimaient avec une sorte d'indulgence ironique et évitaient la brutalité du nom propre ivre, mais l'enfant qui les entendait associait simplement l'idee de l'homme ivre à celle du mot saoul, et c'est ainsi que saoul est devenu le synonyme de mot ivre qu'il a même remplacé dans l'usage familier; par là même le mot saoul est celui qui maintenant exprime la chose avec le plus de crudité. Cette discontinuité de la transmission du langage ne suffirait à elle seule à rien expliquer, mais, sans elle, toutes les causes de changement auraient sans doute été impuissantes à transformer le sens des mots aussi radicalement qui'il l'a été dans un grand nombre de cas: d'une manière générale d'ailleurs, la discontinuité de la transmission est la condition première qui détermine la possibilité et les modalités de tous les changements linguistiques; un théoricien est même allé jusqu'à vouloir expliquer par la discontinuité tous les changements linguistiques (voy. E. Herzog, Streitfragen der romanischen Philologie, I.).

First of all it is necessary to take into account the essentially discontinuous nature of language transmission: the child who learns to speak does not receive a completely formed lan-

guage: he must recreate it completely in
order to adapt it to his use and according to
what he hears around him, and it is a common
fact drawn from experience that young children
start off by giving very different meanings to
words than the same words have for the adults
from whom they learned them. From then on, if
one of the causes which are going to be taken
into account begins to act in a permanent
fashion, and if, later on, the word is often
used in a special fashion in the language of
adults, it is this accepted meaning which
strikes the attention of the child, and the
former meaning of the word, which is still
dominant in the mind of adults, is effaced in
the new generation; thus, for example, the
word drunk whose former meaning is "replete";
now this word is applied to intoxicated people
who are "sated with drink"; the first people to
have used the word drunk in this fashion express themselves with a sort of ironic indulgence and avoided the brutality of the correct
word intoxicated, but the child who heard them
simply associated the idea of a drunkard with
the word drunk and it is thus that the word
drunk has become synonymous with the word
intoxicated which has even replaced it in
current usage; thus the word drunk is the one
which now expresses this state with greater
crudity. This discontinuity in the transmission of language would not suffice in itself
to explain anything, but, without it, all the
causes of change would have doubtlessly been
incapable of transforming the meaning of words
as radically as has been the case in a large
number of instances; moreover, in a general
fashion, this discontinuity of transmission is
the first condition which determines the
possibility and the modalities of all linguistic changes; one theoretician even went so
far as to explain all linguistic changes by
discontinuity (see E. Herzog, Streitfragen der
romanischen Philologie, I.).

Halle's citation is misleading on several counts.
First, it fails to advise the reader that Meillet's
passage is set within a discussion of lexical change
(the essay from which it is drawn is entitled "Comment
les mots changent de sens"). The example of saoul,
which Halle omits, makes this context perfectly clear.

Without it, the reader might incorrectly understand
"le sens des mots" (used towards the end of the para-
graph, and quoted by Halle) to refer to syntactic or
semantic configurations, while its actual domain is
the lexicon. Admittedly, Meillet does speculate that

> d'une manière générale d'ailleurs, la dis-
> continuité de la transmission est la condition
> première qui détermine la possibilité et les
> modalités de tous les changements
> linguistiques.

> moreover, in a general fashion, discontinuity
> of transmission is the first condition which
> determines the possibility and the modalities
> of all linguistic changes.

However, Meillet only suggests this discontinuity as
a <u>principal condition</u>, not as a sufficient explanation
of the change process. For this stronger hypothesis,
Meillet refers the reader to Herzog, a reference which
Halle omits by replacing Meillet's semicolon with a
period.

   Most important, has Halle accurately represented
Meillet's notion of discontinuity? Halle defines the
discontinuity of generations in terms of a child/adult
pair. Yet Meillet is far less categorical. He does,
as Halle suggests, maintain that discontinuity exists
in so far as each individual child must recreate the
language for himself, based upon his linguistic
milieu:

> Pour chaque individu, le langage est ainsi une
> recréation totale faite sous l'influence du
> milieu qui l'entoure (1951:74).

> Thus, for each individual, language is a total
> recreation effected under the influence of the
> milieu in which he lives.

(cited by Halle, p. 344). But what is this milieu?
Meillet nowhere restricts it to adults. In cases in
which language acquisition does not result in a change,
adults must, at some point, provide a direct or in-
direct model. However, Meillet's only restriction
upon conditions for language transmission is preserva-
tion of intelligibility.[11] In order to maintain
communication during periods of what the historical
linguist will, in retrospect, call "linguistic
change", there must exist bidialectal (or biidiolect-
al) speakers:

Que la discontinuité soit la plus petite
possible, dans le cas de transmission de la
langue des aînés aux jeunes, ou relativement
grande, à des degrés divers, dans le cas de
changement de langue, il faut que les hommes
chez qui se produisent ces transmissions
continuent de se comprendre entre eux, il faut
qu'ils aient la volonté de continuer telle ou
telle langue. En ce sens, il y a continuité
de la langue (1951:77).

For discontinuity to be as small as possible, in the case of transmission of language
from elders to the young, or relatively large,
in differing degrees, in the case of change of
language, it is necessary that those people in
whose cases these transmissions take place
continue to understand each other, it is
necessary that they have the will to continue
such or such a language. In this sense, there
is continuity of language

Meillet poses no restriction upon the age of such
"bilinguals".[12]
Even on a metatheoretic level, Meillet's general
approach to language change is ill suited for Halle's
purposes. Although both Halle and Meillet are
interested in linguistic change, they interpret the
term in two distinct senses. Halle is primarily
interested in the changing shape of the underlying
grammar, not in overt differences. To quote Halle
(1962:345):

Since every child constructs his own
optimal grammar by induction from the utterances to which he has been exposed, it is not
necessary that the child and his parents have
identical grammars, for ... a given set of
utterances can be generated by more than one
grammar.

Thus, Mommy proposes (through linguistic innovation)
and Junior disposes (by imposing his own structure
upon the total input), but the output is (eventually)
identical. Compare now Meillet, who seems to use the
term "linguistic change" to refer to surface differences between two stages. I suggest that the kind of
restructuring to which Halle refers, i.e. which yields
the old surface output, is not even considered by
Meillet. Halle and Meillet both maintain that children recreate language anew. Yet the result of that
recreation is interpreted quite differently by each.

What does Halle contribute to the notions of
comparative description and path of actuation? Halle
primarily speaks of simplification, a metatheoretic
aspect of comparative description. Given the distinction between surface and underlying differences
with respect to adult and child grammars, it becomes
clear why transformationalists have appeared to
continue the 19th century view that children simplify
grammars. Actually the "deep structure" of these two
arguments differs, but the "surface structure"
realization is still simplification in each case. As
illustrated by Meillet, the 19th and early 20th
centuries defined "linguistic change" as "surface
change". There is no logical reason for surface
change to involve only simplification. However,
scholars of this early period, focusing much of their
attention upon Indo-European inflection, tended to
conclude that languages in general do tend to become
less complex over time. Early transformational work
in diachrony (e.g. Halle 1962) focused upon changes in
the underlying linguistic structure and in rules,
suggesting that children simplify through restructuring. Within any theoretical framework, there is
normally no reason to assume that children will
produce the same output as their parents by using a
more complicated grammar. This condition is, of
course, possible. Between the ages of two and four,
there are many instances in which children fail to
make generalizations which appear in the adult language, and thus their grammars, at this midpoint, are,
considering only the particular construction in question,[13] more complex than the adult prototypes. However, we assume generalizations are attained before
the acquisition process is complete. But what about
surface changes which children initiate and/or
promulgate? Halle does not deny, on any metatheoretic
basis, that children might introduce complexity. However, the question of added complexity is never considered by virtue of his failure to consider innovations which appear in the surface structure of child
language.
    The next major transformationalist contributions
to ontogenetic/diachronic theory were made by
Kiparsky. In a number of ways, Kiparsky directly ex-
pands some of Halle's notions. However, Kiparsky also
goes beyond Halle in that he considers how children
may initiate change appearing in the surface structure. After presenting Kiparsky's general theoretical
framework (based primarily on Kiparsky 1965),[14] I will
then attempt to interpret Kiparsky's contributions in

relation to Halle's original model and in relation to
the three general parameters of change proposed in
Chapter 1 (i.e. child/adult, initiation/promulgation,
comparative description/path of actuation). While
Kiparsky's discussion focuses upon phonological
change, there is no a priori reason that the same
arguments cannot be applied, with appropriate
modifications, to other types of linguistic variation.[15]

Kiparsky postulates that phonological change can
be characterized by two distinct mechanisms: innovation by adults (which is part of sound change) and
imperfect learning by children. He traces these concepts back to Paul:

> I would regard [as] his [i.e. Paul's] funda-
> mental insight [that] the phonology of a lan-
> guage can change in two ways: by Lautwandel
> and by abweichende Neuerzeugung. I will trans-
> late them as sound change and imperfect learn-
> ing (Kiparsky 1965:1-4).

Kiparsky proceeds to explain briefly what is meant by
sound change and imperfect learning:

> Sound change is brought about by the joint
> operation of innovation and subsequent re-
> structuring. Innovation in phonology is change
> in the way phonological representations are
> executed by speakers of a language; restructur-
> ing is the resulting revision in the phono-
> logical representation .... Imperfect learning
> is due to the fact that the child does not
> learn a grammar directly but must recreate it
> for himself on the basis of a necessarily
> limited and fragmentary experience with speech.
> It is in no way surprising that the grammar
> should change in the process of transmission
> across generations of speakers (1965:1-4).

Each of these concepts -- innovation, restructuring,
and imperfect learning -- may now be examined in some
detail.

Innovations are changes in the surface form of
language. These alterations are, contrary to de
Saussure's belief, part of langue itself rather than
part of parole. Kiparsky does not specify either the
source of these innovations or their distribution
within the speech community. However, from the structure of the discussion, we infer that innovations
constitute the addition of rules at some point in the
phonological system (cf. Kiparsky 1965:1-33). While

there is no mention of where these innovations
originate or which age range adds such rules, we again
infer that the rules are added and used by adults.[16]
Typical examples of innovations are the addition of an
umlaut rule in Old High German and the various steps
of Grimm's Law.

The next concept, <u>restructuring</u>, is also somewhat
amorphous. Kiparsky applies the term to revision
(both in rules and in underlying representations)
which is necessitated by the addition of rules through
innovation. By "rule revision", Kiparsky does not
refer to such fairly recent theoretical types as rule
loss or reordering of rules. Rather, he is referring
to the more general case in which the number of rules
necessary to describe a set of innovations may be
reduced by positing a new underlying representation
and/or changing the structural analysis component or
structural change component of some rule. Kiparsky
does not specify who carries out this restructuring.
However, if the surface output of (a) the original
grammar plus innovation and (b) the restructured
grammar is identical, we assume that children are responsible for the restructuring, in the same fashion
as described by Halle.

Of even greater interest is Kiparsky's discussion
of imperfect learning which is, if I understand him
correctly, the means by which children introduce
change into the language. Superficially, imperfect
learning shares the features of the kinds of restructuring by children which Halle describes, i.e.
simplicity and similarity of child and adult output:

> The possibilities of imperfect learning are
> constrained by the two conditions only that the
> changed grammar should be simpler than the
> original grammar (or, in the case of very small
> changes, as simple as the original grammar) and
> that it should generate nearly the same lan-
> guage (Kiparsky 1965:2-48).

However, the differences between the original adult
grammar and that produced by imperfect learning in the
child, are all-important, as they constitute the linguistic change initiated by the child. Kiparsky
provides an explicit account of what he means by
imperfect learning, which I quote in full:

> Suppose that the child has constructed the
> optimal, "simplest" grammar for a certain body
> of linguistic experience. Further data that he
> encounters may subsequently motivate a re-

analysis. If no reanalysis is made, the
grammar will "congeal" as the child matures
and passes the stage where complex unconscious
skills are easy to acquire. That no reanalysis
is made may be due to the fact that the language in fact has no counter-data. In this
case the child has arrived at the "right"
grammar. But -- and this is of vital impor-
tance-- that is not the only possible reason
why a reanalysis may fail to take place. It
may well be that the language has counter-data
which do not register on the child in the
language-acquisition stage, perhaps because of
their rarity, the child's limited linguistic
experience, some mental or perceptual limitations of the child, or probably most commonly
just because of the inevitably fragmentary and
incomplete nature of the data at the child's
disposal. In that case, linguistic change has
taken place: the child arrives at the "wrong"
grammar, i.e. not the grammar of those whose
speech provided his linguistic experience
(1965: 2-12 — 2-13).

Kiparsky's notion of imperfect learning is very
similar to what I termed "arrested development" in an
earlier paper (Baron 1971) describing the effects of
ontogeny in the simplification of inflectional paradigms in the history of English.

The long-term effect of imperfect learning is
simplification of the grammar. Such simplification
may take the form of rule loss or reordering. When
imperfect learning results from "fortuitous
ignorance", i.e. the absence of crucial data from the
child's input, the resulting simplification is
negligible. However, in cases in which the child
"actually override[s] the data and arrive[s] at a
simpler grammar than his linguistic experience
warrants" (1965:2-13 — 2-14), the resultant changes
yield much greater simplification.

One of Kiparsky's reasons for maintaining the
distinction between innovation (i.e. change in surface
output by addition of a rule) and imperfect learning
(i.e. alteration of surface output by simplifying
rules) is that the two forms of change are manifested
quite differently in the language at large. Innovations spread over large areas quite rapidly, while the
effects of imperfect learning spread slowly and dis-
continuously "because of independent development of
the same change in several speech communities" (1968:

195).

Kiparsky's contributions may be summarized within
the tripartite framework of linguistic evolution. If
I have correctly interpreted Kiparsky's meaning of
innovation and restructuring, then Kiparsky does, in
fact, differentiate between the roles of adults and
children in linguistic change. Adults add additional
rules to the grammar by innovation. Children either
restructure the innovations, yielding the same surface output as their elders, or fail to learn completely their parents' grammar, thereby yielding a
presumably simplified output. Kiparsky also grapples
with the distinction between initiation and promulgation. Both innovation and imperfect learning are
types of initiation. However, due to their different
structures and use in the speech community, they
spread in two distinct patterns. But what about the
third parameter, i.e. comparative description/path of
actuation? Like his predecessors, Kiparsky only considers simplification as a possible description of the
effects of children upon the language (though
presumably rule addition by adults is a form of
elaboration). Kiparsky does give considerable content
to his notion of simplification. In a sense, he
produces a metatheoretic typology of rule types and
rule applications. Children may simplify by losing
rules or reordering them. Certain orders maximize
simplification. Such notions are all critical additions to a general theory of change, yet they are
still insufficient. First, these principles, must,
where possible, be translated into more specific descriptive and processual statements applicable to
syntax and semantics. In addition, it is necessary
to consider the possibility that children not only
simplify (either on the deep or surface level) but
that they may elaborate as well.

Since the appearance of Halle and Kiparsky's
work, interest in ontogeny and diachrony has rapidly
increased. Thus, when Weinreich, Labov, and Herzog
(1968) (henceforth WLH) appeared, the paper had a
significant impact. Within the framework of a general
theory of change, the authors analyze some of the
problems in past and current ontogenetic/diachronic
theory, and propose some future directions that might
be followed in work on those problems. Their
important "position paper" deserves particular attention because of their explicit sociolinguistic
analysis of the structure of linguistic promulgation
as well as their discussion of how a particular change
relates to the rest of the linguistic system. How-

ever, I will restrict my comments to those aspects of
the paper which are directly relevant to the questions
posed in this chapter.
    WLH analyze the "parent-to-child" model of lin-
guistic change offered by Halle and continued by
Kiparsky and others. Their criticisms, substantiated
by historical and sociolinguistic data, are somewhat
reminiscent of Manly's 1930 paper as well as of an
article by Hockett (1950) which assumes a similar
theoretical stance. WLH deny, first, that the
primary input to children is the adult grammar, and
second, that change is accomplished within a single
shift of generations.[17] On the first point, the
authors state that

> there is a mounting body of evidence that the
> language of each child is continually being
> restructured during his preadolescent years on
> the model of his peer group. Current studies
> of preadolescent peer groups show that the
> child normally acquires his particular dialect
> pattern, including recent changes, from child-
> ren only slightly older than himself (1968:
> 145).

Recall Manly's almost identical claim that

> each and every child, during the formative
> period of its speech, is more closely and
> intimately associated with children slightly
> older than itself than with adults, and is
> psychologically more receptive of influences
> from these children than from adults (1930:
> 289).

Or compare Hockett (1950:449):

> The most important environmental force shaping
> the emerging dialect of a child is the speech
> of other children.

While WLH's recognition of the continuity of generations and the implications of this continuity for the
linguistic input to children learning to speak is not
new, its reintroduction into the current ontogenetic/
diachronic debate is important.
    The authors' second point, i.e. that change is
not completed within a generation, is directly linked
to the first. Kiparsky's explanation for gradual
change was that the change must be recreated many
times. But, to rephrase a question WLH ask in a
slightly different context, why should this process be
repeated in this particular fashion and at this point

in time? The authors' answer goes back to the
continuity of generations:

> A continuous process of transfer within the
> peer group, from children slightly older to
> children slightly younger, is consistent with
> such middle-range developments (1968:146).

where by "middle-range developments", WLH are
referring to persistent change in the same direction
over several generations.

How do WLH's comments contribute to characteriz-
ing the three parameters child/adult, initiation/
promulgation, and comparative description/path of
actuation? While the authors do point out that children base their restructuring upon peer rather than
upon adult models, WLH do not otherwise clearly
distinguish the roles of children and of adults in the
initiation and promulgation of change. WLH's examples
suggest that a great deal of innovation originates
among teenagers or adults, and spreads to younger and
younger speakers through peer influence. Without
explicitly saying so, WHL seem to incorporate
Kiparsky's notions of (a) restructuring of an innovation and (b) imperfect learning under a single model
by shifting the major input source to preadolescent
peers who have not "perfectly" acquired the surface
adult model themselves. While some innovative changes
may initiate and spread in the adult grammar, children, within their own preadolescent milieux, are
capable of initiating surface and underlying change,
and of promulgating at least the former. Finally,
WLH's work is particularly instructive for developing
the notion path of actuation. With concrete examples,
the authors illustrate how linguistic variation is
largely determined by sociolinguistic factors, and
also show that it is possible to make predictions
about the direction of change.[18]

During the last three or four years, a number of
linguists have become increasingly dissatisfied with
the rather restricted approaches to ontogeny/diachrony
I have described so far. The most obvious target was
the tacit assumption that children and, by implication, languages, only simplify. In both traditional
and early transformational approaches to diachrony,
adults were said to introduce complexity through the
addition of rules to the grammar. Typically, this
surface elaboration was assumed to be absorbed into
the community language through simplification, which
is the result of children structuring their input in
the best way possible. Yet surely this account is not

sufficient. There may well be cases in which the
child himself, rather than the adult or even an older
peer, initiates increased structural complexity.
While the child's contributions may, in fact, directly
stem from his creation of an "optimal" grammar, the
end result is an elaboration of the previous adult
model. I will later argue that precisely this situation obtained in the evolution of English periphrastic
causatives have and get. For the present, however, I
will briefly mention the work of several other
linguists who have reached independent conclusions
about elaboration.

Traugott (1969) offers various examples of
"additions and elaborations" in the history of English.
Consider the case of relative reduction. In Early
Modern English, any surface subject relative was
deletable. For example,

    (1) Shakespeare, Measure for Measure II.ii.34
        I have a brother is condemned to die.
    (2) Shakespeare, King John IV.ii.69 This is
        the man should do the bloody deed.

In modern English, surface subject relatives may only
be deleted when followed (at a deeper level) by be.
This be, however, must also be deleted on the surface.
Thus, in modern English,

    (3) I have a brother who is condemned to die.
    (4) *I have a brother Ø is condemned to die.
    (5) I have a brother Ø Ø condemned to die.
    (6) This is the man who should do the bloody
        deed.
    (7) *This is the man Ø should do the bloody
        deed.

Bever and Langendoen (1971:436) argued that surface
structure elaboration through the imposition of
stronger restrictions upon modern relative clauses is
explicable in terms of perceptual strategies assigning
syntactic functions to nouns and verbs. Two such
strategies are:

    a string consisting of a nominal phrase is the
        beginning of an internal structure
        sequence (i.e. sentoid)
    the verb phrase (optionally including a
        nominal) is the end of such a sequence

The use of such strategies persists even in strings
lacking the necessary internal structure. For
example, in the line from Measure for Measure, perceptual strategies may incorrectly analyze brother as

only the surface subject of <u>is condemned</u> when it is,
in fact, also the object of <u>have</u>, i.e.

>(8) *I have [$_S$ a brother is condemned to die]$_S$

>(cf. [$_S$ I have a brother]$_S$ is condemned to die)

Bever and Langendoen claim that historically, the
failure of noun-verb strategies to yield correct
analyses resulted in obligatory presence of the surface subject in relative clauses:

>As the number of false <u>NV = Subject Verb</u>
>segmentations determined by [the] perceptual
>strategy ... became too great the independent
>marking of the relative clause became
>obligatory. This development stands as an
>example of the effect of behavioral mechanisms
>on the formal rules, in which the rules changed
>so as to accommodate the perceptual strategies
>(1971:446).

Thus, the simplest set of rules in a formal grammar
need not correspond to perceptual simplicity. Rather,
perceptual considerations may override existing
grammatical rules.

How might this restriction have originated in the
speech community? Bever and Langendoen (1971:451)
seem to imply that such "neologisms" are, according to
the familiar model, still initiated by adults, and
then adopted by children for perceptual reasons:

>linguistic evolution is interpreted as an
>interaction between systematically constrained
>neologisms and an ontogenetically shifting
>filter in the child: those neologisms that are
>appropriate to the particular stage in the
>child "survive"; they are picked up by the
>child and incorporated within the predictive
>grammar of his language.

Yet why must we assume that adults initiated the neo-
logism? It seems equally plausible that the innovation originated in the speech of children trying to
make sense of their elders' cryptic style. In fact,
it is conceivable that even Elizabethan children
initially retained the subject relative, only
beginning to omit it as they gained stronger control
over the nuances of their language. A similar
phenomenon occurs in modern English in the case of
contractions. Many three and four-year-olds use the
full modal plus negative forms such as <u>do not</u> and

cannot in contexts where they will later almost
exclusively use contracted don't and can't.

    Stampe (1969) also argues for elaboration by
children, but from a rather different perspective.
Stampe proposes to explain children's acquisition of
phonology as well as historical phonological change in
terms of a theory of natural phonological processes.
A phonological process is defined as a rule which

> merges a potential phonological opposition into
> that member of the opposition which least tries
> the restrictions of the human speech capacity
> (1969:443).

a definition vaguely reminiscent of Zipf's principle
of least effort (Zipf 1949). Children in their "lan-
guage-innocent state" possess a full set of unlimited
and unordered phonological processes. Such processes
may, however, be contradictory. For example, the
natural process of devoicing obstruents conflicts
with the natural process of assimilation whereby
obstruents are voiced in voiced environments. The
child resolves these conflicts either by suppressing
one process, placing limitations upon a process, or
imposing ordering upon processes. The working of
natural processes in language acquisition may have
consequences for diachrony. When children success-
fully elaborate their grammar to approximate the adult
model (i.e. by suppressing, ordering, or limiting
natural processes), the language of the community
remains unchanged. Failure to make these adjustments
leads to historical change:

> A phonetic change occurs when the child fails
> to suppress some innate process which does not
> apply in the standard language (1969:448).

Viewing acquisition and diachrony as two ends of a
spectrum,

> the child's progressions [i.e. suppressions,
> limitations, and orderings] are essentially
> opposite to the tendencies of change -- we
> might say the regressions -- of the standard
> language (1969:449).

    On an initial reading, Stampe seems to imply that
children only simplify the community model, through
what Sweet, Paul, and Kiparsky have called "imperfect
learning" (or, in Stampe's framework, imperfect
suppression, ordering, or limitation).[19] However, on
closer analysis, the divisions between simplification
and elaboration begin to fade. For example, if the

child only partially alters a set of natural
processes, he may effect changes in the linguistic
community which are not readily classifiable as
simplifications or elaborations. Stampe considers
the two natural processes of (a) devoicing word-final
obstruents and (b) lengthening stressed vowels before
voiced segments. Failure to restrict these processes
results in a great many homonyms, i.e. a form of
phonological simplification. Early child language
illustrates the non-restrictive situation. For
example, Velten (1943) reports that his daughter Joan
originally pronounced both back and bad as [bat],
which Stampe accounts for by ordering the length
adjustment process after devoicing. Later, Joan used
vowel length to distinguish between the two words,
i.e. back [bat], bad [ba:t]. In Stampe's terminology,
the processes have been restricted by imposition of
the new ordering, i.e. (a) length adjustment and then
(b) devoicing. Three weeks later, a second restriction occurs -- suppression of the devoicing process --
whereby Joan attains the standard pronunciation.

    Consider what would happen if only the first
restriction, i.e. ordering, occurred. In Stampe's
schema, this would constitute a condition of imperfect
learning. Yet do the historical consequences of such
a condition result in simplification? Stampe considers certain Appalachian dialects in which the rule
devoicing final obstruents has not been suppressed
and minimal pairs are distinguished only by vowel
length, e.g. bet [bɛt], bed [bɛ:t]. Are these
Appalachian dialects simpler or more complex than
standard English? Stampe (1969:448) suggests that the
latter is the case:

> if an American child fails to suppress the
> process devoicing word-final obstruents, for
> example, his speech -- compared to the adult
> standard -- will exhibit a phonetic change
> corresponding to the "addition" of a process
> to the phonology.

Such an "addition" -- initiated by children --
apparently corresponds to the "innovations" which
Paul, Halle, and Kiparsky maintained only adults can
introduce. Darden (1970:466-467) seems to make a
somewhat similar point about children effecting
historical elaboration:

> What does not seem to have occurred to any-
> one is the possibility that a child, possessing
> a partial grammar, might perform simplification

on that grammar which would actually change his speech, so that it would be impossible ever to formulate a grammar identical to that of the adult. This short-term economy on an incorrect grammar might, from the point of view of an adult grammar, result in a net increase in complexity. We could hope that any radical change in the surface data would be eliminated by the resultant loss of communicative function or by social pressure, but we must admit the possibility of such a change surviving and spreading.

While Stampe's (and Darden's) discussion of acquisition and historical change centers around phonology, the notion that a child's incomplete development may function as the source for eventual elaboration in adult language is directly applicable in syntax. In fact, it is even possible that the concept of natural processes in phonology has some analogue to the concept of path of actuation I will be presenting for syntax. If we believe that syntactic/semantic notions are innate, then the analogy is quite precise: syntactic change results from the failure by children to restrict the syntactic functions of a particular syntactic/semantic notion. If, instead, we hold that these notions develop maturationally, the analogy to Stampe's natural phonological processes still holds, but must be rephrased: syntactic change results from the child's failure to restrict notions which are emerging, epigenetically, in the child's language.

Finally, just as Stampe (1969) has pointed out that natural processes in phonology may be in conflict, Traugott (1972b) illustrates how natural processes in phonology (e.g. syllable reduction) may conflict with syntactic tendencies (e.g. morphological segmentation of tense, mood, and aspect). These particular conflicting phonological and syntactic processes produce what has been called the analytic-to-synthetic cycle (cf. Reighard 1971). In constructing a model of linguistic evolution, it will be necessary to examine how conflicts are resolved within phonology, within syntax, and between phonology and syntax, and then to compare solutions which appear in onto-genetic and diachronic development.

In addition to expanding the notion of comparative description to include elaboration (and, perhaps, paths of actuation to include natural processes in phonology), the recent work of such linguists as Traugott, Bever and Langendoen, Stampe, and

Darden has also contributed to the two other parameters of linguistic evolution (i.e. child/adult;
initiation/promulgation). In Halle's model, only
adults initiated change (elaboration). Kiparsky added
the possibility of children initiating simplification.
The authors I have just discussed interject a third
possibility: that children initiate elaboration.
While promulgation is not a central issue in the
papers mentioned, some of Stampe's discussion may be
extended to the problem of continuity of generations.
In the example of vowel lengthening and devoicing of
obstruents, the Appalachian dialects correspond to a
stage in which the first restriction (or ordering) has
been imposed by children, but not the second (i.e.
suppression). However, it is not necessary to assume
that the relevant set or sets of Appalachian children
did not eventually suppress the devoicing rule in
their own speech. As I have argued elsewhere (Baron
1971:136) the time during which children may effect at
least some language changes is limited to the period
during which they serve as slightly older peers to the
next "generation" one or two years their junior.
Eventually, older Appalachian peers may in fact
suppress devoicing. Yet this further restriction on
their own grammars does not directly affect the
emerging linguistic change, since by this time, their
role as transmitters of language has been taken on by
the new "generation" which does not yet suppress the
rule.[20]

2.3 The Three Parameters of Linguistic Evolution

A survey of ontogenetic/diachronic studies has
revealed a number of theories and empirical observations about the kinds of linguistic change that are
possible, and the mechanisms via which such change
may come about. The examples (and counter-arguments)
permit a fuller understanding of the three parameters
-- child/adult, initiation/promulgation, comparative
description/path of actuation -- on the bases of which
I have proposed studying linguistic evolution. The
description of each of these parameters is still far
from complete. However, by summarizing the findings
thus far, I hope to show that the parameters are not
merely metatheoretic constructs, void of empirical
content. Table I summarizes these findings. Cases
involving more than one parameter are detailed under
the first heading and only noted in the second. The
terms simplification and elaboration refer to the
particular construction under investigation, not to

an evaluation of the entire grammar.

Table I.   Examples of the Three Parameters of
            Linguistic Evolution

child/adult	child: <u>processes within own grammar</u>
	       construct and test a series of hypotheses (grammars)
	       as acquire native linguistic competence (n.b. this
	       series may or may not reflect diachronic processes)
	
	<u>diachronic effects</u>
	   i. simplify language historically by own
	      (a) reorganization of underlying structures or
	          rules, while yielding the same output as the
	          adult model
	      (b) imperfect learning
	  ii. elaborate language historically by own
	      (a) imperfect learning
	
	adult: <u>processes within own grammar</u>
	      lose rules, simplify rules, add rules
	
	<u>diachronic effects</u>
	   i. simplify language historically by own
	      (a) rule loss
	      (b) rule simplification
	  ii. elaborate language historically by own
	      (a) rule addition

initiation/
promulgation
	initiation: both children and adults may initiate change
	                (cf. above)
	promulgation: both children and adults promulgate change
	                (n.b. the nature and speed of promulgation is
	                a function of social and cultural factors)
	
	    adult: (a) rapid spread of adult innovation, potentially
	             at all age levels of the linguistic community
	
	    child: (a) slow spread of child's innovation by indivi-
	             dual children spontaneously producing the
	             same innovation
	          (b) continuous "hand-me-down" process from
	             children to slightly younger peers

comparative
description/
path of
actuation
	description: metatheoretic:
	          (a) simplification
	          (b) elaboration
	
	         specific:
	          (a) phonology: metathesis, assimilation,
	                 dissimilation
	          (b) syntax: reduction of paradigm
	actuation: phonology, syntax: natural processes

Footnotes

[1]Cf. Haeckel 1897, 1:1-2. In this and subsequent
quotations from French and German, I use English
translations where they appear in published English
sources (cf. Bibliography A). Passages cited in the
original French were translated by Reinhard Kuhn.

[2]But cf. Brown 1958.

[3]The following discussion is based upon the 6th
edition (1960). Judging from the English translation
of the Prinzipien (1888), which was based upon the 2nd
German edition, Paul does not appear to have considered the role of children in his early versions.

[4]Cited by Weinreich, Labov, and Herzog 1968:108.

[5]E.g. "l'individu ou les individus de la jeune
génération manifestent une initiative ou une résist-
ance là où le langage normal présente quelque
embarras, quelque rupture d'equilibre apparente ou
cachée" (Cohen 1933:391).

The individual or individuals of the young generation
show evidence of initiative or resistance there where
normal language presents some difficulty, some obvious
or hidden rupture in equilibrium

[6]Since "la langue des auteurs classiques", i.e. 17th
and 18th century classical written French, contains
greater morphological complexity than the early 20th
century spoken cultivated adult standard, it is not
surprising that children's spoken usage is simpler
than that of written archaic language.

[7]My page references will be to the reprinting in
Fodor and Katz (1964).

[8]Cf. Bloom 1971.

[9]This claim, however, depends upon a prior description
of what aspects of adult speech actually constitute
the linguistic input to the child (cf. Farwell 1973).

[10]E.g. Labov 1966; Weinreich, Labov, and Herzog 1968.

[11]Halle also requires intelligibility, but Kiparsky
(1965:1-35) argues that intelligibility is not a sine
qua non for linguistic variation.

[12]Weinreich, Labov, and Herzog (1968) pursue the
question of how this bilingual chain operates in
actual sociolinguistic settings.

[13]Although in terms of the entire grammar, the child's
formulation may be equivalent in complexity or less
complex than the total adult model.

[14]This framework is partially redefined in Kiparsky
1971.

[15]As Halle's misrepresentation of Meillet reveals,
extreme caution is necessary in applying analytic
tools created for one purpose to data falling within
a different theoretical realm.

[16]I base this interpretation, in part, upon Kiparsky
(1968:195): "We can relate the concepts of rule
addition and simplification to adult and child language, respectively. The typical form of rule addition is the borrowing of rules among adults;
simplification typically occurs in the learning of
language by children."

[17]As I have said earlier, Kiparsky, unlike Halle, does
not claim all change is complete within one generation.

[18]In a somewhat different context, cf. also Greenberg
1969.

[19]Stampe (1969:448) even cites the Neogrammarian
theory of "imperfect imitation, by children, of the
speech of adults", referring to Passy (1890:225).

[20]Cf. also Andersen 1969.

Chapter 3
ENGLISH PERIPHRASTIC CAUSATIVES

The model of language acquisition and historical change outlined in Chapter 2 will be tested through a detailed examination of the historical evolution and ontogenetic development of a single construction type in English. The construction selected is periphrastic causative verbs. Chapter 3 presents a rudimentary syntactic and semantic discussion of periphrastic causative constructions (a more detailed analysis appears in Baron 1974). Hypotheses are here presented about a possible paradigmatic analysis of these verbs and about markedness, which are later tested in the chapters on diachrony and language acquisition.

3.1 Periphrastic Constructions

A periphrastic is a grammatical construction using two or more words to express a notion which is typically represented in a given language as a unitary inflected form.[1] This unitary form may have the structure of a single lexical item, a phrase, or, in the case of periphrastic causatives, an entire sentence. Periphrastic constructions may serve to segmentalize (i.e. represent as free morphemes) such notions as verbal tense, aspect, mood; nominal case; or adjectival or adverbial degree. For example, in Latin, temporal relations can be expressed by a unitary, inflected verb, e.g. amavi ("I loved") or by a compound (periphrastic) construction, e.g. habeo amatus ("I have loved"). As an illustration of periphrasis with nouns, consider the Latin genitive singular dei which is translated in English by the periphrastic construction "of god". A third area of periphrasis is adjectives and adverbs. Instead of the unitary inflected form stupidest or oftenest, it is possible to use the periphrastic most stupid or most often.

In the case of verbal periphrasis, the lexical element which is added to the original unitary form generally covers a very broad semantic range. For example, English have (cf. "I have loved") has other functions besides the expression of aspect and tense. It may appear as a main verb indicating possession or location, e.g.

(1) How many volumes does this library have?
    (cf. How many volumes are there in this

library?)

as a dummy element expressing the notion "to
experience", e.g.

> (2) Did you <u>have</u> a good time at Coney Island?
>   (cf. Did you enjoy yourself at Coney
>   Island?)

or as an added element in syntactic (i.e. periphrastic) causative or resultative constructions, e.g.

> (3) The mechanic will <u>have</u> your car finished
>   within an hour.
>   (cf. The mechanic will finish your car
>   within an hour.)

Periphrastic causative constructions are two-part
configurations expressing causation. The first part
is a verb (e.g. <u>have</u>, <u>make</u>, <u>get</u>) and the second is a
complement, which has the underlying structure of a
sentence. For convenience, I will use (interchange-
ably) the terms <u>periphrastic</u>, <u>periphrastic verb</u>, or
<u>periphrastic causative verb</u> to refer to this first
verbal element in a periphrastic causative construction.

The terms <u>periphrastic</u> and <u>periphrasis</u> are to be
distinguished from the more general notions <u>para-
phrastic</u> or <u>paraphrase</u>. <u>Periphrasis</u> is the name of a
particular type of grammatical configuration which
uses several words to express a construction which is
generally expressed in a unitary form. <u>Paraphrase</u>
refers to the broader use of one set of words or
constructions to express (i.e. "paraphrase") a notion
(or notions) represented by other words or constructions. For example, the rather pedantic

> (4) Would you kindly desist from conversing in
>   such a lofty manner?

is roughly <u>paraphrased</u> by

> (5) Ah, come off it!

Most <u>periphrastic</u> causative constructions can be
loosely analyzed as <u>paraphrases</u> of other constructions, e.g. (6) loosely paraphrases (7):

> (6) Martin finally <u>got</u> his income tax forms
>   filled out.
> (7) Martin finally filled out his income tax
>   forms.

However, there are a number of periphrastic causatives
which cannot be reduced to unitary forms, e.g.

(8) The mother made the baby smile.
(9) *The mother smiled the baby.

For this reason, I have chosen the narrower term periphrastic (rather than paraphrastic) to refer to the
normal syntactic mode of expressing causation (but cf.
Babcock 1972:30fn.).

3.2 The Periphrastic Causative Paradigm

What types of elements function as the second
part of the periphrastic causative construction? Consider the following examples:

(10) The doctor made his patient breathe
deeply.
(11) The army will make you a soldier.
(12) The teacher made the student angry.
(13) The candidate had his name cleared.
(14) The provost got the students out of his
office.

Not every periphrastic can occur with every complement. For example, we do not normally say

(15) *The provost made the students out of his
office.

or

(16) ?The teacher had the student angry.
(although cf. The cook had the water hot
in a jiffy.)

Moreover, there are restrictions on which periphrastics take to-complementizers in the noun+infini-
tive construction, and which do not, cf.

(17) The doctor made his patient breathe
deeply.
(18) *The doctor made his patient to breathe
deeply.
(19) The doctor got his patient to breathe
deeply.
(20) *The doctor got his patient breathe
deeply.

Consider a hypothetical grammar in which all
periphrastic verbs could occur with all possible
complements. I will call this matrix of verbs and
complements a periphrastic causative paradigm. A
grammar containing such a paradigm would be optimally

simple and maximally productive with respect to surface syntactic features of periphrastics in that no
restrictions would apply to only certain periphrastic
verbs.
      What would such a periphrastic causative para-
digm look like?   Table II below constitutes an
exemplary matrix based upon the three periphrastic
causatives have, make, and get, and seven different
complement types.   These seven complements are:

          infinitive   adjective
          present participle   past participle
          clause   locative
          noun

Where possible, I have kept examples parallel for each
complement type. Some examples, especially with have,
are predominantly resultative rather than causative
(see Baron 1974).   I have found a large amount of
dialectal and idiolectal variation as to which cells
in the matrix are grammatical. However, this lack of
agreement among native speakers reinforces the
hypothesis I shall make that the paradigm is flexible
and the acceptable cells are subject to variation and
change within the bounds of the matrix (see Chapter
4).

Table II. Periphrastic Causative Paradigm for <u>Have</u>,
           <u>Make</u>, and <u>Get</u>

Complements	Periphrastics		
noun +	HAVE	MAKE	GET
a. infinitive to + V	*The doctor had his patient to breathe deeply	*The doctor made his patient to breathe deeply	The doctor got his patient to breathe deeply
V	The doctor had his patient breathe deeply	The doctor made his patient breathe deeply	*The doctor got his patient breathe deeply
b. present participle	The actress had her director eating out of her hand	*The actress made her director eating out of her hand	The actress got her director eating out of her hand
c. clause	I asked my lawyer to have it so that the case would not come up for another month	I asked all of my subjects to make it so that the blue dot was above the red dot	?I asked my subjects to get it so that the blue dot was above the red dot
d. noun	The army will have you a soldier in two months	The army will make you a soldier	*The army will get you a soldier
e. adjective	The cook had the water hot in a jiffy	The cook made the water hot	The cook got the water hot
f. past participle	The candidate had his name cleared	The candidate made his power felt	The candidate got his name cleared
g. locative	The provost had the students out of his office in ten minutes	*The provost made the students out of his office	The provost got the students out of his office

Having presented the proposed paradigm, it is
useful to clarify my notion of complement as it is
used with periphrastic causative verbs. I have
proposed that the complement of a periphrastic causative verb has the underlying form of a sentence. For
example, the underlying structure of

    (21) The doctor made his patient breathe
        deeply.

might, in <u>Aspects</u> style, be something like

    (22)

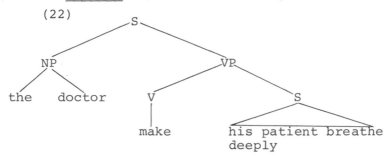

In a more abstract analysis, <u>make</u> might be decomposed
into a set of features or predicates including
INCHOATIVE and CAUSATIVE (cf. Lakoff 1965, 1968;
McCawley 1968). Alternatively, the sentence could be
analyzed into two distinct sentential components "the
doctor does" and "his patient breathe deeply" which
are linked in a causative relationship (cf. Schank
1971; McCawley 1970, 1971; Dowty 1972). In either
case, the same kind of embedding (Lakoff) or predicate
raising (McCawley 1968) or two-sentence analysis
(Schank; McCawley 1970, 1971; Dowty) could be used
for both morphological and periphrastic causatives
(cf. <u>kill/cause to die</u>; <u>walk/make walk</u>).
    There are, however, some instances in which the
dual sentence analysis may, in fact, be questioned.
Consider noun + noun,or noun + locative constructions
(where locative includes both position and direction).
One might wish to argue that it is simplest to analyze

    (23) The army will make you a soldier.
    (24) The provost got the students out of his
        office.

as single sentences. In the case of (23) a simplex
analysis within a case grammar framework (cf. Fillmore
1968) would require a distinction between <u>you</u> and
<u>soldier</u>, though that same distinction is needed anyway
for general <u>N be N</u> constructions.[2] In (24) one might
analyze <u>students</u> as an Object and <u>out of his office</u>

as a Locative, both occurring in a single case frame
with get. This analysis would, however, fail to distinguish between a causative verb plus locative in
(24) and an acquisitive verb and locative as in (25):

(25) I always get my shoes at Kinney's.

One might, of course, counterargue that while
causative get (e.g. (24)) typically takes a directional modifier, acquisitive get (e.g. (25)) typically
takes a positional term. In fact, in all but the
earliest work on case grammar, position and direction
are expressed by distinct case relations.

An additional problem arises with get + noun +
locative constructions in that many get + locative
combinations function as idioms or verb + particle
units rather than as separate grammatical elements.
In many cases, get + locative can be replaced by a
single lexical item, e.g.

(26) The boy got his coat off.
(27) The boy removed his coat.
(28) Jimmy is getting a dance band up.
(29) Jimmy is forming a dance band.

Furthermore, many particles can occur directly following the verb in addition to appearing in final position, e.g.

(30) The boy got his coat off.
(31) The boy got off his coat.
(32) Marilyn got a box down from the shelf.
(33) Marilyn got down a box from the shelf.

The ultimate choice between a simplex or complex
analysis depends upon two factors: how abstract
should representations be in general, and how
important is it to give syntactically similar representations to constructions with close semantic
interpretations (e.g. periphrastic causatives and
their various complements)? In the present study, I
have chosen to use a complex analysis for all complements in order to test the validity of a general
periphrastic causative paradigm.

Finally, it is necessary to say a few words about
my use of the terms adjective and past participle. In
general synchronic analysis, I am using the term
adjective to refer to the traditional "part of speech"
which modifies nouns (and pronouns). In English,
adjectives typically occur before nouns, or after
copulas and inchoatives, e.g.

(34) The salty water is in the glass.

(35) The water is <u>salty</u>.
(36) The water became <u>salty</u>.

Some adjectives may have past participial surface form
(i.e. ending in -<u>ed</u>, -<u>t</u>, -<u>en</u>), e.g.

(37) I found a <u>moth-eaten</u> coat.
(38) I found a coat which was <u>moth-eaten</u>.

(cf. Hirtle 1969). <u>Past participle</u> refers to a verbal
form appearing in periphrasis, e.g.

(39) The witch had <u>mixed</u> a magic potion.
(40) A magic potion was <u>mixed</u> by the witch.

It is, however, often difficult or impossible to distinguish on the surface between adjectival and past
participial functions. For example, a sentence such
as

(41) The police were bewildered.

is ambiguous: it might either mean that the police
were in a state of bewilderment (i.e. <u>bewildered</u> =
adjective) or that someone had bewildered the police
(i.e. <u>bewildered</u> = past participle). There are some
cases in English in which adjectival and past
participial function are differentiated by the
presence or absence of a suffix, e.g.

(42) The casket was <u>open</u> (=adjective).
(43) The casket was <u>opened</u> (=past participle).

However, in most instances, there is no formal
morphological distinction. Historically, past
participles derive from adjectives (see 4.4). In discussion of the diachronic (4.4, 4.5) and ontogenetic
(5.6, 5.7) data, I will argue that surface past
participial complements with periphrastic causative
verbs are often interpreted as adjectives.
     Is there any diachronic or ontogenetic evidence
supporting the proposed paradigmatic analysis of
periphrastic causative constructions? Historical data
suggest that most of the cells in the hypothesized
paradigm have been "filled in" at one point or another
in the history of English. Consider the use of
complementizers with noun + infinitive constructions.
During the Late Middle English and Early Modern
English periods, <u>have</u>, <u>make</u>, and <u>get</u> appeared both
with and without the complementizer <u>to</u>, e.g.

          <u>make</u> (44) c1386 CHAUCER <u>Pars.T.</u> 540 Flaterye..
                    <u>maketh a man to enhauncen</u>
                    his herte (OED 53b)
                    (= Flattery makes a man exalt

his heart)

(45)   1390 GOWER Conf.I. 202 At Knaresburgh
be nyhtes tuo The kinges Moder
made him duelle (OED 53a)
(= The King's mother made him
remain at Knaresburgh for two
nights)

have (46)   1591 SHAKS. Two Gent.III.i.80 What
would your Grace haue me to do
in this? (OED 18b)

(47)   1662 J.DAVIES tr. Olearius' Voy.
Ambass.   28 She would needs have
the young counts..go to the
Inn..to Complement them (OED
17a)

get (48)   1596 SHAKS. Tam. Shr.I.ii.38 I bad
the rascall knocke vpon your
gate, And could not get him for
all my heart to do it (OED 30)

(49)   1598 SHAKS. Merry W.II.ii. 76 They
could neuer get her so much as
sippe on a cup with the prowdest
of them all (OED 30)

In modern English, however, only get may appear with
to. A full analysis of the historical paradigmatic
status of the periphrastic causatives have, make, and
get will be presented in Chapter 4.

Do ontogenetic data support the paradigmatic
analysis? Observers of child language have frequently
commented on children's use of overgeneralization in
morphology. Studies of various languages (e.g.
English: Brown 1973; Ervin [-Tripp] 1964; French:
Guillaume 1927b; Russian: Slobin 1966a) show that
young children typically adopt single morphological
markers of case, number, gender, tense, etc., and
apply these markers productively without much regard
for restrictions in the adult model. Common English
examples are mans for men, sheeps for sheep, and goed
for went. Usually the child's overgeneralization
merely supplants an alternative form which already
exists in the adult language (e.g. men, sheep, went).
However, upon occasion, the child's productive rule
might yield forms for which there are no lexical
equivalents in the adult language. If, for example,
English has dog and doggie, horse and horsie, why not
snake and snakie or elephant and elephantie?

In syntax there are parallel examples in which a
child overgeneralizes a particular construction to one
lexical item where a distinct lexical item or construc-

tion is appropriate. The example in (50) is typical:

> (50) I fall the truck.
>   (cf. The truck falls, I drop the truck.)

on analogy with

> (51) I open the door.
>   (cf. The door opens.)

However, as in morphology, there are also cases in
which children extend syntactic paradigms beyond the
adult paradigm. Consider the use of both make and get
in such constructions as

> (52) The teacher $\left\{\begin{array}{l}\text{made}\\\text{got}\end{array}\right\}$ the girl confused.

> (53) The teacher $\left\{\begin{array}{l}\text{made}\\\text{got}\end{array}\right\}$ the girl $\left\{\begin{array}{l}\text{dance}\\\text{to dance}\end{array}\right\}$.

If both make and get appear in constructions such as
(52) and (53), we might also expect to find a construction such as (54)

> (54) *The teacher made the poster down.

on analogy with

> (55) The teacher got the poster down.

In Chapters 5 and 6 I will examine longitudinal and
experimental data to test the ontogenetic reality of
the paradigm.

3.3 Markedness

The periphrastic causative paradigm in Table II
presents the three verbs have, make, and get without
regard to markedness. It is, however, possible to
argue that make is the least marked of the verbs, get
is more marked, and have most marked. While I do not
have all the necessary empirical data for validating
this hypothesis synchronically, I will outline the
form such an argument might take, and indicate what
implications a synchronic analysis of markedness would
have for diachronic and ontogenetic data.
    Greenberg (1966) proposes a number of criteria
on the basis of which to determine which of two forms
is less marked. While several of Greenberg's observations are limited to particular areas of grammar, at
least three criteria are applicable to causative
periphrasis.
    The first of these criteria is textual frequency:
"In general the unmarked category has higher frequency

than the marked" (p. 64). To test whether make is
most frequent, get less frequent, and have least
frequent as a periphrastic causative, it would be
necessary to examine contemporary texts or recorded
conversation. While raw data are available for
measuring relative textual frequency (e.g. from the
Brown University Standard Corpus of Present-Day Edited
American English -- see 5.4), I have not tabulated
the comparative frequency of periphrastic causative
use. However, I think it is likely that a formal
analysis of texts would support the relative ranking
make - get - have (cf. adult data in Chapters 5 and 6
for evidence that periphrastic causative make is more
frequent than have (and get than have) in adult
speech).

The second criterion deals with neutralization:
"In certain environments the opposition of two or more
categories is suppressed, and it is the unmarked member which appears" (p. 74). Just as, for example, in
morphology, the categories "singular" and "plural" do
not have the same semantic range, although they share
the basic element of "numerosity", the periphrastic
causatives have, make, and get also differ slightly
in meaning. Make is essentially causative, get
basically inchoative, and have basically resultative
(cf. Chapter 4). If make is the least marked of the
periphrastics, then there should be instances in which
have or get is actually appropriate, but make appears,
or where have is appropriate, but get appears (cf.
Chapters 5 and 6 for evidence that make meets the
neutralization criterion).

A third category is defectivation: "The marked
category may simply lack certain categories present
in the unmarked category" (p. 74). It is possible
that this criterion can be applied to periphrastic
causatives by examining the number of complement types
which occur with each verb. If make is least marked,
then it should take the widest range of complements;
if have is most marked, it should take the smallest
range. Looking at Table II, it would appear that
these predictions are not borne out. While three
complement types are ungrammatical (i.e. "defective")
with make, there are two (or possibly three) defective
cells with get, and only one with have. However, two
of the cells (i.e. adjective and locative) are
defective for have when the modifier phrase is
removed. Therefore, it seems that while the
defectivation criterion does not support the markedness hierarchy I have proposed, it also does not
strongly argue against that hierarchy.

On the basis of the three synchronic criteria of
textual frequency, neutralization, and defectivation,
I tentatively hypothesize that make is least marked,
get more marked, and have most marked of the three
periphrastic causatives in modern (adult) English.
Thus far, I have only suggested what kinds of synchronic evidence would be necessary to support this
hypothesis, but have presented no data. However, as
I mentioned above, the conversational and experimental
data on adults which I will report on in Chapters 5
and 6 do support this hierarchy with respect to the
frequency and neutralization criteria.

If the proposed (synchronic) hierarchy is
correct, what predictions can be made about diachronic
and ontogenetic development of periphrastic causative
constructions with make, get, and have? It is tempting to apply literally the synchronic markedness
criteria in predicting the order and manner of
historical and ontogenetic emergence. Literal
historical predictions might say that make would (1)
be the earliest periphrastic causative in English (i.e.
at least among these three verbs), (2) appear more
frequently than get or have, and (3) perhaps develop
a wide range of complement types earlier than the
other two verbs. An inverse set of predictions would
be made for have. The parallel ontogenetic predictions
would be (1) that make appears as the first periphrastic causative, (2) that it appears more frequently than get or have, and (3) that it develops a wide
range of complement types earlier than the other two
verbs. The inverse predictions would hold for
have. In addition, we might predict that (4) children may use make where get or have is appropriate, or
get where have is appropriate. Are there grounds for
making either of these sets of predictions? I will
argue that while the historical predictions are largely untenable, the predictions about language acquisition can and should be tested.

Historically, it is difficult or impossible to
predict how a particular construction will evolve
with respect to markedness. Kiparsky (1965, 1968) and
King (1969) seem to suggest that languages tend to
move from more highly marked conditions to less marked
states, e.g. with respect to rule ordering or
generality within a single rule. However, the tendency to focus upon examples of grammars becoming less
marked through time is partially a function of the
belief that in the long run, languages only simplify
(cf. 2.1, 2.2). Once we recognize that both children
and adults do elaborate language, then there is no

reason why languages cannot become more marked rather
than less marked (cf. Traugott 1972c).

In addition to the general problem of direction-
ality of markedness, there are several specific
factors which make it difficult to predict on the
basis of markedness how isolated lexical items
developed. The first of these factors is borrowing.
Consider the verbs have and get. I have hypothesized
that synchronically, have is more marked than get as a
periphrastic causative. Historically, have existed
in Old English, while get, which is an Old Norse loan-
word, was not borrowed until Middle English times (see
4.5). It is therefore meaningless to speak of have
being more or less marked than get in Old English.
One might, however, be able to argue that in Middle
English get was relatively unmarked as a periphrastic
causative in that once the transitive verb was
borrowed into the English language, it rapidly
developed a number of causative uses (see 4.5).

A second problem about making diachronic markedness predictions about periphrastic causatives is that
such predictions take no account of the rest of the
grammatical system at the time. For example, make may
be the least marked of the three verbs synchronically.
However, although the verb existed in Old English, it
was only rarely used, even as a non-causative (see
4.3). Royster (1922:353) finds only a handful of
examples in hundreds of edited pages of Old English
texts. Rather, both causative and non-causative functions of modern make were typically filled by other
verbs in Old English (see 4.3).

Finally, there is the more general problem of
making inferences about usage on the basis of preserved written texts. As I point out in 4.1, the English
written record may be a poor indicator of relative
frequency of construction types, especially with
respect to colloquial usage. In view of factors such
as these, I will make no formal attempt to discuss
the historical development of the three periphrastics
with respect to markedness.

Are there grounds for making predictions about
markedness with respect to first language acquisition?
The answer here seems to be "yes". While all
historically documented stages of English represent
fully formed linguistic systems, the child learning
English does not yet possess a full-blown language.
Instead, he proceeds in a rather orderly fashion to
achieve native competence by typically beginning with
those constructions which are simplest and most
general, and then expanding his system to include more

complex phenomena (cf. Jakobson 1941; Brown 1973;
Clark 1971). If we assume that less marked constructions are also simpler syntactically and semantically
than more marked constructions, then it is reasonable
to predict that less marked constructions will be
learned before more marked forms. On the basis of
this general assumption, I will test the ontogenetic
predictions about markedness (cf. above) with respect
to longitudinal and experimental data on child
language acquisition.

Footnotes

[1]Some languages may only have what is defined here as
periphrastic forms to express a particular construction. However, if other languages use inflectional
means to express the same construction, it is
simplest in terms of cross-linguistic analysis to
retain the term "periphrastic" in both the former and
latter cases.

[2]Fillmore (1968:84) suggests _essive_ or _translative_.
However cf. Anderson (1968) and Sechehaye (1926) for
arguments in favor of the dual sentence interpretation.

Chapter 4

THE HISTORICAL EVOLUTION OF ENGLISH PERIPHRASTIC CAUSATIVES

4.1 Sources

How did have, make, and get develop periphrastic causative interpretations in the history of English? The answer to this question depends just as strongly upon linguistic theory and interpretation as it does upon raw data from written records. Even if there existed a complete corpus of all spoken and written language during a particular period of time, it would still be the linguist's task to discover structure within these data. Furthermore, the kind of structure he looks for is determined by his interests. An analysis comparing differences between two stages might differ considerably from an analysis of the actuation processes through which the language at stage A was actually replaced by that of stage B.

Of course, such an ideal corpus of English does not exist. The only documentation until quite recently has been of the written, not the spoken language. As linguists have long recognized (e.g. Bloomfield 1933; Royster 1922), innovation generally appears in the spoken language long before it is documented in writing. This was almost universally true before the vast spread of literacy and popular writing in the twentieth century. In fact, until the 15th or 16th centuries, nearly all writing was done in a formal style, leaving even standard colloquial usage largely undocumented.[1] Moreover, the language recorded is almost invariably that of adults. If it is true that linguistic variation in children and adolescents is an important source of linguistic change, it would be of great advantage to be able to compare the variation among immature speakers of a given period with the language as documented at some later stage.

There are numerous other problems with using the English written record. Through the centuries, many manuscripts have been destroyed or lost. Those which remain do not document the development of a single, unified language but rather represent a wide variety of dialects which were recorded not only by English-speaking scribes, but by Celtic and French scribes as well. The sharp regional differences existing in English until at least the 15th century make it impossible to string together in chronological order

all examples of a particular construction and label
the result a single historical progression. While
scholars have classified by dialect area most documents cited in the Oxford English Dictionary (OED) and
Middle English Dictionary (MED), the task of arranging
all data on periphrastics according to dialect has
been too vast for the present study.

Another difficulty with using the OED and MED is
that the examples cited may not be wholly representative of the construction being examined. While the
historical dictionaries do classify citations with
respect to meaning and basic syntactic usage, it is
impossible for them always to reflect accurately other
relevant parameters such as time, aspect, and modifier
restrictions. Furthermore, with the exception of
general comments such as "rare" or "common", the
dictionaries cannot be expected to mirror the relative
frequencies of occurrence of various constructions.
Some of these problems can be overcome by examining
entire texts or even the whole surviving literary output of particular authors.

A final problem is that of dating. I have already alluded to the fact that language innovations
often do not appear in the written record until after
they are well entrenched in the spoken language. It
is therefore highly possible that although innovation
i actually appeared fifty years before innovation j,
innovation j may be documented several decades before
i. Yet the difficulty does not end here. While
scholars have assigned dates to nearly all English
records, the problems involved in dating are complex.
Even cursory comparison between the OED and MED sometimes shows discrepancies of fifty or seventy-five
years for the same textual example. While my discussion of the history of English periphrastic causatives necessarily relies upon dating of documents, the
reader should be aware of the tentativeness of any
chronological differences between the emergence of
constructions which are less than fifty or a hundred
years apart.

4.2 Periphrastic Causatives in Old and Middle English

Periphrastic causatives were already well documented in Old English. As a syntactic type, they
derive from Indo-European as evidenced by parallel
examples in Greek and Latin, as well as in other older
Germanic languages (cf. Royster 1922:333ff). However,
in comparison with morphological causatives, peri-

phrastics had only restricted usage in Old English.
This distribution is to be expected in light of the
limited use of any type of verbal periphrasis (e.g.
tense, aspect, mood) during the early English period.
Royster (1922:331) speculates that at least one reason
for the later spread of periphrastics at the expense
of morphological causatives was that while verbal
morphology often indicated not just causation but
other aspectual properties as well (e.g. inchoative,
frequentative), the analytic use of periphrasis
emphasized causation itself.

Old English had four main periphrastics with
clearly causative meaning: <u>hatan</u>, <u>don</u>, <u>lætan</u>, and
<u>macian</u>. According to Royster, causative <u>hatan</u> is by
far the most frequent in the Old English record, <u>don</u>
somewhat less frequent,[2] causative <u>lætan</u> relatively
infrequent, and <u>macian</u> rare either as a periphrastic
causative or a basic transitive verb. Royster (1922:
355) also mentions <u>biegan</u> ("bend, bow"), <u>berenian</u>
("arrange, cause"), <u>bringan</u> ("bring"), and <u>wyrcan</u>
("do, make") which occasionally had causative interpretations.

Old English also had a large number of periphrastic verbs of implied causation which involved
exhorting, commanding, forcing, permitting, allowing,
etc. The following examples are drawn from Royster
(1918, 1922) and Calloway (1913):

       exhorting, commanding, forcing:
         bescufan ("impel")
         eggian ("egg, incite")
         gedihtan ("direct, order")
         mannian ("suggest, exhort")
         niedan ("force, compel, constrain")
         sprytan ("incite")
         tihten ("exhort")
         þreatnian ("urge, force, compel")

      permitting, allowing:
         forgiefan ("grant, allow")
         lætan ("allow")
         liefan ("allow")

Distinguishing between causation on the one hand
and commanding or permitting on the other is as
difficult in Old English as in modern English. Consider the following modern English sentences with <u>let</u>:

    (1) I'll let Junior go swimming if he cleans
        up his room first.
    (2) I would greatly appreciate your letting me
        know when you have made your decision.

    (3) Let me make one thing perfectly clear.
    (4) I'm going to let you have a piece of my
        mind!
    (5) Lemme outa here!

Sentence (1) is permissive. Junior may or may not
wish to go swimming once the authoritative obstacle is
removed. Sentence (2) is also permissive, although
the polite language actually camouflages a stronger
request of "cause me to know". Sentence (3) is a
borderline case, and sentences (4) and (5) drop all
permissive pretense. Most grammarians (e.g. Kruisinga
1925; Curme 1931; Poutsma 1904-1928; Bøgholm 1939)
recognize the dual permissive/causative status of let.
This ambiguity traces back to early Germanic,
evidenced not only in Old English lǣtan, but also in
Old High German lā33an and Old Norse lāta.[3] Tradi-
tionally, it is assumed that the causative interpretation derives from the permissive.[4] Whatever its
semantic source, the permissive use of lǣtan was far
more frequent than the causative in Old English. In
Middle English, the causative sense became widespread,
though beginning in the 15th century, let was once
again largely restricted to the permissive sense (see
Trnka 1930). Hatan developed from the earlier meanings 'order', 'ordain', 'direct', 'bid', 'command'.
Royster (1918) posits that the imperfective sense of
'order', in which the requested act may or may not be
carried out, gave rise to the perfective sense
'cause', which entails completion of the desired act.
However, one indication of the difficulty in distinguishing between these two senses is the fact that
although Royster classifies hatan as the most frequent
periphrastic causative in written Old English, earlier
philologists almost without exception never translate
the verb as a true causative.

    The major complement types occurring with Old
English periphrastic causatives are (a) (noun) +
infinitive and (b) (noun) + clause.[5] In many cases,
the embedded subject noun, which functions as the
immediate cause, is deleted. For example,

    (6) Bede, Ecclesiastical History of the English
        People p. 116, l.6 (E.E.T.S., O.S.,
        95)
        þā hēt sē cyning sōna Ø neoman þone
        mete (cited by Royster 1918: 84 fn.)
        (= then commanded the king immediate-
        ly to take the food, i.e. then imme-
        diately the king commanded that they
        take the food)

(7) Chaucer, <u>Knightes Tale</u>, 1903-1905
Hē ēst-ward hath upon thē gāte
aboue
. . .
Dōōn Ø māke ān auter and ān
oratorīe (cited by Royster 1918:
84fn.)
(= Eastward upon the gate above
he has caused an alter and an
oratory to be made)

This focus upon the accomplishment of the change in
the state of affairs (i.e. a result) rather than upon
the immediate instigator of that change may be one
factor which helps account for the general rise of
past participial complements with periphrastic causatives, cf. modern English

(8) The secretary had the typewriter fixed.
(i.e. someone besides the secretary fixes
the typewriter)
(9) The executive got his office carpeted.
(e.g. someone besides the executive lays
the carpet)

In Old and Middle English, some subjectless complements appeared as past participles rather than as
infinitives. Many editors in the past have tended to
emend past participial complements to infinitives in
Old and Middle English texts. Royster (1922:89-90),
however, argues that the subjectless past participle
is a perfectly comprehensible, though "mixed",
construction. Consider the following lines from <u>Beo-
wulf</u>:

(10) <u>Beowulf</u>, 991-992
Þā wæs hāten hreþe, Heort innan-weard
folmum gefrætwod (cited by Royster
1918:89fn.)
(= Then was commanded quickly Heorot
within with hands to be adorned, i.e.
then quickly it was commanded that the
interior of Heorot be adorned by hand)

We would normally expect the infinitive <u>gefrætwian</u>
rather than the past participle <u>gefrætwod</u>. Royster
(1918:90fn.) conjectures that

By the time the writer...came to putting
down <u>gefrætwod</u>, his mental image had been
shifted from the giving of the order to the
completely adorned state of Heort that had been
brought about by Hrothgar's command. The

writer, consequently, expressed this latest
idea in his mind by that form of the verb which
indicates completed action, the past
participle.

A phrase in Chaucer's Man of Law's Tale raises a
similar problem:

>(11) Chaucer, Man of Law's Tale, 171
>   han dōn frōught (cited by Royster 1918:
>   90fn.)
>   (= has caused to be loaded)

While Stratmann and others have analyzed frought as an
infinitive which lacks its final -e, Skeat (and
Royster) judge the use of the past participle to be
intentional in the text. I am not suggesting that
subjectless past participial complements necessarily
represent an actual historical stage in the development of periphrastic causatives. Rather, I interpret
these subjectless past participial complements as
surface structure indications that periphrastic causative constructions are also resultative.

The notion that periphrastics may be used to
express result or completion is further supported by
the fact that most periphrastic causative verbs in
both Old and Middle English also could function as
auxiliaries.[6] Some examples of auxiliary use are:

>(12) hatan Genesis xii, 18
>   Faroa þa het clipian Abram
>   (translates simple Latin past:
>   vocavitque Pharoa Abram)(cited by
>   Royster 1922:351)
>   (= Pharoah then commanded to call
>   Abram, i.e. then Pharoah commanded
>   Abram to be called)
>(13) lætan Chronicles E.963
>   and leot macan þone mynster
>   (cited by Royster 1922:353)
>   (= and cause to make the
>   monastery, i.e. and have the
>   monastery built)
>(14) don   Boethius' De Consolatione 14, 17
>   Swa doð nu ða þeostro þinre
>   gedrefednesse wiðstandan minum
>   leohtum larum (cited by Royster
>   1922:338)
>   (= So do now in darkness your
>   trouble to oppose my clear
>   teachings, i.e. so now in darkness
>   oppose my clear teachings with

your trouble)

Hatan as an auxiliary soon dropped out of English, lætan persisted through Middle English, and don eventually developed into a full-fledged auxiliary. Given this integral connection between causativeness and resultativeness as expressed in temporal and aspectual marking it is not surprising that have and get also developed as auxiliaries in addition to assuming periphrastic causative function.[7]

In section 3.2 I introduced the notion of a periphrastic causative paradigm which matched all periphrastics with all complements. Old and Middle English translations of Latin support the interchangeability of lætan, hatan, and macian:

    (15) Latin original: De Consolatione
         Philosophiae, Metrum 6, Book II
         Alfred's translation: sē [cāsere Nēron]
                het...forbærnan ealle Rōmanburg
                ...and eft hēt ofslēan ealle
                wīsestan witan
         Chaucer's translation: Hē [Nēro] lēet
                brennen thē citē of Rōme and māde
                slēēn senatōūrs (cited by Royster
                1910:00fn.)
                (= He had the city of Rome burned
                and the senators slain)

Chaucer replaces Alfred's het with both leet and made. Similar variation between hatan and lætan is evidenced in multiple manuscripts of the same composition (e.g. La3amons Brut, Floris and Blanchefleur). Generally, a form of hatan in the earlier manuscript alternates with a form of lætan in the later manuscript.

One question which inevitably arises in discussions of the history of English syntax is whether foreign languages such as Latin, French, or Celtic may have influenced the development of English. Several scholars (e.g. Trnka 1930) have suggested that Latin facere + infinitive or Old French faire + infinitive served as an immediate source of English causative make + infinitive and perhaps causative do + infinitive as well. However, given the fact that Old English did have native constructions of the form "periphrastic causative (e.g. hatan, lætan) + (noun) + infinitive", it is more likely that Latin and Old French merely served to reinforce an indigenous construction type (cf. Jespersen (1961,5:290). A related hypothesis suggests that the non-causative, auxiliary use of do in Middle English derives from

non-causative, periphrastic use of faire + infinitive
in Old French (cf. Earle 1887, Tobler 1921). However,
Ellegård (1953) and Visser (1969,3) argue that Old
French faire + infinitive constructions were typically
causative, and it is more likely that Middle English
influenced French than vice versa. Preussler (1938,
1939) has suggested that Celtic was actually the
source of English non-causative, periphrastic do.
Both Ellegård and Visser reject this hypothesis:

> To establish a genetical relation between
> parallel expressions in two languages it is not
> enough to show that the expression exists in
> both languages, and is found earlier in one
> than in the other....Celtic influence is
> generally believed to have been fairly insig-
> nificant in English, and I do not see any
> reason why it should have been stronger in the
> 13th century than during all the previous
> centuries that the races had been in contact
> (Ellegård 1953:119).

This brief survey indicates some of the important
aspects of periphrastic causatives as a historical
construction type in English. Most if not all periphrastic causatives[8] seem to develop from verbs with
other dominant semantic elements.[9] Using modern diachronic terminology (cf. Reighard 1971; Traugott
1972a), we might say that the appearance of periphrastic causatives represents a surface realization
of underlying semantic features or predicates which
already existed or were implied in earlier stages of
the language. This same interpretation would also
explain why so many periphrastic causatives assumed
resultative function as auxiliary markers.

The remainder of Chapter 4 will focus upon the
development of make, have, and get as periphrastic
causatives.[10] For further information on Old English
periphrastic causatives hatan, lætan, and don, cf.
Royster (1918, 1922). Causative and auxiliary uses
of Middle and modern English do are treated by Royster
(1915, 1916, 1922); Zilling (1918); Moore (1918);
Engblom (1938); Ellegård (1953); Dahl (1956);
Mustanoja (1960); Smyser (1967); Traugott (1972a).
Gar, the Middle English periphrastic causative
borrowed from Old Norse, is discussed in Trnka (1930)
and Mustanoja (1960). See Trnka (1930) for comments
on the borrowing of cause from French.

4.3 Make

Historically, make precedes both have and get as an English periphrastic causative. However, in both its periphrastic and non-periphrastic uses, Old English macian did not begin to gain prominence until Late Old English and Early Middle English. The non-periphrastic meanings of "create" or "build" were generally expressed in written Old English by wyrcan, (ge)sceapan, aræran, and (ge)timbrian (Royster 1922: 354). The periphrastic causative was typically expressed by hatan, lætan, or later don, e.g.

> (16) Beowulf, 3110
> Hēt ðā gebēodan byre Wihstānes
> (cited by Royster 1918:82)
> (= Commanded then to announce the son
> of Wihstan, i.e. he had the son of
> Wihstan announced)

Use of a form of do as a periphrastic causative rather than make was typical of other older Germanic languages as well. Yoshioka (1908:17) cites Middle High German

> (17) Mai und Beaflor 100,4
> din maere mich hohes muotes tuot
> (=your news makes me [have] high
> spirits)
> (18) Gottfried von Strassburg, Lobgesang 17
> der aller reiner herzen bluot ze
> fröiden tuot(=which makes blood of
> all pure hearts rejoice)

explaining that modern German would use machen rather than tun.

(a) Clause, Noun, Adjective

The earliest complements to be used with periphrastic causative make in English were (a) (noun) + clause, (b) noun + noun, and (c) noun + adjective. All of the following examples are from the 11th or 12th centuries:

> (noun) + clause
> (19) Ælfric, Homilies I 6, 11
> He gemacode ða þæt fyr come ufan
> swilce of heofenum (primary text)
> (= He made then that fire come
> from above as if from heaven)
> (20) Wulfstan, Homilies I 98, 25
> þa he gemacode eac þurh
> drycræft, þæt hy agunnon,

swylce hy cwice w æ ron (primary
text)
(= then he made each through
sourcery, that they begin [to act]
as if they were alive)

(21) Chronicle E 1075
gemacodon þ he naht ne dyde. ac for
to scipe æt Norðwic (n.b. þ =
þæt) (primary text)
(= made that he nothing did but
proceed to ship at Norwich, i.e.
caused that he accomplished nothing
but had to take ship at Norwich)

noun + noun
(22) Ælfric, Homilies II 82, 24
þone ðe he ær ehtende martyr
ȝemacode (primary text)
(= that whom he earlier persecuting
a martyr made, i.e. the one whom he
had earlier made a martyr through
persecution)

(23) Genesis xii, 2
ic macige ðe mycelre m æ gðe
(n.b. translates Latin: Faciamque
te in gentem magnam) (primary text)
(= I shall make you a great people)

noun + adjective
(24) Ælfric, Homilies II 88, 28
and heora lufiȝendne ȝemaciaþ
weliȝne ecelice (primary text)
(= and of them lover make
prosperous forever, i.e. and make
their lover prosperous forever)

(b) Infinitive

The infinitive, which is the most common type of
complement with periphrastic causative make in modern
English, is not documented until the end of the 12th
century:

(25) c1175 Lamb. Hom. 159
Swa makeð þe halie gast þe Mon bi-
halden up to houene (OED 53a)
(= So makes the holy ghost the Man
command up to heaven, i.e. command
the Man up to heaven)

I have no conclusive arguments on the basis of which
to determine whether the infinitive complement with
make derives directly from the clausal complement,[11]

or developed on analogy with other infinitival constructions in Old English. However, there are two kinds of evidence which strongly support the latter hypothesis: first, Old English periphrastic causatives lætan, hatan, and occasionally don were followed by infinitives; and second, available Latin texts often used facere + infinitive constructions.

In Old and Middle English, use of the bare infinitive on the one hand, or inflected or to infinitive on the other, was syntactically and semantically determined. The bare infinitive was used, for example, after a certain set of verbs such as go, hear, think, e.g.

> (26) Gower, Confessio Amantis 3956
> I þenke tellen a partie (in Mossé 1952:315)
> (= I intend to tell a part)

with auxiliaries and models (e.g. shall, will, may, can, dar, mot, lete), cf.

> (27) Dan Michel, Ayenbite of Inwyt: Gluttony 24-25
> 'A, God huet ssole we ete to-day?' (in Mossé 1952:224)
> (= 'Oh, God what shall we eat today?')

in accusative + infinitive constructions, e.g.

> (28) Robert Mannyng of Brunne, Handlyng Synne 4120
> Why wuld þey nat suffre hym lyve? (in Mossé 1952:218)
> (= Why would they not allow him to live?)

and with verbs of motion which follow another motion verb, e.g.

> (29) La3amons Brut 14033
> þa com an guldene leo liðen (primary text)
> (= then came a golden lion to travel, i.e. then a golden lion passed by)

The Old English inflected infinitive or gerundive, and its Middle English descendent, the to infinitive, were used in most other instances. During Middle and Early Modern English, the defining syntactic and semantic criteria became obliterated, and the inflectional ending on the infinitive itself started to decline.

Many verbs began appearing in both forms, even in the
same document. Since make + noun + infinitive did not
become productive until Middle English, it is not surprising that both the bare and the to infinitive are
documented, e.g.

> (30) make + bare infinitive
>   c1175 Lamb. Hom. 159 (cf. (25)   above)
> (31) make + to infinitive
>   c1200 Trin. Coll. Hom. 11
>   Þe deuel..makeð Þe unbilefulle man
>   to leuen swilche wi3eles (OED 53b)
>   (= The devil makes the unbelieving
>   man believe such deceits)

Use of the to infinitive was common and perhaps
dominant up through Early Modern English, e.g.

> (32) 1603 SHAKS. Meas. for M. III.ii. 254
>   I am made to vnderstand, that you
>   haue lent him visitation (OED 53b)

A number of examples are even found in the 19th
century (cf. Van Draat 1897), e.g.

> (33) 1859 F.E. PAGET Curate of Cumberworth 153
>   Making the dust to fly in all direc-
>   tions (OED 53b)

Although make + noun + infinitive is first documented
as a syntactic type at the end of the 12th century,
the "force" interpretation did not develop until much
later. The first examples cited by the OED are at the
very end of the 16th century:

> (34) c1592 MARLOWE Jew of Malta IV, iv
>   I'le make him send me half he has, &
>   glad he scapes so too (OED 54)
> (35) 1592 GREENE Upst. Courtier. Wks. (Grosart)
>   XI. 227
>   I will make thee do me homage (OED
>   54)

(c) Past Participle
   Use of periphrastic causative make with a past
participial complement did not develop until the early
14th century, e.g.

> (36) a1300 E.E. Psalter cii[i].7
>   Kouthe made he to Moises his waies
>   well (OED 48b)
>   (= Known made he to Moses his ways
>   well, i.e. he made his ways well
>   known to Moses)

(37) c1384 CHAUCER <u>H. Fame</u> I.155 ·
    The greke Synon With his fals
    forswerynge.. Made the <u>hors broght</u>
    in-to troye (OED 48b)
    (= The Greek Sinon with his false
    oaths..caused the horse to be
    brought into Troy)

In most cases, the past participial complement seems
to function as a passive rather than a translative +
adjectival, i.e.

(38) He made [Moses knew his ways well]
(39) The Greek Sinon made [someone brought the
    horse into Troy]

although it is not always possible to distinguish
between translative and passive. The causative subjects of (38) and (39) are Agentive. Judging from the
citations in the OED, Instrumental causative subjects
do not appear until Early Modern English or later, e.g.

(40) 1759 JOHNSON <u>Rasselas</u> xvi
    His generosity made <u>him courted</u> by
    many dependents (OED 48b)

Notice that the complement in (40) is still passive,
i.e.

(41) His generosity made [many dependents
    courted him]

Use of the passive complement persisted through the
19th century, e.g.

(42) 1836 J. H. NEWMAN <u>Lett.</u> (1891) II.202
    Their coming from you will make them
    [sc. sermons] <u>read</u> (OED 48b)

and still appears in some semi-fixed phrases, e.g.

(43) The President was determined to make his
    power felt.

However, in general, current usage requires that the
auxiliary <u>to be</u> is expressed when the complement is
passive, e.g.

(44) *The Greek Sinon made the horse brought
    into Troy.
(45) (?)The Greek Sinon made the horse be
    brought into Troy.

It is not clear when the past participial complement used with a translative rather than passive focus
developed in English, cf.

(46) The candidate made the electorate excited.
         [the electorate became excited]

Although noun + adjective complements, cf.

(47) The artist made the sky blue.
         [the sky be(came) blue]

are documented in Old English, I have found no clearly
translative examples of past participial complements
with causative make in the OED.

What is the origin of past participial complements with periphrastic causative make? While lacking
firm evidence,. I postulate that past participial complements with make developed from subjectless infinitives (which are often translated as passives),
and were strongly influenced by passive and resultative constructions with other periphrastic causatives.
For example, hatan frequently appears as a subjectless
infinitive

(48) Beowulf, 198-199
         Hēt him ȳđlidan gōdne gegyrwan (cited
         by Royster 1918:82)
         (= He ordered for him to make ready a
         good ship)

which may be interpreted passively,[12] i.e.

(49) He caused a good ship to be made ready for
         him.

and hatan, lætan, and don are predominantly resultative when they are used with past participial complements (either with or without subjects), e.g.

(50) Chaucer's Clerkes Tale E. 1098
         Hath don you kept (cited by Royster
         1918:90fn.)
         (= Has caused you to be preserved)
(51) Chaucer's Knightes Tale 1055 (A 1913)
         Hath don Ø wroght (cited by Royster
         1918:90fn.)
         (= Has caused to be made)

Given the possible passive interpretation of subjectless infinitives (e.g. (48)), it is not surprising
that many of the early infinitival complements with
make are explicitly passive:

(52) a1225 Juliana 38
         Ich makede þen wittie ysaye beon isahet
         þurh ant þurh to deađe (OED 53a)
         (= I made then wise sayings to be said
         through and through to death)

(53 c1450 <u>Merlin</u> 29
   The kynge made hem alle <u>be Shett</u> in a
   stronge house (OED 53a)
   (= The king had them all shut in a
   strong house)
(54) c1489 CAXTON Blanchardyn xlviii.185
   He shal to morowe make hym <u>to be hanged</u>
   (OED 53b)

   (= He shall tomorrow have him hanged)

While dating of documents is only approximate, the
first passive example of an infinitive complement
(a1225:(52)) appreciably precedes the first use of
past participles (a1300:(36)). If past participial
complements with <u>make</u> did originate in passive
infinitival complements, it is not at all surprising
that translative interpretations of past participles
should develop later than inherently passive constructions.

(d) <u>Locative</u>
  Locative complements with periphrastic causative
<u>make</u> apparently never became productive in standard
English. However, there are a number of citations
which seem to exemplify the paradigmatic type.
Figurative use of the positional interpretation of the
locative appears in the 14th and 15th centuries:

   (55) 1470-85 MALORY <u>Arthur</u> XVIII.xx.761
     Now hath dethe <u>made</u> vs two <u>at debate</u> for
     your loue (OED 48c)
     (= Now death has put the two of us in
     debate for your love)

Or, compare modern English

   (56) Make yourself at home.

Actual directional use of the locative complement is
also documented in the 15th century:

   (57) a1483 <u>Liber Niger</u> in Househ. <u>Ord</u>. (1790) 71
     Noe yoman of this office..to bere or
     <u>make oute</u> of this office any breade but
     <u>by knowledge</u> of the brevour (OED 91a)
   (58) a1483 <u>Liber Niger</u> in Househ. <u>Ord</u>. (1790) 25
     Lett it alwey be remembered to <u>make in</u>
     the Kinges doggettes..as often as it
     pleseth the King the prince to come or
     goe (OED 88a)

The fact that <u>make oute</u> and <u>make in</u> are not separated
by the object suggests that the verb plus particle

may be functioning as a single unit, rather than the
noun plus locative functioning as a reduced clause.
However, in other cases, the noun does intervene between make and the locative, e.g.

    (59) 1760-72 H. BROOKE Fool of Qual. (1809)
         I.142
         They would..make him away by pistol, or
         poison (OED 84a)

(though cf.

    (60) 1593 SHAKS, 2 Hen. VI, III.i.167
         To make away my guiltlesse Life (OED
         84a))

    Table III summarizes the major developments in
the history of periphrastic causative make. Where
possible, complements are arranged in order of
chronological appearance. The earliest citation of a
complement type is marked with "x". Mortality of
construction types in modern English is indicated by
"+".

Table III. Chronological Development of Periphrastic
        Causative Make

approximate date	complements: noun +					
	clause	noun	adjective	infinitive	past. part.	locative
1000	x	x	x			
1100						
				x: bare inf.		
1200				x: to inf.		
1300					x: passive	
						x: fig. (pos.)
1400						x: lit.(dir.)
1500						
				x: force		
1600						
1700						
1800						
1900				+: to inf.	rare: pass.	+: lit.

4.4 Have

Since have (Old English habban) did not exist as
a causative in Old English, it is possible not only to
follow its evolution through examples,[13] but also to
speculate on the kinds of syntactic or semantic restructurings which were necessary to give rise to the
new construction.[14] In addition, the earlier development of have as an auxiliary stimulates conjectures
about a possible relation between the emergence of
causative and auxiliary functions.

Although absent from earliest Old English, use of
habban as an auxiliary appeared by the 8th century,
considerably before the development of causative have.
The tense function developed directly out of a
possessive have + noun + past participle construction,
where the past participle functions as an adjective
modifying the accusative noun. For example, in

> (61) Alfred, Boethius 1.8
> ða (he) þas boc hæfde geleornode
> (= when (he) those books had in-a-
> state-of-learnedness)(cited by Trau-
> gott 1972a:94)

geleornode is a past participle which agrees (cf. -e)
in gender, number and case with the accusative plural
feminine boc.

However, in Old English, not all nominal and
adjectival uses bore surface inflection. The relevant
example here is strong neuter adjectives, which had no
overt marker in the accusative singular (and, in some
dialects, accusative plural). Therefore, in a sentence such as

> (62) Ic hæfde fæt gebrocen.

where fæt is an accusative singular neuter, the past
participial adjective gebrocen lacks surface inflection. This original possessive + adjectival construction was now open to reinterpretation whereby hæfde
and gebrocen came to function as a unit, and the
implied resultativeness of possession was overtly
expressed through perfective aspect:

> (63) I had broken a vessel.

This kind of reanalysis could then spread to other
possessive + adjectival constructions in which inflectional marking was originally obligatory,[15] e.g.

> (64) Alfred, Pastoral Care
> wiotona ðe...ða bec eall æ befullan

geliornod hæfdon
(= of-wise-men who...those books
completely learned had)
(cited by Traugott 1972a:94)

There is additional support for the hypothesis
that have developed into an auxiliary through surface
realization of resultativeness already inherent in the
simple verb. In other Germanic languages (cf. Lockwood 1968:114ff),[16] and in most Romance languages
(cf. Reighard 1971), an earlier form of possessive
have was later reanalyzed as an auxiliary. Moreover,
as was already mentioned, many Old English causative
verbs (i.e. which are also necessarily resultative)
assumed the function of auxiliaries. The important
question to be asked is, given the fact that Old
English habban was an aspectual marker before developing periphrastic causative interpretation, did the
causative develop out of the perfective rather than
directly out of the possessive?

There are several plausible arguments for linking
the causative with the perfective. Semantically, both
ultimately derive from possessive have, and both are
integrally resultative. On the surface, it would seem
that the same original possessive have + noun + past
participial adjective might have been reanalyzed in
two ways, where focus upon resultativeness was restructured as perfect, and focus upon the passive
value of the past participle[17] was restructured as
causative. While the perfective requires a change in
word order[18] in addition to syntactic/semantic restructuring, the causative does not. The surface subject of the original possessive is reanalyzed from an
Experiencer to an Agentive in the case of the perfect,
and also in the case of the true causative,[19] cf.

(65) possessive: Ic hæfde fæt gebrocen.
Experiencer
(I had a having-been-broken
vessel)
(66) perfect: I had broken a vessel.
Agent
(67) causative: I had a vessel broken.
Agent

A close examination of the data suggests, however,
that the development of perfective and causative have
were actually quite distinct. The argument hinges
upon differential use of past and future time. The
English perfective focused upon action which is already completed (i.e. past). Throughout Old and

Middle English, the only existing forms of the perfect
were present perfect and past perfect, e.g.

(68) present perfect: I have picked ten
bushels of apples.
(69) past perfect: I had picked ten bushels
of apples.

Future perfect constructions with auxiliary <u>shall</u> and
<u>will</u>, e.g.

(70) future perfect:[20] I will have picked ten
bushels of apples by the
time you return.

did not appear until the 15th century (cf. Traugott
1969). Compare now causative <u>have</u>. Semantically, the
causative is composed of not only resultativeness but
also inchoativeness, i.e. the change itself from state
of affairs X at time T_1 to state of affairs X' at time
T_2. While semantic analyses of modern English (cf.
McCawley 1968) make the inchoative explicit, the
notion of change is not normally expressed in surface
structure. However, in Middle English, when causative <u>have</u> first originated, the inchoative aspect of
causation was almost universally expressed through use
of expressed or implied futurity, that is, reference
at time T_1 to some point in the future (T_2).[21,22]
I hypothesize that the linguistic "vehicle" via which
causative use of <u>have</u> arose was the overt realization
of inchoativeness through the expression of futurity.
Once causative <u>have</u> became established within the language, use of implied or expressed futurity became
optional. This hypothesis does not deny the importance of a passive or happenstance feature associated
with the rise of causative <u>have</u>. However, I believe
that the role of future is <u>more</u> critical than that of
passive or happenstance.

Because of the high degree of ambiguity in so
many historical citations with <u>have</u>, the chronological
order I propose for the development of causative <u>have</u>
is only tentative. I will begin with a summary of my
findings, and then present examples and arguments
supporting the proposed chronology.

Causative <u>have</u> derives directly from possessive,
resultative <u>have</u>. While the emerging perfect focused
upon the resultative aspect of possessive <u>have</u>, causative <u>have</u> focused upon both resultative and inchoative. Possessive <u>have</u> + noun + past participial constructions are, in general, one syntactic source of
causatives, though there is no evidence of their being
either the sole or primary origin of causative <u>have</u>.

Have is first documented as a causative with clausal,
locative, adjectival, and past participial complements at approximately the same date (cl200). Infinitive and noun complements are not documented for at
least another century (late 14th century). The overwhelming majority of the early examples of all
complements (with the exception of locatives) involve
explicit or implied futurity. Although passive or
happenstance interpretations are particularly
prevalent with past participial constructions, they
also dominate a number of locative and infinitival
constructions.

(a) <u>Clause</u>
     Causative <u>have</u> is first cited with a clausal
complement at the end of the 12th century:

> (71) cl175 (?OE) <u>Bod. Hom.</u> 68/25
>   Þe wæl3a rice..walde þa habban
>   Lazarum..þæt he mid his fingræ hure
>   his tunga drypte (MED 10a)
>   (= The mighty rich man..would then
>   have Lazarus..that he with his fingers
>   at least moisten his tongue)

Subsequent use of clausal complements with <u>have</u> is,
however, very limited, supporting Macháček's (1969)
generalization about the decline of content clauses
in Middle English (though cf.

> (72) 1653 H. COGAN tr. <u>Pinto's Trav.</u> xlviii.185
>   Good luck would have it that this young
>   Damosel came hither (OED 18b))

Note the presence of futurity markers (<u>walde</u> and
<u>would</u>) in both clausal examples.

(b) <u>Locative</u>
     Locative complements with <u>have</u> also appeared
about the same time, persisting through the end of the
19th century, e.g.

> (73) al225 (?al200) Lay. <u>Brut</u> 759
>   Brutus hæfde his <u>folc</u> <u>bi-foren</u> & <u>bi-</u>
>   <u>hinden</u> (MED 10b)
>   (= Brutus had his people before and
>   behind)
> (74) cl430 <u>Arte Nombryng</u> E.E.T.S. 11
>   Euery part of the nombre multiplying is
>   to be hade <u>into</u> euery part of the
>   nombre to be multipliede (OED 16)
> (75) al475 <u>Ludus C.</u> 361/184
>   I askyd the aungyl to haue you <u>present</u>

(MED 10c)

(76) 1749 FIELDING Tom Jones XVII.iii
There I was had into a whole room full
of women (OED 16)

(77) 1889 STEVENSON Master of B. vi.176
A little later he was had to bed (OED
16)

Futurity is by no means obligatory (cf. (73), (76),
(77)), though it is present in at least one quarter
of the examples cited in the OED and MED. As in
modern English, many of the examples are resultative
in focus and positional in meaning (e.g. (73)), though
in other cases (e.g. (76),(77)) the force of the
locative does seem both causative (i.e. resultative
and inchoative) and directional. Finally, a significant number of the examples are passive (e.g. (74),
(76), (77)), though, judging from the dates, this
seems to be a 15th century development. What is of
primary importance for the present analysis is that
locative complements were originally productive and
often occurred with reference to future time.

(c) Adjective
Causative have with adjectival complement is
documented in the same general period as clausal and
locative complements:

(78) a1225 (?a 1200) Lay. Brut 8163
Þe oðer wolde him habben dæd (MED 10b)
(= The other wished to have him dead)

(79) c1325 (c1300) Glo. Chron. A 11221
So þat þe clerkes adde þe stretes
sone iler (MED 10b)
(= So that the clerks soon got the
streets cleared)

(80) c1390 Chaucer CT.NP.B. 4091
A beest..wold han maad areest Vp on
my body and han han me deed (MED 10b)
(= A beast would have taken prisoner
of my body and have had me dead)

As in the case of locative complements, its focus is
largely resultative, and an overt copula tends to have
been inserted in the complement, e.g.

(81) 1535 COVERDALE Jer. i.17
I will not haue the to be afrayd of
them (OED 18b)

While the adjectival complement does not seem to have
been particularly productive, it is significant that

all but one of the examples cited by the historical
dictionaries refer to future time. Modern English
resultative have + noun + adjective, e.g.

> (82) (?) The cook had the water hot last
>   Friday.

also tends to be used in the future, cf.

> (83) The cook will have the water hot in a
>   jiffy.

(d) Past Participle

Past participial complements begin to appear at
the end of the 12th century, becoming increasingly
productive with time. Many of the earliest examples
are happenstance passives; the clearly causative citations are predominantly implied future.[23]

> (84) cll75 (?OE) H Rood 4/24
>   He hæfde an fet to ðam anum iwroht (MED
>   10a) (= He had a deed to that one done)
>   (happenstance passive)
> (85) c1205 LAY. 32197
>   Þa com him ufel on, Swa godd hit wolde
>   habben idon (OED 18b)
>   (= Then evil came upon him, as god
>   wished to have it done)
>   (implied future)
> (86) al225 (?OE) Lamb. Hom. 37
>   Þu scalt et god seolf habben þine
>   sunne for3euene[24]   (MED 10a)
>   (= You shall eat god himself to have
>   your sins forgiven)
>   (implied future)
> (87) 1489 CAXTON Faytes of A. II.xxxv 150
>   Hanybal..cam by fore the cyte for to
>   haue hyt dystroyed (OED 17a)
>   (= Hannibal came before the city in
>   order to have it destroyed)
>   (implied future)
> (88) al533 LD. BERNERS Huon ciii.343
>   I haue had slayne mo then xx M. men,
>   besyde my thre neuewes and my yonger
>   brother (OED 18)
>   (happenstance passive)
> (89) 1604 SHAKS. Oth. II.iii.258
>   To haue their Balmy slumbers wak'd
>   with strife (OED 17a)
>   (implied future; happenstance passive)

What is the source of past participial complements
with causative have? Trnka (1924) derives the causa-

tive from passive subordinate clauses, e.g.

(90) clause: He would not have it that
               [someone stained his honor]

past participle: He would not have his
                  honor stained.

This interpretation seems reasonable, especially in
view of the fact that Old English causatives frequently occurred with passive infinitives, and in both Old
and Middle English, subjectless past participial
complements sometimes occurred where infinitives were
to be expected. Note, however, that the past
participial complement with have could not have
developed directly from have + noun + passive
infinitive, since infinitival complements with have
had not yet emerged.

Another relevant factor in the rise of past
participial complements may be the development of
happenstance passives. While it is not clear whether
happenstance passive have developed before causative
have (i.e. Trnka's thesis), the surface similarity and
frequent ambiguity of the constructions suggests some
sort of cross influence. Trnka (1924:26) associates
the rise of happenstance passive with the general
shift from impersonal to personal constructions in
Middle English. In both (91) and (92)

(91) Me hungrede.
     (=It hungered to me)
(92) I was hungry.

the personal pronoun is an Experiencer, yet in (92)
the Experiencer is subjectivalized. Consider now

(93) A book was given to me.
(94) I was given a book.
(95) I had a book given me.

While me is a Goal in both (93) and (95) and I is an
Experiencer in both (94) and (95), the writer or
speaker's interest in the subject I is stronger in
(95) than in (94) (see Baron 1974).

(c) Infinitives
    Infinitive complements do not appear until at
least the late 14th century. All of the examples I
found dated before the 17th century involve future:

(96) 1470-85 Malory, Morte d'Arthur 92, 21
             and [they] wold haue had Balen leue
             his swerd behynde hym (primary text)
             (= and [they] would have had Balen

> leave his sword behind him)
> (implied future)
> (97) 1591 SHAKS. <u>Two Gent</u>. III.i.80
>   What would your Grace haue me <u>to do</u>
>   in this? (OED 18b)
>   (implied future)

Early non-future citations seem to be examples of happenstance <u>have</u> rather than causative, cf.

> (98) 1641 HINDE J. Bruen xxxiv. 107
>   Jacob had his wife Rachel <u>to dye</u>
>   suddenly in his journey on his hand
>   (OED 18)

Finally, use of the <u>to</u>-complementizer with <u>have</u> may have been dominant in Late Middle and Early Modern English (cf. (96), (97)) though it drops out by the 19th century, cf.

> (99) 1860 <u>Grandmother's Money</u> I.119 (Hoppe)
>   I had a horse <u>run</u> away with me (OED
>   18)

What is the source of infinitive complements with causative <u>have</u>? Trnka (1924:22) historically derives infinitive (and present participial) constructions from active subordinate clauses, e.g.

> (100) clause: he would have it
>   that [I help him]
>
>   infinitive: he would have me help
>   him
>   present participle: he would have me
>   helping him

Semantically, Trnka associates the infinitive with a purpose clause, cf.

> (101) He would have me for to help him.

This derivation of the infinitive from the clausal complement would then be parallel to the case of <u>make</u>. Another factor in the growth of infinitives with <u>have</u> may be the extensive use of Old French <u>faire</u> + infinitive, which may have strengthened the already existing causative complement type in English (cf. 4.2). Alternatively (though less plausibly), the infinitive might represent an elaboration of the earlier <u>have</u> + noun + past participial construction (cf. Macháček 1969).

(f) <u>Noun</u>
Noun complements are first documented in the 15th century:

> (102) 1470-85 Malory, Morte d'Arthur 221,21
>   You wold haue me a <u>coward</u> (primary
>   text)
> (103) 1630 B. JOHNSON <u>New Inn</u> III.i.22
>   Sir Pierce, <u>I'll have him a <u>Cavalier</u></u>
>   (OED 18b)

As in modern English, all examples are basically resultative and refer to future time.

The following diagram (104) summarizes the relation between possession, causation, time, aspect, and mood with respect to <u>have</u>. Constructions are entered at the approximate date at which they first appear.

(104)   HAVE

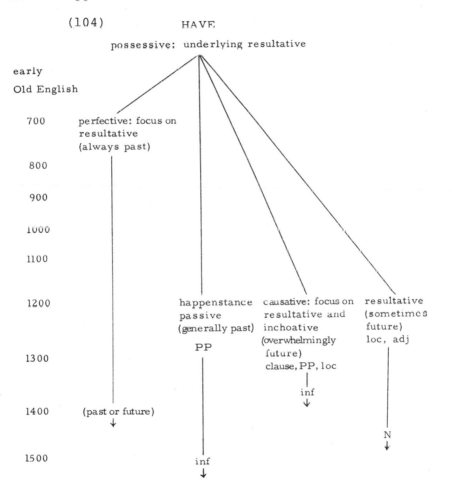

Table IV summarizes the development of causative
have. Basically resultative uses are also indicated
because of their integral relation with causative
have. Constructions which are, in modern English,
generally restricted to future use or are predominantly resultative are marked F and R, respectively.
Complement types are listed in chronological order as
far as is possible. The earliest citation of a complement type is marked with "x". Mortality of construction types at later periods is indicated by "†".

Table IV.   Chronological Development of Periphrastic
            Causative Have

approximate date	complements: noun +					
	clause	locative	adjective	past. part.	infinitive	noun
1100	x			x		
1200		x	x			
1300						
1400					x: to inf.	
					x: bare inf.	x
1500						
1600						
1700						
1800						
1900		F, R	F, R		†: to inf.	F, R

4.5 Get

Historically, get is the last of the three verbs
make, have, and get to acquire causative status. The

main verb get is a loan-word borrowed from Old Norse
(O.N. geta "to get, obtain, beget"). Although the
first documentation is not until Early Middle English
(c1200), the verb must surely have already appeared
in colloquial Late Old English. The following examples are classified with respect to two basic English
meanings of the main verb get:

"fetch, acquire (through one's own agency)"

(105) c1200 ORMIN 10219
        Forr whase itt iss þatt gredi3 iss
        To winnenn erþlic ahhte, A33 alls he
        mare & mare gett A33 lisste himm
        affterr mare (OED 1)
        (= For whosoever it is that is greedy
        to gain earthly goods, always as he
        gets more and more he desires more
        and more)
(106) c1330 R. BRUNNE Chron. (1810) 276
        Þider 3e alle salle ride, a faire
        prey salle 3e gete (OED 1)
        (= Thither you all shall ride, a fair
        prey shall you get)

"receive (without subject's own agency)"

(107) c1250 Gen. & Ex. 1497
        'Broðer,' quad he, 'sel me ðo wunes,
        ðe queðen ben ðc firme sunes, ðat ic
        ðin firme birðehe qete (OED 10)
        (= 'Brother,' he said, 'sell me that
        dwelling which is said to be the
        first son's, that I receive your
        rights of the first-born)
(108) c1300 Havelok 908
        Wel is set þe mete þu etes And þe
        hire þat þu getes (OED 10)
        (= Well is placed the food you eat
        and the payment that you receive)

    Unlike causative have, the development of English
causative get has received comparatively little attention in the literature (cf. Yamakawa 1958:175).
Crowell (1955) does trace the evolution of four "core
meanings" of get in English: "obtain", "effect (the
change to the position or state expressed by the
modifying complement)", "possess", and "must", but
includes causatives as a subtype of "effect" without
explicitly identifying their causative semantic function. Jespersen (1961,5:292) and Trnka (1930:60) mention the causative construction, but only Yamakawa

(1958)[25] attempts to trace its syntactic and semantic
origins. Most other treatments of the verb are
devoted either to a comparison of the get and be
passives (e.g. Hatcher 1949; R. Lakoff 1971), or to
defending or condemning use of get in the senses
"effect", "possess", or "must".[26]
      What are possible syntactic and semantic sources
of causative get? Given the comparatively late entry
of the verb into English (i.e. approximately 1200),
one reasonable hypothesis might be that causative get
developed on direct analogy with causative make and
have. A second alternative (if one subscribes to the
hypothesis that causative have basically emerged
through reanalysis of a possessive have + noun + past
participle construction) is that causative get arose
through a similar restructuring of a basic acquisitive
or receptive get + noun + past participle, cf.

      (109) acquire, receive: The dog got the dirty
                                rug.
      (110) causative: The dog got the rug dirty.

While the first hypothesis may help explain the later
spread of causative get, I will argue that causative
get first originated not in past participial but in
get + locative constructions. This "precausative"
(i.e. immediate precursor to causative) get + locative
construction later became an overt causative by insertion of a noun between get and the locative element.
Infinitival constructions followed soon after, though
past participial complements did not develop for at
least a century after get + noun + locative.
Adjectival complements (both causative and non-causative) did not become productive until about the same
time as past participles. Use of get + past
participle in the sense of "become", as a possessive,
and as a tense marker were also late developments,
and happenstance get passives only emerged in the 18th
and 19th centuries.[27]

(a) Locative
      Simple intransitive get + locative constructions
(what I am calling "precausative") are first documented in English in about the year 1300, i.e. approximately   a century after the earliest citation of
transitive get:

      (111) a1300 Cursor M. 7902
                  In batail sua he suld be sette, þat
                  he awai suld neuer gette (OED 54a)
                  (= In battle so he should be set,
                  that he away should never get, i.e.

> In battle he should thus be situated
> so that he should never get away)
>
> (112) a1300 Cursor M. 17350
> Þai..did to sper þe dors fast.. þat
> he suld noþer-quar get vtc (OED 64a)
> (= They had the doors made fast..
> that he should nowhere get out)

The first true causative constructions with get differ
from the precausative only by the presence in underlying structure of a noun between get and the locative. The earliest citations date back to the mid
14th century, e.g.

> (113) c1350 Will.Palerne 2895
> Þe grettest of þe grim bestes he gat
> to prison sone (OED 27)
> (= The greatest of the grim beasts
> he got to prison soon)
>
> (114) c1400 (?c1390) Gawain 1571
> He gete þe bonk at his bak, bigynez
> to scrape (MED 3b)
> (= He got the hillside at his back,
> begins to paw the ground)

Jespersen (1961,3:325,331) suggests that get +
locative constructions derive from transitive,
reflexives, cf.

> (115) transitive, reflexive: I got myself down.
>
>   intransitive: I got down.

While the theory is appealing (and perhaps ultimately
correct), the first documentation in the OED and MED
of get + reflexive + locative constructions occurs not
only after the appearance of simple get + locative
(i.e. 1300), but also later than initial examples of
get + noun + locative (i.e. c1350). The first citations of get + reflexive + locative do not appear
until the mid 15th century:

> (116) c1450 Alph. Tales 132/20
> Sho gatt hur vp into a tre (MED 4a)
> (= She got herself up into a tree)
>
> (117) 1513 MORE in Grafton Chron. (1568)II.765
> [She] got her selfe in all the hast
> possible..out of the palace of
> Westminister (OED 27b)

In fact, the familiar "get thee hence" is not cited by
the OED until the 16th century:

(118) 1530 PALSGR. 562/I
       Get the hence (OED 27b)

Is it semantically reasonable to hypothesize that
get causatives originated in simple intransitive
locative constructions? I will argue that such a
derivation is, in fact, plausible in that the locative
merely gives surface realization to an underlying
inchoative element which is present in the original
transitive verb.

As a transitive verb, get, in either its acquisitive or receptive sense, implies possession, result,
and change in the state of affairs (i.e. inchoative).
If it is the case that

(119) My son got a tricycle for his birthday.

then my son now possesses a tricycle as the result of
a change in the state of affairs. The underlying element of result by itself is given surface realization
in constructions using get as a perfective auxiliary,
e.g.

(120) I got finished with my housework.

(cf. below). The underlying possessive aspect of get
receives two types of expression: get as a past
participle, and got as a main verb (in non-standard
English), e.g.

(121) past participle: I haven't got a dime
                         to my name.
(122) main verb: I got something to tell
                         you, Buster.

The past participial construction developed during the
16th century (cf. below). The use of got as a main
verb meaning "possess" is non-standard, occurring in
some dialects (e.g. New York City). Crowell (1955:
171) dates the construction back to the 17th century
(cf. 5.6).

One surface realization of the notion of a
change in the state of affairs is use of a locative
construction.[28] In the sentence

(123) Get your dirty shoes off the table!

off specifies the desired change in the state of
affairs (i.e. on at time T_1, off at time T_2). A
similar general analysis also applies to have with
locative complements in future contexts. In (124)

(124) I'll have the storm windows up by 5 this
           afternoon.

the initial state of affairs at time T_1 is that the
storm windows are down, while at time T_2, they are,
presumably, properly in place.

Why should locatives be the source of causative
get but not of causative have? Have is primarily a
resultative verb: not only is the verb itself
stative, but its locative complements are, at least in
modern English, normally positional. Get, however,
is primarily an inchoative verb. Not only is the main
verb non-stative, but its locative complements are
basically directional. Given these inchoative/
resultative, non-stative/stative, directional/posi-
tional contrasts, it is not unreasonable that locative complements might serve as the sole origin of
causative get, while with have, locative complements
were at best supportive of semantically future constructions with clauses and past participles.
Historical citations of precausative (i.e. get +
locative) and causative get frequently express
futurity (cf. (111), (112) above; (126), (137) below).
However, I would argue that futurity was not originally obligatory since the directional locative already
implied a change in time.

(b) Infinitive

The next documented complement type with causative get was the infinitive. The earliest examples
appear at the beginning of the 15th century.

   (125) a1400 Floris (Suth) 107/1007
             Yf it were þy wylle, Þou ne qetest
             not þat maide to spylle (MED 8b)
             (= If it were your will, do not have
             that maid perish)
   (126) c1430 (a1410) Love Mirror 106
             Abideth a litell, and I schal getc
             3ow to haue more (MED 8b)
             (= Wait a while, and I shall get you
             to have more)
   (127) 1596 SHAKS. Tam. Shr. I.ii.38
             I bad the rascall knocke vpon your
             gate, And could not get him for my
             heart to do it (OED 30)

Although use of the to-complementizer appears in the
earliest examples as well as in modern English, the
complementizer was apparently optional in Early
Modern English, e.g.

   (128) 1598 SHAKS. Merry W. II.ii.76
             They could neuer get her so much as

sippe on a cup with the prowdest of
them all (OED 30)

(129) 1647 W. BROWNE tr. Gomberville's
Polexander IV.v. 339
By the helpe of a great tumult which
he heard in the lower towne, hee got
slide some troopes into the enemies
intrenchments (OED 30)

Passive infinitival complements with causative
get do not appear until the late 16th century, e.g.

(130) c1592 MARLOWE Jew of Malta III.iii.
Abig. I am bold to sollicite thee.
Fry. Wherein?
Abig. To get me be admitted for a Nun
(OED 30b)

(131) 1681 H. MORE Exp. Dan. 166
Laodice..got him to be poisoned
(OED 30b)

(132) 1736 LEDIARD Life Marlborough I.20
His Father got him to be made Page of
Honour (OED 30b)

All of these examples are causative, rather than
happenstance passive, in that the higher subject is an
Agent who intends the action of the complement, i.e.

(133) [You] get [someone admit me for a nun]
(134) Laodice got [someone poison him]
(135) His father got [someone made him page of
honor]

However, these passive infinitives may, as was possibly the case with causative have (cf. Trnka 1924) have
supported the development of get + noun + past
participle, which did not arise until the early 16th
century (cf. below). While the earliest citations of
passive infinitives occur at least 50 years after
those for get + noun + past participle, the dates are
close enough to warrant an investigation of the
spoken rather than written style.
What is the source of infinitival complements
with causative get? Unlike infinitival complements
with make and have, there is no possibility of the
infinitive developing out of a clausal complement,
since there is no historical evidence of causative get
with clausal complement -- at any period -- in either
the OED or MED. I conjecture that infinitival clauses
with get arose through direct analogy with Middle
English have and make (and also don, perhaps the most
popular Middle English causative).

(c) <u>Past Participle</u>
    Use of past participial complements did not
develop until the 16th century, e.g.

>   (136) 1500-20 DUNBAR Poems xliii.43
>   Thay get <u>indoist</u> Alhaill thair evidens
>   (OED 28a)
>   (137) 1548 <u>Invent. Ch. Goods</u> (Surtees) 119
>   I can get no such some [=sum]
>   <u>confessed</u> (OED 28a)
>   (138) 1779 R. GRAVES <u>Columella</u> I. 184
>   Poor Barty had applied and got himself
>   <u>appointed</u> a writer to the East India
>   Company (OED 28a)

Beginning in the 19th century, there are some examples
where <u>get</u> is itself made passive, although the causative action is still intentional, e.g.

>   (139) 1843 CARLYLE <u>Past & Pr.</u> IV.i
>   The Bravest men..had here..<u>been got
>   selected</u> (OED 28a)
>   (140) 1870 CARLYLE <u>Corr. W. Emerson</u> (1883) II.
>   331
>   I am by no means certain..that the
>   whole of this amendatory programme
>   will <u>get</u> itself <u>performed</u> to equal
>   satisfaction (OED 28a)

Up until the 18th century, all examples are
clearly causative, i.e. the higher subject is an
Agent or Instrument, and if an Agent, the causative
action is intentional. The first example of a
happenstance passive, with either an Experiencer as a
subject or an Agent who does not intend the results
of his action, is in 1787:

>   (141) 1787 T. JEFFERSON <u>Writ.</u>(1859) II 249
>   I <u>got</u> my right wrist <u>dislocated</u>
>   (OED 28b)
>   (subject = unintending Agent or
>   Experiencer)
>   (142) 1790 J. B. MORETON <u>Mann W. Ind.</u> 23
>   To avoid heats and colds..as well as
>   <u>getting</u> your feet <u>wet</u> (OED 28b)
>   (subject = unintending Agent)

Thus, the development of causative <u>get</u> + noun + past
participle differs from that of <u>have</u> + noun + past
participle in that with <u>get</u>, happenstance interpretation of the complement is a late development, while
with <u>have</u>, the causative and happenstance interpretations seem to have emerged simultaneously.

What is the source of past participial complements with causative get? Yamakawa (1958:156)
suggests ultimately deriving the construction from the
main transitive verb "acquire". As Yamakawa does not
mention locative complements at all, and only refers
in passing to the fact that infinitival complements
with causative get emerged before past participial
complements, it is difficult to know how direct a
relation Yamakawa is actually positing between get +
noun + past participle and transitive, acquisitive
get.

(d) Perfective
    At approximately the same time past participial
complements were emerging with causative get, get also
began to assume the function of a perfective
auxiliary. The construction appears as early as
Shakespeare, e.g.

> (143) SHAKS. Per. IV.ii.66
>   And by the time I had got this all
>   done,..the day was tiptoe on the
>   threshold of the east (OED)
>
>   (cf. by the time I did this all)

As with the case of perfective have, as well as with
the use of Old English hatan and lætan as auxiliaries,
get as a perfective functions as a surface realization
of underlying resultativeness.[29]

(e) Possession
    In addition to its causative and perfective
functions, get also came to be used as a possessive
towards the end of the 16th century. In this case,
however, it was get itself which functioned as the
past participle in a have + got + noun construction,
e.g.

> (144) 1596 SHAKS. Merch.V. II.ii.99
>   What a beard hast thou got; thou hast
>   got more haire on thy chin, then
>   Dobbin my philhorse has on his taile
>   (OED 24)
> (145) 1738 SWIFT Pol.Conversat. 68
>   Miss, you have got my Handkerchief;
>   pray, let me have it (OED 24)

(cf. Crowell 1955).

(f) Adjective
    The first instance of causative get + noun +
adjective is not documented until the late 16th century,[30] cf.

(146) 1590 SPENSER F.Q. I.i.19
      He..knitting all his force, got one
      hand free (OED 29)
(147) 1605 SHAKS. Lear I.iv.8
      Let me not stay a iot for dinner, go
      get it ready (OED 29)
(148) 1847 MARRYAT Childr. N. Forest xi
      Let us first get him all right again
      (OED 29)

A related construction employing an adjectival pre-
positional phrase began to appear earlier in the 16th
century, e.g.

(149) 1530 PALSGR. 562/2
      I get a wench with chylde, je engrosse
      (OED 27c)
(150) 1748 Anson's Voy. II.iv.161
      We exerted ourselves in getting our
      ships in readiness for the sea (OED
      27c)

In view of this latter construction which is locative
in surface form, it is plausible that get + noun +
adjectival causative constructions historically derive
directly from the earlier locative complements (compare (150)("in readiness") with (147)("ready")).
Alternatively, past participial complements, which
appear almost a full century before surface adjectives,
may be the immediate source. Another possibility, of
course, is that both locatives and past participles
provided relevant models.

(q) Inchoative
      Towards the end of the 16th and beginning of the
17th centuries, the verb get began to assume another
new overt function, that of "become". As in the case
of locatives with causative get, the underlying
inchoative element became dominant in surface structure. The first examples appear in get + adjective
constructions:

(151) 1596 SHAKS. Merch. V. I.i.134
      How to get cleere of all the debts I
      owe (OED 33)
(152) 1659 B. HARRIS Parival's Iron Age 169
      Having, with very much adoe, gotten
      loose from their Enemies [etc.] (OED
      33)

Syntactically, the surface inchoative might be analyzed as a surface variation of the causative get + noun
+ adjective construction, where the nominal element is

a reflexive which has been deleted, i.e.

>(153) How to get (myself) clear of all the
>   debts I owe
>(154) Having...gotten (themselves) loose from
>   their enemies

The second construction using get with the meaning "become" was get + past participle. The earliest
example is documented in the mid 17th century:

>(155) 1652 GAULE Magastrom. 361
>   A certain Spanish pretending
>   Alchymist..got acquainted with foure
>   rich Spanish merchants (OED 34b)
>(156) 1823 SCORESBY Whale Fishery 183
>   We got entangled among a quantity of
>   heavy drift-ice (OED 34b)

Inchoative get + past participle could easily have
derived from causative get + noun + past participle by
deletion of a reflexive object, cf.

>(157) A certain Spanish pretending alchemist
>   got (himself) acquainted
>(158) We got (ourselves) entangled

A third inchoative construction, get + noun,
appeared in the 18th century:

>(159) 1768 STERNE Sent. Journ. (1778) II. 158
>   (Paris)
>   I had got master of my secret just in
>   time (OED 33)
>(160) 1874 DASENT Half a Life III.88
>   You must not suppose we got very great
>   friends with Honora Tailby all at
>   once (OED 33)

Since English never developed a causative get + noun
+ noun construction, e.g.

>(161) *The army will get you a soldier

it is not possible to derive the get + noun construction in the same fashion as the other inchoatives.
However, this need not create a problem in analysis,
since the nominal seems to be a late variation on the
adjective construction in that the substantive, like
the adjective, qualifies a change in the subject, cf.

>(162) *I got master
>(163) I got master of my secret[31]
>(164) *We got friends
>(165) We got very great friends[31]

(h) <u>Passive</u>
      The final stage in the evolution of <u>get</u> which is
relevant here is the emergence of a true passive,
happenstance <u>get</u> + past participle. This construction
is extremely recent in English, not being documented
until the 19th century:

> (166) 1826 DISRAELI <u>Viv. Grey</u> II.i
>   His Lordship was voted a bore, and
>   <u>got shelved</u>   (OED 34b)
>   (cf. was shelved)
> (167) 1887 RIDER HAGGARD <u>Jess</u> vi
>   I..<u>got caught</u> in the storm (OED 33b)
>   (cf. was caught)

It is possible that this passive use of <u>get</u> derives
directly from the adjectival and past participial
inchoative constructions.[32] This hypothesis is
supported not only by surface similarity and chronological ordering, but also by the fact that the <u>get</u> +
past participle construction is frequently ambiguous
between inchoative and passive interpretations (cf.
Hatcher 1949). There is, however, an alternative
hypothesis. Given the close proximity between the
emergence of happenstance <u>get</u> + noun + past participle
(i.e. late 18th century) and the first examples of
passive <u>get</u> + past participle (early 19th century), it
is conceivable that happenstance <u>get</u> + noun + past
participle is the immediate source of the <u>get</u> passive.
      The following diagram (168) summarizes the
emergence of causative, perfective, possessive,
inchoative, and passive interpretations of <u>get</u>. The
left-to-right ordering used is based upon chronology
and order of discussion in the text. I have not
attempted to represent the historical origins of each
construction. Constructions are entered at the
approximate date at which they first appear.

(168)

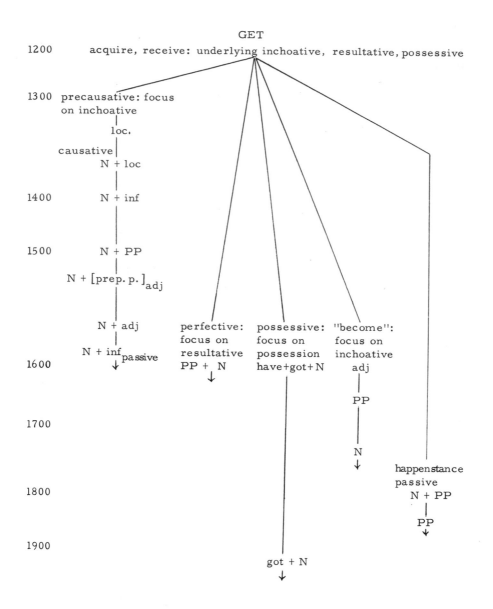

Table V summarizes the development of causative
get. Complement types are listed in order of chronological emergence. The earliest citation of a
complement type is marked with "x". Mortality of
construction types at later periods is indicated by
"†".

Table V.   Chronological Development of Periphrastic
           Causative Get

approximate date	complements: noun +				
	precausative	locative	infinitive	past participle	adjective
1300	x (get + loc)	x			
1400			x: to inf.		
1500			x: bare inf.	x	(x: prep. p) x
1600					
1700					
1800					
1900			† :bare inf.		

Footnotes

[1] But cf. Langenfelt (1933) on colloquial Late Middle English. Also cf. Salmon (1965) on colloquial Shakespearian English. Royster (1922:342-343) suggests that colloquial Middle English documents may help illuminate "habits and practices of the widely used Old English language that do not appear in one of our formal Old English literary compositions."

[2] However, Royster (1922) argues that causative <u>don</u> was far more widespread in spoken Old English than is suggested by literary documentation.

[3] In modern German, <u>lassen</u> is the normal periphrastic causative, e.g.
        Ich lasse ein Haus bauen. (=I am having a
        house built)
though it also indicates permission, e.g.
        Der Oberst liess die Soldaten zwei Stunden
        ruhen. (=The colonel let the soldiers rest
        two hours)

[4] But Royster (1918) argues that causative and permissive meanings developed separately from an Indo-European root *$l\tilde{e}$-i meaning 'strike', i.e.

[5] And also, with some periphrastics, occasional uses of noun + predicate adjective. In general, use of content clauses was more widespread in Old English than infinitives throughout the syntactic system. In later periods, the infinitive has become dominant (cf. Macháček 1969).

[6] Royster (1922:353) notes a similar function as auxiliary in Old Norse: hann let hana verða takna (=he caused her to be taken i.e. he seized her).

[7] Cf. Traugott (1969) for a discussion of the development of auxiliaries in Middle and Early Modern English.

[8] The obvious exception in English is <u>cause</u>.

[9]Cf. Royster (1918, 1922), Yoshioka (1908), and
Gzhanyants (1958) for discussion of the semantic
development of hatan, lætan, don, and macian.

[10]I will omit discussion of present participial
complements, but will discuss each of the other major
complement types listed in Table II.

[11]Macháček (1969) argues more generally that Middle
English infinitives developed out of substantive
rather than clausal constructions.

[12]An alternative (active) interpretation would be
        He caused [someone] to make ready a good ship
        for him.

[13]Cf. Trnka (1924, 1930); Kruisinga (1925,II.i:310ff);
Poutsma (1929, 1.2:804ff); Yamakawa (1958); Poldauf
(1967).

[14]Cf. Trnka (1924); Van der Gaaf (1931); Yamakawa
(1958); Traugott (1972a).

[15]Although restructuring became quite widespread in
subsequent centuries, modern English still retains the
original possessive have + noun + past participial
adjective construction, e.g.
        If you eat any more carrots, you won't have
        any left for the salad.
(cf. Yamakawa 1958:170).

[16]While have occurs as an auxiliary in all the old
West Germanic languages, Gothic evidences only the
synthetic preterite

[17]I.e. in the surface structure, the underlying
(active) complement appears in the passive, e.g.
        The custodian had the windows washed
            [someone washed the windows]
not in the sense of happenstance passive, which may be
active in surface structure cf.
        I had two goldfish die on me
            [two goldfish died on me]

[18]Change in word order did not regularly occur until
at least Late Middle English, cf.
        Dan Michel, Ayenbite of Inwit
                Hwanne þe kempe heþ his vela3e y-veld
                (when the champion has his fellow

                         struck down, i.e. has struck down his
                         fellow)
(cf. Bøgholm 1939:227).   In other forms of Germanic,
the word order shift did not regularly occur, cf.
         Modern German: Ich habe einen Brief geschrieben
                         (=I have written a letter)
         Dutch: De kommandant had de soldaten
                         bij de mensen van het dorp
                         ingekwartierd
                         (=The commander had quartered the
                         soldiers with the people of the
                         town) (cf. Kruisinga 1940)
         Anglo-Irish: O'Flaherty, The Black Soul
                         He has my heart broken
                         (= He has broken my heart)
                         (cited by Yamakawa 1958)
The Dutch hebben + noun + past participle is, as
Kruisinga (1940) observes, ambiguous between
perfective and causative.   In modern German, the
problem of ambiguity does not arise because lassen,
not haben, is the periphrastic used to form causatives.

[19] In the case of happenstance have, the subject
remains Experiencer.   Trnka (1924) seems to imply that
happenstance have developed before causative have,
though I have found it difficult either to
substantiate or refute this claim.

[20] Curme (1931:372) notes that in colloquial American
speech, the original word order of the possessive
construction is more natural, i.e.
         I will have ten bushels of apples picked
         by the time you return.

[21] Trnka (1924:20ff) maintains that causative have
actually originated in a will + have + $\begin{Bmatrix} \text{infinitive} \\ \text{participle} \end{Bmatrix}$
construction, while Yamakawa (1958:181) interprets
the use of will or would as an "external means" helping to disambiguate between perfective and causative
(n.b. Yamakawa implies that causative have derives
directly from the perfect).   Several other grammarians (e.g. Poutsma 1929, 1.2; Kruisinga 1925,II:
310) have also commented upon the frequency with
which some marker of the future historically appears
with past participial and infinitival complements of
causative have.

[22] In Old English, future time was indicated like the present. Old English will<u>an</u> was nearly always a main verb meaning "to inten<u>d</u>, to want". Not until Middle English did <u>will</u> assume auxiliary status as a regular marker of <u>future</u> time. Yet semantically, Old English will<u>an</u> already implied futurity through prediction or request.

[23] According to Trnka (1924:22) futurity was probably obligatory with causative <u>have</u> + past participial complements until at least <u>the</u> time of Shakespeare.

[24] Note use of the (adjectival) ending -<u>e</u> on for3euene agreeing with <u>sunne</u>.

[25] However, also cf. Hatcher 1949:433 fn.

[26] Since the late 18th century, prescriptivists have held in disdain many of the extended uses of <u>get</u>. Even in the 20th century, Kennedy (1920:42) writes with respect to the "effect" meaning of <u>get</u> that

> one hesitates to encourage too freely the use of many of these combinations because of the responsibility of the trained and farsighted student of English for the maintenance of certain standards in usage.

However, such writers as Mencken (1938:604) defend colloquial usage as an acceptable norm:

> Why should a foreigner be taught to say that he has <u>disembarked</u> from a ship? Isn't it sufficient for him to say that he <u>got off</u>? And why should he be taught to say that he has <u>recovered</u> from the flu, or <u>escaped</u> the police, or <u>ascended</u> a stairway, or <u>boarded</u> a train, or <u>obtained</u> a job? Isn't it enough to say that he has <u>got over</u> the first, <u>got away</u> from the second, <u>got up</u> the third, <u>got on</u> the fourth, and simply <u>got</u> the fifth?

(Cf. Crowell (1955:Chapter 1) for a review of the arguments supporting or condemning the extended uses <u>get</u>). Despite the lack of concrete evidence, it is conceivable that similar negative sanctions against causative <u>get</u> by prescriptivists are partly responsible for grammarians' general failure to accord causative <u>get</u> the same in-depth analysis as other causatives.

[27]I have no data on the development of causative <u>get</u>
with clausal complements. However, unlike the case of
<u>make</u> and <u>have</u>, where the clausal complement is one of
the first causative constructions to develop, it
appears that <u>get</u> + it + clause, if grammatical at all,
is a 19th or 20th century construction which developed
on analogy with <u>have</u> and <u>make</u>.
    There are also no data on the construction type
causative <u>get</u> + noun + noun, which apparently has
never been grammatical in English. However, cf. discussion below of inchoative <u>get</u> + modified noun.

[28]The other type is use of <u>get</u> in the sense of "become" (cf. below).

[29]Yamakawa (1958:186) seems to suggest that the
causative use of <u>get</u> + noun + past participle emerges
directly from the perfective. However, given the
slightly earlier historical dating of the causative as
well as the prior existence of past participial
complements with causative <u>have</u> and <u>make</u>, this
hypothesis is in need of supporting evidence.

[30]The MED cites the following passive example over a
century earlier:

        c1450 <u>Pilgr. LM</u> 206
                The flesh shal first be roten and
                neewe geten ayen at the general
                assemblee (MED 8a)

However, the editors interpret this use of <u>geten</u> as
meaning "produce, create", rather than "cause", cf.

        ?c1400 (c1340) *Rolle <u>Psalter</u> (Sid) Cant. Mo.
                2.27
                God þat þe gate [UC 64: gast] þou
                forsoke, & þou hathe forgetyne lord
                þi maker (MED 8a)

[31](163) and (165) are not grammatical in 20th century
English.

[32]According to Hatcher (1949:433 fn.), this is the
position of the OED.

Chapter 5

ONTOGENETIC DEVELOPMENT OF PERIPHRASTIC CAUSATIVES
IN (AMERICAN) ENGLISH: LONGITUDINAL STUDIES

In the last chapter, we traced the semantic and
syntactic development of the three English periphrastic causative verbs have, make, and get. We can
now place along side these data longitudinal and
experimental studies on the acquisition of these constructions by children learning English as a native
language. The longitudinal data (i.e. speech samples
of conversation collected over a period of time) on
the three verbs are presented in Chapter 5, with the
experimental studies being discussed in Chapter 6.

5.1 Ontogenetic Hypotheses

The major purpose of the longitudinal analysis
is to discover how children begin to use make, get,
and have as periphrastic causative verbs, and to trace
the order in which the various complements emerge with
each verb.
What kinds of hypotheses might be made about the
ontogenetic development of these periphrastic causative constructions on the basis of general knowledge
about diachrony and first language acquisition? I
have hypothesized (cf. Chapter 1) that children may
effect linguistic change through the natural process
of learning to speak. Before analyzing acquisition
data, it is therefore useful to ask what kinds of
changes have taken place over time, and whether these
are the sorts of changes for which children may have
been responsible. This approach does not entail
literally predicting ontogenetic recapitulation of
phylogenetic processes. Rather, it proposes that
prior knowledge of diachrony may suggest particular
ontogenetic hypotheses which might otherwise never
have been posed (cf. Sinclair 1971) much the same way
as ontogenetic data may suggest the plausibility of
new diachronic hypotheses (cf. 1.4 above).
In tracing the diachronic development of make,
have, and get I hypothesized that periphrastic causative uses of these verbs historically evolved from
non-periphrastic, non-causative make, have, and get.
If we assume that (a) in English, periphrastic causative constructions are syntactically and semantically
more complex than their non-causative counterparts,
and (b) children generally learn simpler constructions
before more complex ones, then it is reasonable to

predict that children will learn non-causative uses of make, have, and get before learning causative uses. This hypothesis may be tested with respect to all three periphrastics.

Chapter 4 traced the order in which complement types historically emerged with periphrastic causative make, have, and get. However, before asking what similarities these three chronologies have to their ontogenetic counterparts, it is necessary to consider what is already known about child language acquisition processes in general. These data may suggest that while some historical changes may have originated in child language (in that the historical processes involved are parallel to normal linguistic behavior of children), there are other types of changes which almost certainly must have originated in adult speech (in that the processes involved are not at all typical of child language).

Consider first infinitival and clausal complements. Historically, clausal complements emerged as one of the first periphrastic causative expressions with make and have (cf. Tables III and IV). Similarly, diachronic development of infinitival complements with make and get followed within approximately a century of the first periphrastic construction with each verb (cf. Tables III and V). Are there any grounds for postulating that young children may have been the source of these innovations? Ontogenetic studies clearly argue against such a hypothesis. In general, clausal complements of any type are rare in the speech of preschool children, although, as the data in this chapter will illustrate, preschoolers do use periphrastic causatives with other complements. Infinitival complements (in general) begin to appear in the speech of two-year-olds (cf. Limber 1973). However, infinitives are far less productive than other complement types (e.g. locative, adjective, past participle). In light of such ontogenetic evidence, there is therefore no reason to believe that historically, young children may have initiated or spread these early clausal or infinitival complements with periphrastic causative verbs.

While clausal and infinitival complements with periphrastic causatives are not likely to have originated in the speech of two or three-year-old children, one might argue that other complement types, such as locatives, may be historically based in the language of children. A large number of ontogenetic studies (e.g. Leopold 1939; Braine 1963; Brown and Fraser 1964; Miller and Ervin 1964) have pointed out

that overt locatives (as a construction type) are
among the earliest productive forms which children use
at the one and two-word stages of language acquisition. On the basis of this observation, we may turn
to the historical data and ask whether the diachronic
development of locative complements with periphrastic
causatives is conceivably related to the natural
process of language acquisition.

In analyzing the development of get in the
history of English I attempted to show that causative
use of get emerged from a "precausative" get +
locative construction by insertion of a noun between
the verb and locative, rather than directly from
transitive get + noun. Given the importance of locative constructions in early child language, I predict
that children also develop a causative use of get
from non-causative (though, I would argue, precausative) get + locative. While locatives seem to have
been less important in the development of make and
have as periphrastic causatives, it is still possible
that the historical emergence of locative complements
with these verbs might also be traced to first language acquisition, despite the fact that make + noun
+ locative is ungrammatical in standard adult usage
today.

In addition to tracing the order and manner in
which the three periphrastic causatives emerge, I also
wish to examine the ontogenetic data in terms of
first, the periphrastic causative paradigm and second,
the markedness hierarchy which I proposed in Chapter
3.

5.11 Periphrastic Causative Paradigm

A grammar containing a periphrastic causative
paradigm is optimally simple and maximally productive
in that there are no restrictions against particular
verb-complement combinations. In 3.2, I presented
morphological and syntactic evidence that children
often overgeneralize constructions, i.e. fail to apply
restrictions to particular morphological or syntactic
configurations. One purpose of longitudinal analysis
of child speech is to find out whether children
spontaneously produce periphrastic causative constructions which are inadmissible in standard adult
English, e.g.

     (1) *Grandma made her sweater off.
     (2) *Daddy had the girl to dance.

The appearance of such sentences would suggest that
children learn periphrastic causative constructions by
beginning with the general strategy of matching all
causative verbs with all complements, and only later
adding restrictions.

My hypothesis is that children do begin with
something like this general strategy. There are, however, a number of factors complicating this hypothesis.
I will discuss these factors in terms of complement
types.

Infinitive
If a child's grammar is characterized by an unrestricted paradigm with respect to infinitival
complements, then we would expect to find errors with
to-complementizers. Either the child might not use to
in obligatory contexts, cf.

(3) *The doctor got his patient breathe deeply.

or he might use it inadmissibly, cf.

(4) *The doctor made his patient to breathe
    deeply.

This paradigmatic strategy is more readily testable
with respect to the presence of to (e.g. (4)) than to
its absence (e.g. (3)). In general, children initially learning infinitival complements do not use the to-
complementizer, regardless of what the main verb is.
For example, it may be fortuitous that a child's use
of (5) is grammatical but (6) is not:

(5) I helped Mommy cook.
(6) *I wanted Mommy cook.

If a child is still at the stage of not using to-complementizers, then failure to use to with periphrastic
causative get, i.e.

(3) *The doctor got his patient breathe deeply.

tells us little about the child's analysis of periphrastic causatives. However, a child's correct use
of the to-complementizer with some verbs but not with
periphrastic causative get would lend ontogenetic
support to the proposed paradigm with respect to
infinitival complements.

Present Participle, Clause
Present participial and clausal complements, e.g.

(7) The actress had the director eating out
    of her hand.
(8) I asked all of my subjects to make it so

that the blue dot was above the red dot.

are fairly sophisticated constructions which normally do not appear in the speech of preschool children. I therefore will not discuss overgeneralizations with respect to the ontogenetic appearance of these complement types.

Noun
The paradigmatic hypothesis predicts that children who use nominal constructions such as (9)

(9) The army will make you a soldier.

may overgeneralize the nominal complement to periphrastic causative get, e.g.

(10) *The army will get you a soldier.

With periphrastic causative have, a temporal modifier is a necessary condition for grammaticality,[1] cf.

(11) ?The army will have you a soldier.
(12) The army will have you a soldier in two months.

Use of have + noun + noun without a temporal modifier (e.g. (11)) would support the paradigmatic analysis of periphrastic causative verbs and nominal complements.

Adjective
Adult use of periphrastic causatives with adjectival complements is restricted in two ways. First, have does not occur with all adjectives, e.g.

(13) ?The teacher had the student angry.

Second, in those cases in which have is admissible, a temporal modifier is required, e.g.

(14) ?The cook had the water hot.
(15) The cook had the water hot in a jiffy.

If the child is using an unrestricted paradigm, we might find examples in his speech of sentences such as (13) and (14).

Past Participle
Because all three periphrastic causative verbs are grammatical with past participial complements, children's use of such complements with make, get, and have neither supports nor refutes the paradigmatic hypothesis.

Locative
Locative complements with periphrastic causative

make are not grammatical in standard adult usage, cf.

> (16) *The provost made the students out of
>   his office.

However, children's use of such constructions would
lend support to the notion of a periphrastic causative
paradigm.

In summary, the following overgeneralizations
would constitute support for the ontogenetic periphrastic causative paradigm:

> Infinitive
>   i. no use of to in get + noun + infinitive
>   caveat: the child must already use to-
>   complementizers with other verbs
>
> ii. use of to in$\left\{\dfrac{\text{make}}{\text{have}}\right\}$ + noun + infinitive
>
> Noun
> iii. use of get + noun + noun
> iv. use of have + noun + noun without temporal
>   modifier
>
> Adjective
>   v. use of have + noun + adjective with inad-
>   missible adjectives
> vi. use of have + noun + adjective without
>   temporal modifier
>
> Locative
> vii. use of make + noun + locative

5.12 Markedness

In 3.3 I made four basic ontogenetic predictions
about the acquisition of periphrastic causative make,
get, and have on the basis of a synchronic theory of
markedness. These four predictions are:

> (1) make will appear as the first periphrastic
>   causative
> (2) make will appear more frequently than get
>   or have (frequency)
> (3) make will develop a wide range of comple-
>   ment types earlier than get or have
>   (defectivation)

(with the inverse predictions for have)

> (4) children may use make where get or have
>   is appropriate, or get where have is
>   appropriate (neutralization)

All of these predictions can be tested with
respect to longitudinal data. To test prediction (1),
it is necessary to have acquisition data from the very
earliest stages of syntactic development so that it is
possible to identify the initial use of each verb as
a periphrastic causative. Predictions (2) and (3) may
be tested by identifying all periphrastic causatives
in the data, and then classifying each example with
respect to complement type. The frequency and range
of usage for each verb may then be compared. Prediction (4) overlaps with the notion of a periphrastic
causative paradigm. Use of make where get or have
would be appropriate would be exemplified by a construction of the type make + noun + locative, in that
get and have, but not make, appear in this construction in standard adult English.

5.2 Registers and Individual Differences

In comparing the speech of children with that of
their immediate adult interlocutors or of the adult
community in general, it is important to ask how these
three speech modes (i.e. adult-to-adult, adult-to-
child, child-to-adult) differ from or relate to one
another. Do adults speak differently to children than
to other adults? Does the language of a given child
directly reflect the idiosyncrasies of his adult
model? Students of child language are just beginning
to try to answer these questions.[2]
Drach (1969), using a pilot sample of adult-child
and adult-adult conversation, found several clear
differences between the language used in addressing
children and that used in speaking with adult peers.
Utterances addressed to other adults averaged two and
a half times the length of those addressed to children; the adult-adult speech was considerably more
rapid than that of adult-to-child; and the lexical
content was more diverse in adult-adult than in adult-
child interchange. Pfuderer (1969) reports upon a
study in which the complexity of a mother's child-
directed speech gradually increases during the child's
second and third years of life. And, in an analysis
dealing with slightly older children, Gleason (1973)
concludes that adults in her sample used one style of
speech in addressing children less than about age
four, but a rather different register in addressing
children between four and eight years old.
If it is the case that adults modify their language in speaking to children, is it also true that
children somehow mirror the models addressed to them?

The strongest negative evidence against this
hypothesis has been the data reported by Brown (1973)
on three children's acquisition of 14 grammatical
morphemes (e.g. plural, possessive, regular past tense,
articles). While the order of emergence of the 14
morphemes was highly correlated across children, and
the frequency of use in adult speech addressed to
children highly correlated across parents, there was
no correlation between adult frequency on the one hand
and order of acquisition in children on the other.3
However, order of acquisition did correlate with
degree of syntactic and semantic complexity.

Given Brown's finding that syntactic and semantic
complexity are better predictors of order of acquisition than parental frequency, it would be interesting
to compare the complexity of periphrastic causative
constructions with their ontogenetic emergence. However, with the exception of predictions about markedness (cf. 3.3 and 5.12) I have not distinguished
levels of complexity with respect to either periphrastic causatives or their related complements. In
fact, I have argued that all periphrastic causative
constructions have the same basic underlying structure
in a synchronic model (cf. 5.11). Admittedly, the
relative complexity of periphrastic causatives in an
abstract synchronic grammar may have little relation
to complexity from the point of view of the child,
particularly since the synchronic model posits a number of transformations and deletions, while the child
might well interpret the surface structure as an
underlying form (cf. Watt 1970). Lacking an
appropriate model of complexity, I will not be able
to compare syntactic or semantic complexity with order
of acquisition.

In Brown's study of grammatical morphemes, there
is no obvious markedness hierarchy along which to rank
the 14 types. For example, while it is possible to
speak of singular as being less marked than plural, it
is difficult to know how to compare markedness between
plurality in nouns, and, for example, verb tense. The
case of periphrastic causative constructions is somewhat different. While periphrastic causative constructions with make, get, and have do have distinct
syntactic and semantic parameters (cf. Baron 1974),
they share the same basic underlying configuration and
most semantic properties. The essential similarity of
these constructions makes it possible to posit a
relative markedness hierarchy with make, get, and
have. I have already hypothesized that frequency in
child speech is one measure of ontogenetic markedness.

If the same markedness hierarchy exists in the adult speech addressed to the child, then frequency in onto- genetic data should correlate with frequency in adult speech directed to the child. However, it may not be possible to demonstrate that the child's frequency is actually a function of adult frequency rather than a function of an independent ontogenetic markedness hierarchy.

Even if frequency in adult speech addressed to children does not directly determine the basic order of ontogenetic development, it may still be the case that relative frequency in child use is partially related to frequency in adult speech to the child.[4] This hypothesis could be tested by comparing the speech of several children and their adult interlocu- tors.

I shall make the following predictions with respect to adult speech registers and individual differences in child speech:

1. adult use of periphrastic causatives is different when speaking to adults than when speaking to children

2. adult frequency of periphrastic causatives in language addressed to children is an accurate predictor of order of acquisition (although the correlation may only reflect parallels in markedness hierarchies in adult and child speech)

3. idiosyncrasies in adult use of periphrastic causative constructions addressed to child- ren will predict some idiosyncrasies in child speech

To test prediction 1 it is necessary to compare

(a) adult speech addressed to children (P)[5] versus adult speech addressed to adults (A)

Testing of prediction 2 requires comparison of

(b) adult speech addressed to children (P) versus child speech (C)

For the third prediction, it is necessary to compare the speech of several adults and several children, i.e.

(c_1) the speech of adult P_n versus child C_n

(c_2) the speech of adult P_n versus adult P_m

(c_3) the speech of child C_n versus child C_m

5.3 Previous Ontogenetic Analyses

In the literature on the acquisition of English as a first language, there is almost no discussion of causative constructions in general or of periphrastic causatives in particular. A few linguists have made anecdotal reference to overextension of suppletive causatives (e.g. Braine 1971) though no one has analyzed the various types of morphological causatives as an emerging system. Several sources do, however, treat the three verbs make, get, and have to varying extents.[6]

Bloom (1970) chooses the verb make to illustrate the use of reduction transformations by Kathryn (one of her subjects) at age 2;10. Kathryn's mean length of utterance was then 1.92 morphemes, although sentences with make were among the longest in the corpus. Bloom (1970:143-145) lists a total of 45 utterances with make which appeared in the sample taken at age 2;10. The majority are simple transitive sentences in which make means "create, build" or "prepare", e.g.

>   "create, build"
>   (17) make another bridge
>   (18) made ə[7] choochoo train
>   (19) Kathryn make ə house
>
>   "prepare"
>   (20) make ə vegetable
>   (21) make pineapple

However, seven utterances are periphrastic causatives:

>   (22) make ə[8] sit down again
>   (Kathryn trying to seat second wire man,
>   after seating first one)[9]
>   (23) make this sit down
>   (Kathryn trying to seat man again)
>   (24) make it sit
>   (Kathryn picking up her car)
>   (25) Kathryn ə make ə under bridge
>   (Kathryn taking lamb to bridge. Adult
>   interlocutor has just said, "I know who's
>   going under the bridge....Let's make him
>   go under the bridge)
>   (26) make ə more under bridge
>   (Kathryn pushed first lamb under bridge;
>   picking up another lamb)
>   (27) make ə more under more
>   (bridge collapsed as Kathryn was about to
>   push lamb through)

(28) make ə   car under bridge
(Kathryn pushing car under bridge)

In the first three utterances (i.e. (22), (23), (24)), periphrastic causative <u>make</u> takes an infinitive complement, i.e.

(29) make + $\left\{\begin{matrix} ə \\ this \\ it \end{matrix}\right\}$ + sit (down (again))

The next four examples, all ungrammatical in standard English, illustrate a locative complement, i.e.

(30) make + $\left\{\begin{matrix} ə\ more \\ ə\ car \end{matrix}\right\}$ +(ə) + under $\left\{\begin{matrix} bridge \\ more \end{matrix}\right\}$

The immediate adult model for these locative sentences is the grammatical construction <u>make</u> + noun + infinitive:

(31) Let's make him go under the bridge.
(cf. (25))

At first glance, the child's utterances might be interpreted as reductions of (31), i.e. dropping out the subject and verb of the complement. The question is, why should this particular reduction occur. Or, to rephrase the question, is <u>make</u> + noun + locative a reduction of an infinitival complement, or is it rather a non-reduced structure which the child generates on the basis of an underlying periphrastic causative paradigm with respect to locative constructions and a markedness hierarchy? In 5.5 and 5.8, I will argue in favor of the non-reduced structural analysis.[10]

Two studies have examined the development of <u>get</u> in passive sentences. Bates (1970) used a forced choice picture task to determine how well children comprehend passives. Fifty three year old children were asked to identify the correct picture going with full (i.e. agent expressed in <u>by</u> phrase) or truncated <u>be</u> and <u>get</u> passive sentences spoken by the experimenter. For example, the illustration of a girl spanking a clown is accurately described by each of the following sentences:

(32) full <u>be</u> passive: The clown was spanked
                          by the girl.
(33) truncated <u>be</u> passive: The clown was spanked.
(34) full <u>get</u> passive: The clown got spanked
                          by the girl.
(35) truncated <u>get</u>   The clown got spanked.
     passive:

The incorrect picture would be that of a clown spanking a girl. Bates found that children did better in
identifying truncated get passives than truncated be
passives, and full get passives better than full be
passives, i.e.

> (36) truncated get > truncated be > full get >
>   full be

Fischer (personal communication) also found that
preschool children are, in some sense, more responsive
to get passives than be passives. Fischer presented
four-and-a-half to five-year-old children with full
get and be passives, and asked the children to say
which one sounded better. Four out of five of the
children preferred the get passive. For example,
given the pair

> (37) Jimmy got run over by a car.
> (38) Jimmy was run over by a car.

the children selected (37). When the verb is non-
stative (e.g. run over), either sentence is admissible
in adult English. When the verb is stative, only the
be passive is acceptable. However, when presented
with the stative pair

> (39) *The girl got loved by the boy.
> (40) The girl was loved by the boy.

children still selected the get passive (i.e. (39)).
Cromer (1968) discusses the development of have
as an auxiliary. Drawing upon the longitudinal
corpora of Adam, Eve, and Sarah collected by Brown's
group at Harvard in the early 1960's, Cromer finds
that have does not appear unambiguously as an
auxiliary until age four or five.[11] Moreover,
Cromer's appendix on "Uses of Have" lists no causative
examples. One possible interpretation of these data
would be that causative have develops out of perfective have; examples of causative have probably
develop very late, since periphrastic have is itself
a late development. However, I will argue in section
5.7 that the kind of structures from which periphrastic causative have develops ontogenetically are
present before the appearance of perfective have.
Limber (1973), in a study of the origins of
complex sentences, discusses what main verbs two and
three-year-old children use with infinitival and
clausal complements. Make appears in the age range
1;11-2;5. While neither get nor have appears in the
range 1;11-2;5 or 2;5-3;0, a larger, unpublished word
list based upon the same data does include get.

5.4 Sources

(a) <u>Nina and Erica</u>
   The primary source of longitudinal data was two
separate copora made available to me by the Stanford
Institute for Mathematical Studies in the Social
Sciences. Each corpus represents twenty hours of
recorded conversation between a child and one or more
adult interlocutors. All recordings were made in the
children's homes under naturalistic conditions.
   The first corpus follows the linguistic development of Nina. The first hour was recorded when Nina
was 1;11 and the twentieth when she was 2;4. All 20
sessions were evenly spaced over the five month
period, approximately one week apart. Each one-hour
session took place on a separate day. Collection and
editing was done by Nina's mother, Florence Yager,
who was a member of the staff of the Stanford
Institute for Mathematical Studies in the Social
Sciences. In addition to a transcription of the text,
the Nina corpus includes appropriate extra linguistic
context noted during the taping session, as well as a
brief "diary" at the beginning of each hour describing
Nina's mood and physical health, and summarizing
Nina's relevant activities since the last recording
session. The corpus has a total of 26,476 intelligible
utterances[12] of which half (13,255) were spoken by
Nina and the other half (13,221) by her mother or some
other adult. The child portion of the Nina corpus has a
total of 35,478 tokens, of which 1,514 were distinct
lexical items.
   The second corpus records the speech of a girl
named Erica. Erica was 2;7 when the project began and
2;9 at its completion. Most recordings were of one-
hour sessions, scattered throughout the three month
period, though some sessions were two hours in length,
and several one-hour samples extend over several days.
Much of the data were collected and edited by Arlene
Moscowitz. However, the later hours were recorded by
Erica's parents and edited by Robert Smith. The data
include almost no extralinguistic context. The
corpus contains a total of 19,613 intelligible
utterances[13] of which 8,918 were made by the child and
the remainder (10,695) by the adult interlocutor. The
child portion of the Erica corpus contains 27,922
tokens, of which 1,853 were distinct lexical items.
   Table VI summarizes the important features of the
Nina and Erica corpora.

Table VI.   Nina and Erica Corpora

	Nina	Erica
CHILD		
1. age	1;11 - 2;4	2;7 - 2;9
2. sex	female	female
CORPUS		
1. number of hours	20	20
2. number of utterances		
a. total	26,476	19,613
b. child	13,255	8,918
c. adult	13,221	10,695
3. child's lexicon		
a. types	1,514	1,853
b. tokens	35,478	27,922
4. adult's lexicon		
a. types	1,898	2,867
c. tokens	67,437	51,848
5. extralinguistic context	diary, extralinguistic context recorded during session	--

Both corpora were transcribed in standard English orthography. The symbol <xxx> was used to indicate the unintelligibility of all or part of an utterance. If it was possible to determine at least the grammatical category of an otherwise unintelligible segment, that segment was transcribed in angular brackets, e.g. <n>, <v>, <adj>. When the editor judged that a string of segments was functioning as a single word rather than a productive syntactic construction, the segments were joined by hyphens and counted as a single word in the lexicon, e.g.

    (41) Nina: raggedy-ann
    (42) Erica: squishy-squashy

Both corpora were typed into an PDP-10 computer and
extensively analyzed by Robert Smith as part of his
dissertation research (cf. Smith 1972).

Smith wrote and executed all programs used in my
own study of Nina and Erica. Three general listings
were made:

(43) a. alphabetical type/token lexicon:
    i.   child Nina (i.e. child portion
        of Nina corpus)
    ii.   child Erica
    iii. adult Nina (i.e. adult portion
        of Nina corpus)
    iv.   adult Erica

   b. numbered listing of all child and
      adult utterances:
    i.   Nina (child and adult combined)
    ii.   Erica (child and adult combined)

   c. chronological listing of all utterances,
      extralinguistic context, and diary
      (Nina corpus only)

In addition, Smith designed a special program which
provided numbered listings of all child and all adult
utterances containing any morphological form of have,
make, and get. In analyzing these data, it was
possible to refer back to the numbered listing of the
complete corpus (cf. (43.b) above) to determine linguistic (and, in the case of Nina, extralinguistic)
context and to identify spontaneous imitations by
either child or adult.

I did not attempt to divide the total corpora
into stages, either with respect to age, mean length
of utterance, or some other syntactic or semantic
measure. The Erica corpus covered too short a span of
time and was too sporadically collected to show general progression with age. While progression of mean
length does correlate with age in the case of Nina
(cf. Suppes and Smith, forthcoming), I decided to
postpone a general stage analysis of the Nina corpus
until more data become available.[14] Nevertheless, because the data are numbered in the order in which the
utterances were spoken within the twenty hours of
recorded conversation, I was able to make some
observations about which constructions seem to emerge
only towards the end of the corpora.

(b) Adam I
A secondary source of longitudinal data on child
language acquisition was the earliest sample (I) on

the child Adam in Roger Brown's Harvard study. At the
time, Adam was aged 2;3. The corpus represents two
hours of naturalistic conversation recorded in the
child's home. The Stanford Institute for Mathematical
Studies in the Social Sciences has formated the Adam I
corpus on the PDP-10 system, and I obtained my data
directly from the Institute. The corpus I used, containing only Adam's speech (i.e. no adult interlocutor,
no extralinguistic context), totals 2,729 utterances.
The Adam I corpus contains a total of 4,963 tokens,
with a lexicon of 591 distinct items.

The Adam I lexicon contains a large number of
compounds which Brown's group has analyzed as simple
lexical items,[15] e.g.

      (44) mottapplejuice
      (45) marchingbear
      (46) overthere
      (47) rightinhere
      (48) getout

It is difficult to determine whether such compounds
are as yet unanalyzed in the child's speech. For
example, both marching and bear occur as distinct
items in Adam's lexicon, as do over and there, right
and in and here, and get and out. In the Nina and
Erica corpora, the compound analysis is reserved for
strings in which all segments do not occur separately.

The corpus of Adam I was selected to supplement
the Nina and Erica corpora because it represents a
less highly developed period of acquisition. Although
Adam was 2;3 at the time of recording (cf. Nina: 1;11,
Erica: 2;7), many of his utterances are limited to
one or two words. It is not possible to compare
precisely the mean length of utterance (MLU) of Adam,
Nina, and Erica. In the case of Adam, the MLU is
based upon morphemes,[16] while the analysis of Nina
and Erica is based upon distinct lexical items.
Furthermore, the analysis of Adam recognizes far more
compounds than does that of Nina and Erica. Nevertheless, even a rough comparison (cf. Table VII) suggests
that Adam I represents an earlier period of development than Nina or Erica, and Nina an earlier period
than Erica.

Table VII.   Mean Length of Utterance (MLU) of
             Children in Longitudinal Corpora

Child	Average MLU in First of 20 Hours (Nina and Erica only)		Average MLU of All Hours in Sample (Nina, Erica: 20 hrs; Adam: 2 hrs)	
	age	MLU	age	MLU
Adam I (MLU measured in morphemes)	--	--	2;3	2.06
Nina (MLU measured in lexical items)	1;11	1.83	2;2	2.54
Erica (MLU measured in lexical items)	2;7	3.26	2;8	3.05

Ideally, all the data should have been collected on a
single child or on several children over a span of two
or three years.   However, given my limitation on
available corpora, I decided to include the Adam I
corpus as an empirical check upon my extrapolations
from the Nina and Erica corpora to the earlier stages
of the acquisition of periphrastic causatives.

(c) Ten Plays
     Crowell (1955) analyzes the function of the word
get in ten plays produced in New York between the
period 1932 and 1950.[17]   The plays, all comedies, were
selected by the criterion "that the dialog should
reflect as much as possible standard present-day
General American colloquial English" (1955:24).   The
dialogue generally represents adult-adult conversation.   Crowell does not list the total number of
tokens or utterances in the corpus.   Moreover, he
provides selected examples rather than a complete
listing of all utterances containing forms of the verb
get.

(d) Brown University Standard Corpus of Present-Day
     Edited American English
     The Brown University corpus is a collection of
500 samples of written American English, totaling

1,014,232 tokens and 52,248 utterances. The 500
samples are divided into fifteen categories, ranging
from daily newspapers to science fiction to humor.
They represent a variety of prose styles and include
a sizeable percentage of dialogue which appears to be
almost exclusively between adults. The entire corpus
is coded for IBM processing. For a description of the
corpus and analysis of the lexicon, cf. Kučera and
Francis (1967).

With the assistance of ᵣW. Nelson Francis and
Jerry Rubin of Brown University, I obtained a
concordance listing of every third passage containing
the verbs make, get, and have.[18] The concordance
program is organized by rows of print-out rather than
by utterances. A single entry consists of three
lines: the line in which the concorded word appears,
the preceding line, and the following line. In nearly
all cases, it is possible to determine the syntactic
function of the concorded item from this amount of context. Because of time limitations, I will restrict my
discussion in the present study to the data on get.

The next three sections (5.5 - 5.7) will present
and analyze the data on make, get, and have,
respectively. Each section will take the following
form:

   1. data
      a. summary of Adam, Nina, and Erica's use
         of the verb
      b. summary of use of the verb in adult
         portions of Nina and Erica corpora
      c. summary of Crowell and Brown University
         data (get only)
   2. discussion
   3. outline of chronological emergence of
      periphrastic causative and related uses of
      the verb

5.5 Make

DATA

Adam I
Adam uses make a total of four times. While
three of these are uninterpretable without adult or
extralinguistic context, i.e.

   216[19]   make mosquito
   1915   make cromer
   1916   make cromer doctordan

one instance seems to function as a periphrastic
causative with infinitival complement:

     1409   daddy make go
            (cf. daddy make it go)

Child Nina
In the child portion of the Nina corpus, there
are 134 instances of make. Most uses have the basic
transitive senses of "create", "build", or "prepare",
e.g.

     19536 i make a monster
     23198 make a pony tail

However, 16 are clearly causative.[20] The most common
causative complement is the infinitive, all instances
of which are intransitive, e.g.

      2129 make duck drink
     26588 made me cry
     26981 i make it fall

Half (i.e. 6 out of 12) of the infinitive complements
contain locative markers, e.g.

      8119 make it stand up
     20543 make him sit down
     26982 i make it fall down

As in Bloom's data on Kathryn, there are also several
examples of make + noun + locative:

     15992 i made a basket on
     17314 oh, i make a seat over
     25375 i, i make cream on dolly's hair

Finally, there is one utterance which may exemplify
the adjectival complement, though the surface order is
make + adjective + noun rather than the normal make +
noun + adjective:

     26747 i make that purple home

The surrounding context does not make it clear whether
Nina is going to make a home become purple (i.e.
causative) or build a home which will also happen to
be purple (i.e. non-causative). Table VIII summarizes
Nina's use of make.[21]

Table VIII.   Causative/Non-Causative Distribution of
             Make in Child Nina

$$\Sigma N = 134$$

	N	%
CAUSATIVE		
1. make + N + inf		
a. with locative phrase	(6)	(4)
b. total	12	9
2. make + N + loc	3	2
3. make + N + adj	1	1
4. make + N + N	0	0
Total	16	12
NON-CAUSATIVE, MISCELLANEOUS	118	88

Child Erica

The verb make occurs 133 times in Erica's speech.
A total of 120 instances have non-causative complements or are unclassifiable. Of the remaining lines
seven are causative with intransitive infinitival
complements, e.g.

    1206   mommy, make her stand
    8095   now i make you eat some

(although five out of seven citations have the
identical complement her stand, and occur within the
same 100 lines of text). One infinitival complement
contains a locative element, i.e.

    5595   made it all go down

Causative make appears twice with a noun+locative
complement, i.e.

    1257   make my hand on her hand
    15977 i made queen on my head

and four times with an adjectival complement:

    1274   gonna make her taller
    2719   making them loud
    13968 make it hot
    14499 that makes me warm

Table IX summarizes Erica's use of make.

Table IX. Causative/Non-Causative Distribution of Make in Child Erica

$$\Sigma N = 133$$

	N	%
CAUSATIVE		
1. make + N + inf		
a. with locative phrase	(1)	(1)
b. total	7	5
2. make + N + loc	2	2
3. make + N + adj	4	3
4. make + N + N	0	0
Total	13	10
NON-CAUSATIVE, MISCELLANEOUS	120	90

Adult Nina
In the adult portion of the Nina corpus, there are 293 citations with make, almost one quarter of which are syntactically causative. The vast majority of causative complements (i.e. 62 out of 78 causative utterances) are intransitive and transitive infinitives. Some examples are:

  8154 you going to make the nurse say hi?
20773 you need a hard surface like a book to make the mouse go
25317 can you make her close her eyes?

Of the 62 infinitival constructions, 25 contain locatives, e.g.

  8874 let me see if i can make it stand up
19590 that was a nasty chair that made you fall over
22522 let's see if i can make it go all the way round

Despite its ungrammaticality in adult English, causative make + noun + locative occurs three times in the adult portion of the Nina corpus:

    13347   no, what did mommy make on top of the
            box?
    19204   make the blanket to be on the pillow[22]
    26154   there, shall we make a train on there?

Causative adjectival complements of the form <u>make</u> +
noun + adjective appear in three utterances:

     8127   can you make her feet straight?
    18017   i'll kiss it and make it all better
    18550   what shall we do to make her warm?

In addition, there are eight examples in which an
overt verb is expressed, e.g.

    11441   so is the sun making the girl get hot?
    15657   did he make nina feel better?
    15681   make your tummy feel better to have a
            lollipop?

I have classified these examples with adjectival
complements rather than with infinitives since the
predicate of <u>get</u> or <u>feel</u> is an adjective rather than
a noun or locative. Finally, there are two lines in
which the complement is a nominal construction:

    23439   you make this snoopy's cup, ok?
    23679   shall we make this box into his house?

Table X summarizes the adult use of <u>make</u> in the Nina
corpus.

Table X.   Causative/Non-Causative Distribution of
           <u>Make</u> in Adult Nina

$$\Sigma N = 293$$

	N	%
CAUSATIVE		
1. make + N + inf		
a. with locative phrase	(25)	(8)
b. total	62	21
2. make + N + loc	3	1
3. make + N + adj	11	4
4. make + N + N	2	.5
Total	78	26.5
NON-CAUSATIVE, MISCELLANEOUS	215	73.5

Adult Erica

Causative complements account for 49 of the 191 citations of make in the adult portion of the Erica corpus. A comparatively small number of these (15) involve intransitive and transitive infinitives, e.g.

    12079   what makes you think you may do that?
    15877   he made the girls all cry

Of these 15, three examples have locative elements:

    1203   you're making that go back and forth
    6805   oh, sure, if you make it fall down
    6819   oh, you made it fall down

There are no citations of make + noun + locative. The majority of causative complements in the adult Erica sample are adjectives. There are 24 examples of the type make + noun + (be) + adjective:

    11022   and coal will make you very black
    12252   there this will make it really be pretty
    19213   did it make me angry

Two utterances are of the form make + noun + feel + adjective:

    13370   don't you think that will make it feel
            better?
    14411   that'll make it feel better

In addition, there are seven examples in which the complement is formally a past participle, one with the word embarrassed and the other six with all gone, e.g.

    15882   he made them all embarrassed
    13508   sure made that all gone, didn't you

Because there is no evidence that these past participial forms are functioning as verbs rather than as adjectives, cf.

            he made them all wet
            sure made that all empty

I have classified all of these examples among the adjectives. Finally, there is one citation with a nominal complement:

    6826   shall we make this the door?

Table XI summarizes the use of make in the adult portion of the Erica corpus.

Table XI.   Causative/Non-Causative Distribution of
             Make in Adult Erica

$\Sigma N = 240$

	N	%
CAUSATIVE		
1. make + N + inf		
a. with locative phrase	(3)	(1)
b. total	15	6
2. make + N + loc	0	0
3. make + N + adj	33	14
4. make + N + N	1	.5
Total	49	20.5
NON-CAUSATIVE, MISCELLANEOUS	191	79.5

DISCUSSION

I will first discuss infinitive constructions, then treating in turn locatives, adjectives, and nominals, and then past participial and clausal complements.

Infinitive
The longitudinal data suggest that causative make with infinitival complement appears quite early in the young child's speech. There is already one example in Adam I, and multiple examples in the child samples from Nina and Erica. In fact, the make +(noun) + infinitive construction is probably one of the earliest expressions in which infinitives appear in child language.

Locative
Locative constructions, though less well documented, also appear in child Nina and Erica. As causative constructions in their own right (i.e. make + noun + locative), these non-standard constructions are syntactically parallel to grammatical get + noun + locative, a construction which also appears quite

early (cf. 5.6). These examples offer supporting
evidence for the reality of the periphrastic causative
paradigm with respect to locatives, as well as
evidence for the unmarked status of make.

From the data, it is not obvious what the source
of this syntactic overgeneralization might be. In
addition to the citations in both children, there are
three examples in the adult Nina corpus. One explanation would be that causative make + noun + locative
originates in child speech and is then picked up by
parents when addressing children. Alternatively, the
construction might be "invented" by adults as a baby
talk form, which is then readily adopted by children
because of its paradigmatic similarity to get + noun
+ locative. One apparent problem with this latter
theory would be the absence of make + noun + locative
in the adult portion of the Erica corpus. However,
since the primary adult interlocutor in the Erica
corpus was an outside observer, it is an open question
whether the model was ever established in the speech
of Erica's mother, who was her primary language model.
Furthermore, since Erica is older than Nina, it is
possible that at some earlier period, make + noun +
locative appeared in the speech of the primary adult
interlocutor, but was now no longer deemed appropriate
(cf. Pfuderer 1969).

In the adult portion of the Nina corpus, there is
one example of the make + noun + locative construction
with an overt copula:

    19204   make the blanket to be on the pillow

While the copula does not render the sentence
grammatical, it may provide a surface structure cue
that what follows the verb make is actually a sentence
rather than simply a particle. Similar clues appear
in adult speech with adjectival complements (cf.
section immediately below on adjectives, and also discussion of get (5.6)).

Locative elements also appear in a large proportion of the causative infinitive constructions in the
child and adult portions of the Nina corpus.[23] Among
Nina's 12 uses of make + noun + infinitive, all six
infinitives without locative elements consist of
simple intransitive verbs. Nina's mother, who used
37 infinitive causative constructions without locatives, did use a large number of intransitive infinitives, yet nearly one-quarter (i.e. nine) contained
transitive verbs with expressed objects (i.e. verb +
noun). Thus, although the transitive model was
available, Nina's own infinitives with make are

limited to verb (+ locative). One might argue that in
general, intransitive verbs plus locatives are less
complex or more semantically useful to a child than
verb plus object. Another alternative would be that
the notion of location is an integral part of all
verbs of causation, and it is therefore natural that
children should begin to use locatives in infinitive
complements with causative make quite early.

Adjective

While adjectival complements with causative make
are well documented in the adult portion of the Nina
corpus, there is only one (questionable) example in
Nina's speech. Given the ample examples of infinitive
constructions in child Nina (along with the presence
of one infinitival complement but absence of
adjectival examples in Adam I), I conclude that adjectival complements are acquired later than infinitival
complements with causative make.

In both adult corpora, there are adjectival
complements with overt verbs linking the noun and
adjective, e.g.

        Adult Nina: 11441 so is the sun making the
                              girl get hot?
        Adult Erica: 14411 that'll make it feel better

These same types of utterances frequently appear in
English without the surface verb, cf.

        so is the sun making the girl hot?
        that'll make it better

While get and feel do provide overt semantic information, they also function to make clear the sentential
structure of the adjectival complement.

There is an interesting discrepancy between use
of adjectival and infinitival complements in the two
corpora. Table XII summarizes the data.

Table XII.   Use of Adjectival and Infinitival
             Complements with Make

	Nina		Erica	
	Child	Adult	Child	Adult
Adjectives	1 (1%)	11 (4%)	4 (3%)	33 (14%)
Infinitives	12 (9%)	62 (21%)	7 (5%)	15 (6%)

While both children use adjectival complements about
one quarter as often as their adult interlocutors, the
proportion for adult and child Erica is over four
times that of adult and child Nina. In adult Erica,
adjective constructions are over twice as frequent as
infinitival expressions. Although the rank order is
reversed in child Erica, we must consider that five of
Erica's seven infinitives were identical (i.e. her
stand), while all four of her adjectival constructions
were unique. These data suggest that in Erica's
speech, adjectival complements were at least as productive as infinitives. In the Nina corpus, the
numerical dominance of infinitives over adjectives is
clear in both child and adult samples. I suggest that
these data provide the kind of evidence necessary to
establish that the character of a child's syntax is
dependent upon the model he hears (cf. 5.2 above).

Noun
Nominal complements appear infrequently, and only
in the adult corpora. Although their structure is
probably no more complex than adjectival or locative
complements, I surmise that their comparatively limited usefulness in the child's (and adult's) world as
well as their restricted role in the periphrastic
causative paradigm determine their late acquisition.

Past Participle, Clause
With the possible exception of two examples in
adult Erica (i.e. embarrassed and all gone), no past
participial complements occur with periphrastic causative make in any of the four samples. In addition, no
clausal complements appear in either of the corpora.
I conclude that both of these constructions (especially the clausal complement) are very late ontogenetic
developments.

CHRONOLOGICAL EMERGENCE OF CAUSATIVE MAKE

I tentatively postulate the following chronological emergence of causative constructions with the verb
make. Various of these stages necessarily overlap:

Stage 0: transitive "create", "build",
"prepare"
Stage 1: make + noun + infinitive$_{intrans.}$
Stage 2: (a) make + noun + locative
(b) make + noun + infinitive$_{intrans.}$
+ locative
Stage 3: make + noun + adjective
Stage 4: make + noun + infinitive$_{trans.}$

Stage 5: (a) <u>make</u> + noun + noun
         (b) <u>make</u> + noun + past participle
Stage 6: <u>make</u> + noun + clause

5.6 <u>Get</u>

DATA

<u>Adam I</u>
Adam uses the verb <u>get</u> a total of 54 times. In most utterances (i.e. 41), <u>get</u> has the simple, transitive meaning "acquire" or "fetch", e.g.

     415 get you ball
    1406 get car

However in 11 utterances, <u>get</u> is used in constructions relevant to the emergence of the periphrastic causative. There are eight instances of the <u>get</u> + locative construction,[24] a construction which I have earlier labeled "precausative" in that it serves as the immediate precursor of causative <u>get</u> + noun + locative (cf. 4.5):

     428 getin kitty
     429 kitty getin
     430 getin
     559 getout
    1444 adam getover ball
    1445 adam getover
    1515 getaway
    2005 get back[25]

         locatives: away (1)   out (1)
                    back (1)   over (2)
                    in   (3)

While there are no instances of causative <u>get</u> + noun + locative, <u>get</u> + noun + past participle, or <u>get</u> + noun + infinitive, there is one example of <u>get</u> + noun + adjective:

    2619 get supper ready

         adjective: ready (1)

Finally, there are two non-causative uses of <u>get</u> + past participle,[26] both involving the past participle <u>stuck</u>:

     986 getstuck
     987 adam getstuck

These data are summarized in Table XIII.

Table XIII.   (Pre)Causative/Non-Causative
Distribution of Get in Adam I

$\Sigma N = 54$

(Pre)Causative	N	%	Non-Causative	N	%
get + loc	8	15	A. get + adj.	0	0
get + N + loc	0	0	get + PP	2	4
get + N + adj	1	2	must	0	0
get + N + PP	0	0	possessive	0	0
get + N + inf	0	0	B. acquire, fetch	41	76
get + N + Prs. P	0	0			
			C. miscellaneous	2	4
Total	9	17	Total	45	84

Child Nina
Nina employed the verb get a total of 208 times.
Get occurs with the meaning "acquire" or "fetch" 123
times, e.g.

    1384   get it mommy
    14576 don't get a horsie

In at least two of these instances, the verb takes a
position locative phrase, but the construction remains
non-causative, i.e.

    17009 i got balloons in the zoo
    26675 got that airplane in the, in the store

There are 58 precausative or causative uses of
the verb get. Thirty-seven are precausative, i.e.
get + locative. Some examples are:

    9733   you get up
    12031 don't you get in
    17043 get away
    20431 get out of the zoo
    26467 oh, it's hard to get into the hole

The following locatives occur in the 37 get + locative
constructions:

    away   (3)
    in   (4)
    into   (1)
    out   (14)
    up   (15)

In 17 cases, _get_ appears in the causative construction
get + noun + locative, e.g.

     8624   get it down
    17042   get away this[27]
    24586   get it down

The locatives occurring in these 17 examples are

    away   (1)
    down   (1)
    in   (5)
    off   (1)
    on   (6)
    out   (3)

Causative _get_ + noun + adjective does not occur in the
corpus, although there is one instance of causative
get + noun + past participle:

    5592 <xxx> get these all twisted in back

              past participle: twisted (1)

Three examples of the causative _get_ + noun +
infinitive construction appear:

    20437   get those animals don't go to zoo
    20833   i'm going get the piggy sleep on mommy's
            lap
    22035   get a bed fit in there

The obligatory _to_-complementizer is absent in all
three instances.
   Among the relevant non-causative uses, _get_ +
adjective occurs six times:

     9834   shoes got muddy
    11431   this get hot
    12695   they got dirty
    19389   some my get wet
    19391   some my, some of my clothes get wet
    19496   nina get wet in the ocean too
            (spontaneous imitation)

            adjectives: dirty (1)
                         hot   (1)
                         muddy (1)
                         wet   (3)

In addition, there are five cases of _get_ + past
participle:

     6841   these clothes they get put in the suitcase
     8028   get hurt
    21986   it get twisted, mommy (spontaneous imita-
            tion)

```
21990  yogi bear get twist, twist (partial
       imitation)
25094  i will get tired
```

```
past participles:  hurt     (1)
                   put      (1)
                   tired    (1)
                   twist(ed) (2)
```

Finally,there are four cases in which get means "must":

```
5600   got to go upstairs
5711   these guys got to go to bed
6724   i gotta go all the way around three times
21789  got to be careful
```

In the corpus, Nina does not use get to signal possession.
These data are summarized in Table XIV.

Table XIV.   (Pre)Causative/Non-Causative Distribution
             of Get in Child Nina

$$\Sigma N = 208$$

(Pre) Causative	N	%	Non-Causative	N	%
get + loc	37	18	A. get + adj	6	3
get + N + loc	17	8	get + PP	5	2
get + N + adj	0	0	must	4	2
get + N + PP	1	.5	possessive	0	0
get + N + inf	3	1.5	B. acquire, fetch	123	59
get + N + Prs.P	0	0	C. miscellaneous	12	6
Total	58	28	Total	150	72

Child Erica

The verb get occurs 276 times in the child portion of the Erica corpus. Of the total 276, 136 instances have the meaning "acquire" or "fetch", including at least seven cases with positional locatives, e.g.

```
6529   i just get a hurt on my eyebrow (loc)
10276  he get a bath in that (loc)
19891  'cause he has to go get his bowl
```

Precausative and causative uses total 101. Over half (i.e. 59) are precausative get + locative, e.g.

```
  8925   me get on that horsey
 11792   i'll get up in the morning...and i will
         finish
 12769   no, i want to get down
```

The following locatives are represented:

```
     close   (1)
     down    (4)
     home    (1)
     in     (11)
     into    (1)
     off     (2)
     on     (11)
     out     (9)
     over    (2)
     to      (1)
     up     (16)
```

There are 35 examples of causative <u>get</u> + noun + locative, e.g.

```
  9738   me try to get it in
 12294   i'm going to get all the bubbles away
 12922   want to get my fingernails off
```

These utterances employ the following locatives:

```
     away    (3)
     from    (2)
     in      (2)
     off     (3)
     on     (11)
     out     (9)
     to      (1)
     up      (4)
```

Four utterances exemplify causative <u>get</u> + noun + adjective:

```
  2021   i get my boots muddy
  4400   i get it dirty
 13579   daddy get her warm
 18243   getting you all warm and fuzzy
```

```
         adjectives:  dirty   (1)
                      fuzzy   (1)
                      muddy   (1)
                      warm    (2)
```

In addition, there are three causative uses of <u>get</u> + noun + past participle:

```
  4172   she might get her head stuffed
  7527   got my hair cut
 13514   i get a orange juice all gone
```

           past participles: cut (1)
                               (all) gone (1)
                               stuffed (1)

There are no examples of causative get + noun +
infinitive.
     Non-causative get + adjective is found in 17
utterances.   Some examples are:

       780   he get sick, sick dead
       782   he gonna get blue
      6538   it will get better soon
     17367   when i get a big girl[28]

Erica uses a total of 12 adjectives in this construction.   They may be classified into four categories:

general	colors	comparative[29]	adjective + noun
angry (1)	black (4)[30]	better (2)	(a) big girl(1)
dead (1)	blue (2)	smarter (1)	
dirty (1)	green (2)		
mad (1)			
ready (1)			
sick (1)			

There are eight examples of get + past participle:

       674   he will get hitten by a bus, won't he?
      5523   i'm not going to get burned by humidifier
     10794   this time they don't get lost
     11519   get married
     16736   i wanna get married sometime
     17529   get hurt
     19137   getting dressed
     19139   getting dressed

            past participles: burned   (1)
                                dressed (2)
                                hitten   (1)
                                hurt   (1)
                                lost   (1)
                                married (2)

Get appears with the meaning "must" in six cases, e.g.

      5209   i gotta put the apples away
     13532   i got to get new shoes

and as a possessive in two:

      3541   lookit, he's got stripes
      4822   what you got this time?

These data are summarized in Table XV.

Table XV.   (Pre)Causative/Non-Causative Distribution
             of <u>Get</u> in Child Erica

$$\Sigma N = 276$$

(Pre)Causative	N	%	Non-Causative	N	%
get + loc	59	21	A. get + adj	17	6
get + N + loc	35	13	get + PP	8	3
get + N + adj	4	1.5	must	6	2
get + N + PP	3	1	possessive	2	1
get + N + inf	0	0	B. acquire, fatch	136	49
get + N + Prs. P	0	0	C. miscellaneous	6	2
Total	101	36.5	Total	175	63

<u>Adult Nina</u>
In the adult portion of the Nina corpus, there
are 283 instances of <u>get.</u> Over half (150) of all
instances of <u>get</u> have the basic meaning "acquire" or
"fetch", e.g.

      15900   shall i get you some crayons and paper?
      19381   did gail come and get you right away?

Of these 150, at least 15 use positional locative
phrases, e.g.

      12783   will get some bread at the store soon
      26661   oh, i get such nice hugs from my little
              one

Also included within this total of 150 are two cases
in which <u>get</u> takes a purpose clause:

      26897   get something to put around the house
      27099   will get you something to drink as soon
              as i go to the store

There are a total of 69 precausative and causa-
tive instances of <u>get.</u> Precausative <u>get</u> + locative
occurs in 40 utterances, e.g.

      17403   do you want me to get up and cook at the
              stove?
      26423   oh, the car knocked down the tree to get
              by

Six different locatives are represented:

        back   (3)
        by   (1)
        in   (6)
        out   (7)
        there (1)
        up   (22)

Causative get + noun + locative appears 25 times, some examples being

        13277 did you get some clay on your nose?
        19253 she has to be careful not to get the
               ball in the flowers, right?
        25260 is it hard to get your arm through?

These utterances include seven types of locatives:

        away   (1)
        in   (8)
        off   (1)
        on   (9)
        out   (4)
        through (1)
        up   (1)

There are two cases of causative get + noun + adjective:

        13235 oh, did you get it open?
        26112 oh, now you're getting my chin all
               dirty

               adjectives: dirty (1)
                            open (1).

Causative get + noun + past participle and get + noun + infinitive each occur once:

        get + noun + past participle: 10143 did you get
                          your finger stuck in there?
               past participle: stuck (1)

        get + noun + infinitive: 26589 they got
                          you to cry, the chickens

     The non-causative construction get + adjective occurs 22 times, e.g.

        6274   are you getting all yucky?
        9833   and what else got muddy?
        19392 did all your clothes get wet?

Within these 22 examples, nine different adjectives are used. These may be classified as general and comparative:

general		comparative
angry	(2)	more comfortable (1)
cold	(2)	
dirty	(3)	
hot	(2)	
hungry	(1)	
muddy	(5)	
wet	(5)	
yucky	(1)	

Non-causative get + past participle is found in 29 utterances. Some examples are:

    21983 did it get twisted?
    23112 let's get dressed now
    25779 she got hurt on her head when she fell
           out of the train?
    27364 remember when snoopy's neck got broken?

A total of ten different past participles appear:

    broken   (2)
    colored   (1)
    covered   (1)
    dressed   (5)
    hurt   (11)
    messed(up)   (1)
    stepped(on)   (1)
    stuck   (3)
    torn   (1)
    twisted(up)   (3)

Two examples of get carry the meaning "must":

    19983 you got to be very quiet
    21790 got to be careful?

Finally, there are six instances of get used to indicate possession, e.g.

    15118 he's got a funny face, doesn't he?
    15455 i got my picture here to show you

The uses of get in the adult portion of the Nina corpus are summarized in Table XVI.

Table XVI.   (Pre)Causative/Non-Causative Distribution
of Get in Adult Nina

ΣN = 283

(Pre)Causative	N	%	Non-Causative	N	%
get + loc	40	14	A. get + adj	22	8
get + N + loc	25	9	get + PP	29	10
get + N + adj	2	.5	must	2	.5
get + N + PP	1	.5	possessive	6	2
get + N + inf	1	.5	B. acquire, fetch	150	53
get + N + Prs. P	0	0	C. miscellaneous	5	2
Total	69	24.5	Total	214	75.5

Adult Erica

In the adult portion of the Erica corpus, there
are a total of 313 instances of get. Less than half
(i.e. 124) of the citations have the basic meaning
"acquire" or "fetch". These include at least six
instances of non-causative get with positional locative phrases, and three examples of get with a
purpose clause, e.g.

3043   i think we should go get a tissue
7102   go get your automobile puzzle on the
kitchen table (loc)
12894   you sit here and i will get something to
clean out your fingernails (purpose)

Of the 109 instances of precausative and causative get, there are 48 examples of precausative get
+ locative, e.g.

7060   that's right, daddy will get home before
it rains too
12960   erica, would you get back to the table
and eat your lunch?
17498   how did a rock get in your eyebrow?

The full list of locatives occurring in this construction is:

back   (3)
close   (3)
down   (1)
home   (2)
in   (4)
into   (2)
off   (2)

```
on        (6)
over      (1)
out       (10)
'round    (1)
up        (13)
```

Adult Erica contains 45 instances of causative <u>get</u> + noun + locative. For example,

```
 1769  what did you get on your hand?
13060  you better eat your big people's food
       or i'll get you back on the baby food
18752  well, you get all your talking out
```

The complete list of locatives is:

```
away  (1)   in   (4)   underneath  (2)
back  (1)   off  (5)   up          (2)
down  (1)   on   (15)
from  (1)   out  (13)
```

There are seven examples of causative <u>get</u> + noun + adjective:

```
 6965  you'll get your pants all wet
12049  you are getting yourself all wet
12923  am i getting them off or getting them
       clean?
12926  i am getting them clean
13580  the soap gets her warm
18190  it gets you all bloody
18244  you are getting me all warm and what?
       (partial imitation)

       adjectives:  bloody  (1)
                    clean   (2)
                    warm    (2)
                    wet     (2)
```

Nine utterances contain <u>get</u> + noun + past participle, e.g.

```
 7528  helen got her hair cut, didn't she?
11923  ok, let me get it untangled first
13366  let's get your hands washed
```

The complete list of past participles occurring in this construction is:

```
changed           (1)
cut               (1)
finished          (1)
fixed             (1)
put (together)    (1)
untangled         (1)
washed            (3)
```

There are no examples of causative get + noun +
infinitive.

Get + adjective appears 37 times. Some examples
are:

> 10349 he didn't get all white again
> 12352 you're getting to be a grown up girl
> 12968 so we won't get too hot
> 17564 when you get older you will have long
>   hair

The range of adjectives may be classified into four
cagegories: general, colors, comparative, and
adjective + noun:

general		colors		compar- ative	adjective + noun
angry	(1)	ready	(4)	black	(5)	better(1)	(to be a)
(to be)big	(1)	sick	(1)	blue	(1)	bigger(1)	big girl
dark	(1)	silly	(3)	green	(1)	older (1)	(1)
dirty	(1)	soft	(1)	white	(1)	smarter(1)	(to be a)
drunk	(1)	sticky	(1)				grown up
hard	(1)	warm	(1)				girl (1)
hot	(3)	wet	(3)				

There are 24 examples of the construction get + past
participle, e.g.

> 12045 are you going to get dressed this
>   morning?
> 14702 someone left it on the floor and it got
>   stepped on
> 16863 yes, you might get stuck in it

The full list of past participles occurring in this
construction is:

burned	(3)	recorded	(1)
dressed	(2)	rid	(2)
hurt	(2)	stepped(on)	(2)
lost	(2)	stuck	(2)
married	(2)	tired	(1)
mixed	(3)	used	(1)
put	(1)		

Finally, the adult portion of the corpus contains nine
examples of get used with the meaning "must" and five
in which get signals possession, e.g.

> "must": 6264 for a while it's got to be one
>   or the other
>   12215 got to keep your head down,

```
                          don't you?
    "possessive":   2646  he's got bare feet
                    3447  you have now got five of
                          them
```

The various occurrences of get in the adult portion of the Erica corpus are summarized in Table XVII.

Table XVII.   (Pre)Causative/Non-Causative Distribution of Get in Adult Erica

ΣN = 313

(Pre)Causative	N	%	Non-Causative	N	%
get + loc	48	15	A. get + adj	37	12
get + N + loc	45	14	get + PP	24	8
get + N + adj	7	2	must	9	3
get + N + PP	9	3	possessive	5	1.5
get + N + inf	0	0	B. acquire, fetch	124	40
get + N + Prs.P	0	0	C. miscellaneous	5	1.5
Total	109	34	Total	204	66

The Ten Plays

Crowell reports finding a total of 1588 citations of get in the ten plays he examined. In combining the frequencies of each of Crowell's four core meanings of get, I was only able to account for 1561 instances. I have calculated all percentages on the basis of the lower statistic. While listing all locatives, adjectives, and past participles occuring with get, Crowell does not indicate which occur in causative and which in non-causative syntax. I therefore have excluded the lists from the presentation of data below.

The total number of uses of get in the transitive sense "acquire" or "fetch" is 342. Some examples are:

        Plenty of girls are tickled to death you got
        what was coming to you ("The Women")
        What'd my Romeo do? Got himself another girl
        ("The Women")

There are 472 examples of precausative and causative get, with precausative get + locative appearing 318 times, e.g.

How did your generation ever get through the
1920's? ("The Male Animal")
I've worked hard to get where I'm at ("Boy
Meets Girl")

Causative get + noun + locative has 110 citations,
e.g.

I'm going to get her away from all this! ("The
Male Animal")
You'd never get the damn thing through the
mails ("Season in the Sun")

The construction get + noun + adjective only occurs
five times, e.g.

I'll get the window open ("Arsenic and Old
Lace")
Please get our room ready immediately
("Arsenic and Old Lace")

Causative get + noun + past participle appears 27
times, e.g.

Why must you come here to get your picture
painted? ("Biography")

This crew got you transferred ("Mister
Roberts")

and get + noun + infinitive is cited 11 times, e.g.

Let's get Jascha to send a cable ("Boy Meets
Girl")
You'll never get me to believe that... ("Dream
Girl")

In addition, there is one causative use with the
present participle:

I've just got Cynthia entering the monastery
("You Can't Take It with You")

   Non-causative get + adjective appears 65 times,
e.g.

I'm getting hungry ("Boy Meets Girl")
It is getting much darker, isn't it? ("Season
in the Sun")

There are 162 cases of get used in the sense of "must",
e.g.

I've got to do something ("Arsenic and Old
Lace")
You've got to ask yourself where you're going
("Biography")

and 381 examples of <u>get</u> indicating possession, e.g.

My, you have got the jitters, dear ("The Women")
Say, what time you got? ("Arsenic and Old Lace")

Table XVIII summarizes the causative and non-causative uses of <u>get</u> in the ten plays surveyed by Crowell.

Table XVIII. (Pre)Causative/Non-Causative Distribution of <u>Get</u> in Ten Plays

$$\Sigma N = 1561$$

(Pre) Causative	N	%	Non-Causative	N	%
get + loc	318	20	A. get + adj	65	4
get + N + loc	110	7	get + PP	116	7
get + N + adj	5	.5	must	162	10
get + N + PP	27	2	possessive	381	25
get + N + inf	11	.5	B. acquire, fetch	342	22
get + N + Prs. P	1	0	C. miscellaneous	23	1.5
Total	472	30	Total	1089	69.5

Brown University

I analyzed every third instance of <u>get</u> in the Brown University corpus (cf. fn. 18), yielding a total of 488 distinct entries; 155 of these examples have the meaning "acquire" or "fetch", e.g.

...he never got that chance (0300 EIN 11)
Hiding out like this won't get him anything except more trouble or a bullet (1370 EIL 20)

Of these 155, at least 19 employ positional locative expressions, e.g.

Dwellers thereabouts preferred to get their apple pies at the local bakery... (1580 EIE 11)
...I got a letter from home... (1050 EIF 18)

There are 135 instances of precausative <u>get</u> + locative, some examples being

She got to her feet, staggered, and almost fell (1280 EIN 01)
Actually, all a man in uniform has to do is to go get by (1540 EIP 05)

Causative <u>get</u> + noun + locative appears 55 times, e.g.

> Nadine's constant nagging had finally gotten
> Wally out of bed (1590 EIP 18)
> She was in good health and spirits, but still
> determined to get the money from Forbes
> (0420 EIL 21)

<u>Get</u> + noun + adjective is cited only twice:

> I've got her as neat as I can... (0240 EIN 15)
> I did a week of research to get the details
> just right (0150 EIP 10)

However, <u>get</u> + noun + past participle is used 13 times,
e.g.

> In each city civic and educational leaders have
> been working hard to get public opinion
> prepared to accept the inevitability of equal
> treatment (0870 EIB 09)

> I guess he spent the morning getting himself
> all organized, then headed for home (0010 EIN
> 22)

and <u>get</u> + noun + infinitive yields six examples, e.g.

> Preoccupied with his own defense and his
> attempts to get Robinson to fight... (0660 EIG
> 52)
> To get him to pose, Mrs. Coolidge would feed
> him candy... (0420 EIG 41)

Non-causative <u>get</u> + adjective appears in 25 lines,
e.g.

> ...where they can amuse each other until we
> get ready to merge sides (0950 EIE 19)
> ...to determine what might be done if things
> get worse... (0240 EIE 28)

<u>Get</u> + past participle occurs 38 times. For example,

> Incest is still a durable theme, but if it
> wants to get written about it will have to
> find ways to surprise the emotions... (0360
> EIG 26)

> ...to be sure that they didn't get lost, Prevot
> had placed Warren and White in the center of
> the patrol as it filed out (0640 EIK 02)

In the sense of "must", <u>get</u> is used 14 times, e.g.

> But I've got to take a chance on it... (1600
> EIN 27)

> Now look here lady, I know you got to entertain
> these kinds and all (0100 EIR 07)

and the possessive interpretation occurs 25 times,
e.g.

> I've got this cold (1000 EIP 23)
> ...you've got Prussian blue all over your
> shirt... (0500 EIP 10)

　　　Table XIX summarizes the sample of <u>get</u> drawn from
the Brown University corpus.

Table XIX.　(Pre)Causative/Non-Causative Distribution
　　　　　　　　of <u>Get</u> in Brown University Corpus

$$\Sigma N = 488$$

(Pre)Causative	N	%	Non-Causative	N	%
get + loc	135	28	A.　get + adj	25	5
get + N + loc	55	11	get + PP	38	8
get + N + adj	2	.5	must	14	3
get + N + PP	13	3	possessive	25	5
get + N + inf	6	1	B.　acquire, fetch	155	32
get + N + Prs.P	0	0	C.　miscellaneous	20	4
Total	211	43.5	Total	277	57

DISCUSSION

　　　I will begin with a few remarks on transitive <u>get</u>
in the sense of "acquire" or "fetch", and will then
analyze the emergence of precausative and causative
locative expressions.　The remainder of this subsec-
tion will discuss causative and non-causative <u>get</u> with
adjectival and past participial complements and then
causative <u>get</u> with an infinitival complement.

　　　<u>"Acquire", "Fetch"</u>

　　　In all of the corpora, the transitive construction
with the meaning "acquire" or "fetch" accounts for a
large percentage of all instances of <u>get</u>.　These data
are summarized in Table XX.

Table XX.   Use of <u>Get</u> with the Meaning "Acquire" or
            "Fetch"

	Adam I	Nina		Erica		Ten Plays	Brown University
		Child	Adult	Child	Adult		
"acquire", "fetch"	41 (76%)	123 (59%)	150 (53%)	136 (49%)	124 (39%)	342 (22%)	155 (32%)

The highest percentage occurs in Adam I.   Nina, who is
younger and less linguistically advanced than Erica
(cf. Table VII), uses <u>get</u> in this basic meaning less
frequently than Adam, yet more frequently than Erica.
While the relative frequency of this basic transitive
use of <u>get</u> is very close between child and adult
portions of the Nina corpus (i.e. 59% vs. 53%), there
is a somewhat larger difference between child and adult
use in the Erica corpus (i.e. 49% vs. 39%).   The
Crowell and Brown University corpora show less than
one third of the instances with <u>get</u> to have the meaning "acquire" or "fetch".   In the case of Crowell's
ten plays, the percentage is very low (i.e. 22%).
     In 5.2, I presented the general hypotheses that
(a) adults speak differently to younger children than
they do to older children, and (b) adults speak
differently to young children in general than they do
to other adults.   While the present data are only
suggestive, they do seem to support these hypotheses.
The adult speaker in the Erica corpus only restricts
39% of her use of <u>get</u> to this basic transitive function
(Erica = older child), while the adult in the Nina
corpus uses <u>get</u> with this meaning 53% of the time
(Nina = younger child).   Comparing the adult portions
of the Nina and Erica corpora on the one hand, and the
Crowell and Brown University corpora on the other, it
is clear that the latter two adult-to-adult corpora
show more syntactic and semantic diversity with <u>get</u>
(i.e. less restriction to transitive uses meaning
"acquire" or "fetch") than do the adult-to-child
samples in the two longitudinal corpora.
     Given the high percentage (76%) of transitive <u>get</u>
in the Adam I corpus, it is tempting to conclude that
this basic use of <u>get</u> is the first meaning to be
acquired by the child.   However, since Adam also uses
<u>get</u> in some locative constructions (cf. below), it
will be necessary to examine the speech of even less

linguistically developed children before this
hypothesis can be confirmed or rejected. It is also
possible that transitive get (i.e. get + noun) and
get + locative develop simultaneously.

Locative
Do the three longitudinal corpora support the
hypotheses that (a) get first acquires causative
function in locative constructions and (b) causative
get + noun + locative develops directly out of what I
have been calling precausative get + locative? I will
argue that the data offer strong evidence in favor of
both of these hypotheses.

In the child samples of Adam, Nina, and Erica,
precausative get + locative is the second most
frequent construction type with get, surpassed only
by the transitive construction meaning "acquire" or
"fetch". This is also true of all four adult corpora.
Table XXI summarizes the data on precausative and
causative locative expressions.

Table XXI.   Use of Locatives with Precausative and
             Causative Get

	Adam I	Nina Child	Nina Adult	Erica Child	Erica Adult	Ten Plays	Brown University
Precausative get + loc	8 (15%)	37 (18%)	40 (14%)	59 (21%)	48 (15%)	318 (20%)	135 (28%)
Causative get + N + loc	0 (0%)	17 (8%)	25 (9%)	35 (13%)	45 (14%)	110 (7%)	55 (11%)

There is, of course, no necessary relation
between the present frequency and date of acquisition
of constructions. However, if it can be established
that a particular construction type is both frequent
and productive while other constructions are at best
sporadic, there would seem to be grounds for calling
the first construction linguistically prior in the
child's productive system.

The relevant data here are in Adam I. Adam's use
of get is highly restricted. However, of the 11
classifiable instances which are not transitive verbs
with the meaning "acquire" or "fetch", eight are of
the form get + locative. Even if one argues that the
majority of these are as yet unanalyzed into a verb
and a locative component, it is important to recognize
that (a) Adam does use all the locative elements as

distinct lexical items, and (b) all of the same
locatives are used in the Nina and Erica corpora in
get + locative constructions. To conclude the argument that get + locative is the earliest source of the
get causative, it is also necessary to explain the one
appearance of causative get + noun + adjective, i.e.

2619   get supper ready

and the two instances of get + past participle

986   adam getstuck
987   getstuck

in Adam I.

One hypothesis is that both get supper ready and
getstuck are imitations or unanalyzed idioms. Without
adult linguistic context, it is impossible to
substantiate either of these proposals. However, there
is some supporting evidence for the idiomatic status
of getstuck in that multiple occurrences of get +
stuck appear in the adult portions of both the Nina
and Erica corpora.

Given the high plausability that get + locative
constructions are the first precursor to causative
uses of get, we may now examine the hypothesis that
causative get + noun + locative develops from precausative get + locative. If it is actually true that
the causative construction initially derives from the
non-causative by the insertion of an object noun, then
there should be a high degree of overlap between the
locatives used in precausative and causative expressions. Table XXII compares the locatives appearing in
precausative and causative expressions in both child
and adult portions of the Nina and Erica corpora.
Locatives are arranged in order of frequency.

Table XXII.　Locatives in Precausative and Causative
　　　　　　　　Expressions in the Nina and Erica
　　　　　　　　Corpora

Nina Corpus				Erica Corpus			
Child		Adult		Child		Adult	
precaus	caus	precaus	caus	precaus	caus	precaus	caus
up 15	on 6	up 22	on 9	up 16	on 11	up 13	on 11
out 14	in 5	out 7	in 8	in 11	out 9	out 10	out 9
in 4	out 3	in 6	out 4	on 11	up 4	on 6	off 5
away 3	away 1	back 3	up 1	out 9	away 3	in 4	in 4
into 1	down 1	by 1	away 1	down 4	off 3	back 3	up 2
	off 1	there 1	off 1	off 2	from 2	close 3	under- 2
			through 1	over 2	in 2	home 2	neath
				close 1	to 1	into 2	away 1
				home 1		off 2	back 1
				into 1		down 1	down 1
				to 1		over 1	from 1
						'round 1	

　　　　A high degree of overlap is obvious between
constructions, between children, between adults, and
between children and adults.　The most salient
locatives in both precausative and causative expressions are up, on, in, and out.　In child and adult
Erica (both precausative and causative), each of these
locatives occurs at least twice.　On is absent from
the precausative locatives in child Nina, although
this omission may be a function of the model Nina
predominantly hears:　get + on is also absent in the
adult portion of the corpus.　There are no examples
of up in Nina's causative constructions, though that
may, again, be a function of Nina's adult model (i.e.
only a single citation appears in adult Nina).
　　　　There are several possible syntactic "routes" by
which causative get + noun + locative might evolve
from non-causative constructions.　The first, and most
obvious, involves the separation of verb and particle
in get + locative combinations.　As we saw in Adam I,
verb + locative is a typical expression in the early
stages of first language acquisition.　Consider now
the following hypothetical phrases:

    (a) get off
    (b) get off shoes
    (c) get shoes off

The phrase get off is parallel to several of the
utterances found in Adam 1 (e.g. get back, getin).
Also, expressions of the form get off shoes are
reflected in Adam's getin kitty or getover ball. At
this point in development, the child has two choices.
If he is, in fact, analyzing the get + locative
construction into two elements where get is functioning as a causative in the underlying get + noun +
locative construction, he may recognize the basic
synonymy of

    (b) get off shoes

and

    (c) get shoes off

and extrapose off in (b) to form (c).[31] The child's
other alternative is to treat get + locative as a
single verb which may take objects. In some cases
this choice will be correct (e.g. get off + "clothing"
is largely synonymous with the transitive verb
remove) while in other cases it is not. The Nina
corpus provides a potential example of mistaken interpretation. The conversation between Nina and her
mother proceeds as follows:

    17041 Mother: what are you going to do?
    17042 Nina: get away this
    17043   get away (Nina pushes away the
                    blocks)
    17044 Mother: get away the...blocks?

In line 17042, Nina has apparently failed to place the
particle away at the end of the sentence,[32] which
suggests she is treating get away as a unit like get
off. Unfortunately, there is no way to determine from
the data whether or not this utterance is acceptable
in Nina's own grammar. Linguists are well aware that
adults often produce sentences which the speaker, upon
reflection, would judge to be ungrammatical. Children
also sometimes make errors with respect to their own
grammar, but unless they correct their errors, we have
no way of identifying an utterance as ill-formed vis-
à-vis the child.
    A second potential source of causative get + noun
+ locative constructions is parental models in which
the object is preposed, leaving get immediately
followed by the locative, as in the precausative construction. The following example appears in the adult

portion of the Nina corpus:

    10587   what did you <u>get out</u>? (cf. you <u>got what out</u>?)

Similarly, in the adult portion of the Erica corpus:

    19819   what do you want me to <u>get off</u>?
            (cf. you want me to <u>get what off</u>? you want me to <u>get off what</u>?)

A third contributing construction might be precausative <u>get</u> + locative constructions with non-volitional subjects. For example, the adult in the Erica corpus says

    17498   how did a rock get in your eyebrow?

though she might just as likely have used the causative (or perhaps resultative)

         how did you get a rock in your eyebrow?

    Finally, of what relevance to causative <u>get</u> + noun + locative are the non-causative examples of <u>get</u> meaning "acquire" or "fetch" which have positional locative modifiers, e.g.

    Child Erica:
    causative   9738   me try to get it in
    non-causative 10276   he get a bath in that

In theory, there are three distinct possible interpretations: either the two constructions are unrelated, or the non-causative is the source of the causative, or the causative is the source of the non-causative. In practice, however, there seems to be evidence supporting only the first and last hypotheses. It is likely that surface similarity is more important here than underlying linguistic differences. In underlying structure, causative <u>get it in</u> is composed of at least two sentences while non-causative <u>he get a bath in that</u> contains, at least on some analyses, only one. In actual use, it is often difficult to distinguish between the two constructions. Percentagewise, the causative construction is more frequent in Nina and Erica's speech. Given the higher frequency of the causative construction, it is possible that the causative does in fact provide the initial surface syntactic model for the non-causative construction. Another possibility, however, is that the distribution of causative and non-causative configurations is not a function of derivational priority but rather only reflects the pragmatic choices the speaker has made as to what

aspects of the extralinguistic situation he wishes to
encode linguistically. The fact that approximately
the same ratio of causative to non-causative constructions in Nina and Erica's speech appears in all four
adult corpora lends support to this pragmatic explanation.

Adjective
There are two questions to be asked about the
development of get with adjectives: (a) what is the
connection between causative get + noun + adjective
and inchoative get + adjective? and (b) how is causative get + noun + adjective related to causative get
+ noun + locative?

Consider first the two adjectival constructions.
Table XXIII summarizes the use of both inchoative and
causative configurations in all corpora.

Table XXIII. Use of Adjectives with Inchoative and
              Causative Get

| | Adam I | Nina | | Erica | | Ten Plays | Brown University |
		Child	Adult	Child	Adult		
Inchoative get + adj	0 (0%)	6 (3%)	22 (8%)	17 (6%)	37 (12%)	65 (4%)	25 (5%)
Causative get+N+adj	1 (2%)	0 (0%)	2 (.5%)	4 (1.5%)	7 (2%)	5 (.5%)	2 (.5%)

The causative never represents more than two or three
percent of a given corpus, though the inchoative is
well documented in all but Adam I. Although the
distribution of adjectives is quite diffuse, there is
evidence that various of the adjectives occurring in
the non-causative frame later appear in the causative
frame as well. Most of these tend to be basic adjectives for describing the child's world, e.g. wet,
warm, muddy, dirty. For example, Erica uses dirty in
both non-causative and causative constructions:

          inchoative: 13227 get dirty
          causative: 4400 i get it dirty

(cf. adult Nina for a parallel example with dirty).
The adult portion of the Erica corpus reveals similar
pairs with wet and warm:

inchoative: 12219   then you don't get wet, do
                      `you?
causative: 12049   you are getting yourself
                      all wet
inchoative: 16288   no, they're getting warm by
                      the fire
causative: 13580   the soap gets her warm
                      (imitation of child)

While Nina does not yet use causative get + noun +
adjective, wet, muddy, and dirty all appear in her
utterances with inchoative get + adjective.

The adjectival data seem to suggest that causative
use of get + noun + adjective develops from addition
of a noun to an already established inchoative get +
adjective construction. Syntactically, the ontogenetic
origin of causative get + noun + adjective would be
parallel to that of get + noun + locative (cf.
immediately preceding section on locatives). Descrip-
tively, what appears to be happening is that the child
generalizes the surface syntactic construction of
causative get + noun + _____ from only allowing locative elements in final position to allowing adjectives
as well.

Why should the first expansion be to adjectives?
One obvious factor is that adjectives are already to
be found with get in the child's speech at this time,
unlike past participles or infinitives (cf. **Tables
XXIII - XV**). However, there is also some evidence
that adults speaking to children may provide helpful
models which group adjectives and locatives into the
same complement slot with causative get. Consider the
following lines from the Erica corpus:

adult   12923   am i getting them off or getting
                them clean?
adult   12926   i am not taking them off, i am
                getting them clean

Through this conjoined expression, the adult interlocutor signals to Erica that at least some locatives
and adjectives have similar privileges of occurrence.

Past Participle
Parallel to the case of adjectives, two crucial
questions to be asked about past participle constructions are (a) what is the connection between causative
get + noun + past participle and inchoative get + past
participle, and (b) how is causative get + noun + past
participle related to causative get + noun + locative
or adjective? An additional important topic is the
distinction between inchoative and passive interpreta-

tion of non-causative <u>get</u> + past participle. Table
XXIV summarizes the uses of past participles with <u>get</u>
in each corpus. For reasons which will become clear,
I include inchoative and passive examples in the same
category.

Table XXIV. Use of Past Participles with Inchoative
             and Causative <u>Get</u>

		Nina		Erica		Ten	Brown
	Adam I	Child	Adult	Child	Adult	Plays	University
Inchoative get + PP	2 (4%)	5 (2%)	29 (10%)	8 (3%)	24 (8%)	116 (7%)	38 (8%)
Causative get + N + PP	0 (0%)	1 (.5%)	1 (.5%)	3 (1%)	9 (3%)	27 (2%)	13 (3%)

In all samples, the number of inchoative constructions
is at least twice that of the causative. The absence
or extreme rarity of <u>get</u> + noun + past participle in
Adam and Nina, respectively, strongly suggests that
inchoative <u>get</u> + past participle is developmentally
prior to the causative construction.
     As in the case of locative and adjectival
expressions, there is some overlap between the past
participles used in inchoative constructions and those
appearing in causative frames. For example, Nina uses
the past participle <u>twisted</u> in both contexts, e.g.

          inchoative: 21986   it get twisted, mommy
                                (spontaneous imitation)
          causative: 5592   <xxx> get these all twisted
                                in back

Similarly, in the adult portion of the Nina corpus,
<u>stuck</u> appears in both frames:

          inchoative: 16560   your foot get stuck?
          causative: 10143   did you get your finger
                                stuck in there?

While this dual function accounts for the single
examples in the child and adult portions of the Nina
corpus, it applies to only one of the 11 past participles appearing in causative <u>get</u> expressions in the
combined child and adult portions of the Erica corpus:

          Adult Erica:
             inchoative: 11801   i think that kitty get put
                                  outside if he scratches

causative: 5162   we will do that as soon as we
                      get these put together

These data do formally link inchoative and causative
get with past participles, though the connection is
not as clear as in the case of locatives, and, to a
lesser extent, adjectives, in that there are relatively few past participles which occur in both inchoative
and causative function within a single sample.   However, if causative constructions with locatives and
perhaps adjectives are already productive before
causative get + ·noun + past participle constructions
appear, then it is not necessary for the same past
participles to appear with inchoative and causative
get as was the case with locatives in precausative and
causative expressions, and adjectives in inchoative
and causative constructions.   While it is probably
true that the appearance of causative get + noun +
past participle also implies the prior emergence of
inchoative get + past participle, the actual development of the causative is likely to be as much a direct
extension of the causative get + noun + $\begin{Bmatrix} \text{locative} \\ \text{adjective} \end{Bmatrix}$
pattern (cf. above discussion of adjectives) as an
elaboration of inchoative get + past participle.

     In comparing the relative frequencies of
inchoative and causative get, there are several
differences with respect to adjectival and past
participial complements between conversation between
children and adults (i.e. Nina and Erica corpora) and
conversation just between adults (i.e. ten plays and
Brown University corpus).   The comparative data are
summarized in Table XXV.

Table XXV. Inchoative and Causative <u>Get</u> Expressions
with Adjectives and Part Participles

	Nina		Erica		Ten Plays	Brown University
	Child	Adult	Child	Adult		
Inchoative						
get + adj	3%	8%	6%	12%	4%	5%
get + PP	2%	10%	3%	8%	7%	8%
Causative						
get + N + adj	0%	.5%	1.5%	2%	.5%	.5%
get + N + PP	.5%	.5%	1%	3%	2%	3%

Table XXV shows that among both children and adults of
the longitudinal samples, the percentage of inchoative
and causative adjectival constructions is either very
close to or greater than the comparable past participial constructions.[33] However, in the Crowell and Brown
University corpora, the reverse is true: past
participial constructions are uniformly more prevalent
in both causative and inchoative contexts. However,
all of the percentages are small, and the differences
are probably not statistically significant.

In general, Nina and Erica use relatively few
past participial forms. Where they do occur, there is
often no evidence in surface structure that these past
participles are analyzed by the children as verbal
constructions rather than as simple adjectives (cf.
3.2). Listed below are some examples from the child
samples which are normally analyzed as past participles
in an (adult) synchronic model, yet conceivably are
functioning as adjectives in the child's grammar:

                  Nina: 17355 they're tired (cf. they're happy)
                         21765 that's fixed (cf. that's pretty)
                         26119 it's all finished (cf. it's all
                                dirty)
                  Erica: 5056 they're all covered (cf. they're
                                all empty)

18107   he was scared (cf. he was angry)

Watt (1970:185) makes a similar hypothesis that
children construct sentences of the form <u>Those cookies
were baked</u> by the same rules used to form simple
predicate-adjective sentences such as <u>Those cookies
were good</u>: "The surfaces are very similar, and
participles like "baked" are quasi-adjectival" (also
cf. Harwood 1959).

   None of the discussion of past participles thus
far has distinguished between inchoative and passive
interpretations of <u>get</u> + past participle. If the
hypothesis is correct that past participles are first
interpreted as adjectives and only later reanalyzed as
verbal forms, then it should also be true that the
inchoative use of <u>get</u> + past participle develops
before the passive interpretation. The thesis is,
however, not easily proven or refuted, since it is
frequently impossible to determine whether an expression is being used inchoatively or passively. In some
cases, the meaning is clearly inchoative, e.g.

        Child Nina: 25094   i will get tired
        Adult Nina: 21092   let's get dressed to go to
                             justin's house, ok?

In other examples, the presence of a <u>by</u>-phrase clearly
identifies an example as passive, e.g.

        Child Erica   674   he will get hitten by a bus,
                            won't he?
                     5523   i'm not going to get burned
                            by humidifier
        Adult Erica 5535   you would get burned by the
                            humidifier if it were turned
                            on

or the context is a sufficient clue, e.g.

        Adult Erica 14702   someone left it on the
                             floor and it got stepped on

However, in most examples, the distinction is
necessarily subjective. In a sentence such as

        Adult Erica: 12045   are you going to get
                              dressed this morning?

the <u>get</u> construction is inchoative if Erica (i.e. <u>you</u>)
clothes herself, but both inchoative and passive if
she is dressed by, for example, her mother. It is
true that a large number of the <u>get</u> + past participial
constructions involve the kinds of adverse actions
which are typical of true <u>get</u> passives, e.g.

broken
burned
hitten
hurt
stepped on
torn

However, there is no real evidence in these data that
either Nina or Erica has learned that past participles
in get + past participial constructions which express
adverse action must be analyzed as verbs derived from
underlying active sentences.

In section 5.3, I cited data from Bates and
Fischer showing that children both comprehend the get
passive earlier than the be passive, and also prefer
the get passive to the be passive in a judgment task.
These findings imply two conditions: first, that be
and get passives are acquired separately, and second,
that the get passive is acquired earlier. The
longitudinal data on get provide evidence for at least
the first condition. The statistics on Nina and Erica
suggest that the surface construction get + past
participle is a natural extension of the construction
get + locative or get + adjective. I have argued that
get + past participle first functions as an
inchoative, but easily assumes a passive interpretation especially when the subject is disadvantaged by
the action (see Baron 1974). The get passive, is
therefore, not a new construction, but rather represents a change in the semantic focus of the earlier
inchoative. With the be passive, however, there is a
somewhat different ontogenetic history. The recent
literature (e.g. Watt 1970) suggests that the be
passive evolves from a stative, predicate adjective
construction, in which the past participle is
originally analyzed as an adjective, only later
assuming verbal function, e.g.

(a) he was [happy]$_{adj}$

(b) he was [confused]$_{adj}$

(c) he was [confused]$_{verb}$ by the loud noises

There is also some evidence in the longitudinal
corpora that get passives are acquired first. Neither
the child Nina nor the child Erica samples provides
any evidence of the full be passive (e.g. he was con-
fused by the loud noises), although Erica does offer
two examples of full get passive (cf. above). Moreover, there are very few examples in either child

sample which might even tentatively be analyzed as
truncated be passives, cf.

> Child Nina: 6693   yeah, after we get these
>   two more people that's
>   locked downstairs and fell
>   on their head
> Child Erica: 17184   they need a be fixed
>   17185   they need to be fixed

Infinitive
Infinitival complements with causative get are
very infrequent in dialogue between adults and
children. There are no citations in Adam I, child
Erica, or adult Erica, and only three examples in
child Nina, and one in adult Nina. Yet in the two
written adult corpora, infinitival constructions are
sufficiently documented, being twice as frequent as
causative get + noun + adjective in Crowell's data,
and three times as numerous as get + noun + adjective
in the Brown University corpus. These data constitute
additional informal evidence for distinguishing
between the language adults speak to children and the
language of adult conversation, although the
differences between adult-to-child and adult-to-adult
use are not statistically significant. Table XXVI
summarizes the distribution of infinitives with
causative get.

Table XXVI. Infinitive Constructions with Causative
             Get

	Adam I	Nina		Erica		Ten Plays	Brown University
		Child	Adult	Child	Adult		
causative get + N + inf	0 (0%)	3 (1.5%)	1 (.5%)	0 (0%)	0 (0%)	11 (.5%)	6 (1%)

The only anomaly is Nina's three examples of
causative get with infinitival complement. Admittedly, three examples (1.5%) constitute only a very small
portion of the total corpus, and all three appear in
the last month of the sample. Furthermore, Nina does
not yet have full productive control over the construction: in all instances, she fails to use the
complementizer, i.e.

> 20437   get those animals don't go to zoo
> 20833   i'm going get the piggy sleep on mommy's

```
                      lap
       22035     get a bed fit in there
```

However, the omission of to is characteristic of
Nina's infinitives in general, rather than peculiar to
her use of infinitives with get. For example, Nina
uses the verb want with an infinitive five times (all
towards the end of the sample), and to is absent in
all examples:

```
       19428   i want me read the other way
       22659   want me feed her
       22690   i want you hold her eyes, ok?
       22795   you want cover her and i feed her
       22819   want you read her story?
```

There is a possible explanation of why infinitive
constructions with get should emerge only at the end
of the sequence of get causative expressions. In the
case of causative get with adjectives and past
participles, a child is able to substitute either
filler in the same surface slot already established
by the causative locative construction. This
generalization of structure is natural in that locatives, adjectives, and past participles have somewhat
similar distributions in English in general and in
child/adult interchange in particular, cf.

```
       Adult Erica  12923   am i getting them off or
                            getting them clean?
                    12212   <xxx> getting her hair
                            washed
```

Infinitive complements, however, are conceptually more
complex in underlying structure and more distinctly
marked in surface structure in that an overt content
verb appears (e.g. go, sleep, fit, read). In none of
the causative locative, adjectival, or past
participial examples is the underlying copula "relation" expressed, e.g.

```
       Child Erica  4400   i get it dirty
                           (cf. i get it to be dirty)
```

In fact, even in those inchoative uses of get +
adjective in which the copula is obligatory, cf.

```
       Adult Erica  16188  you are getting to be a big
                           girl, aren't you?
```

Erica does not use the to be, i.e.

```
       Child Erica  17367  when i get a big girl
```

CHRONOLOGICAL EMERGENCE OF CAUSATIVE <u>GET</u>

I tentatively postulate the following chronological order of emergence of causative and related <u>get</u> constructions in the acquisition of English as a first language. Some of these stages necessarily overlap:

Stage 0: transitive "acquire", "fetch"
Stage 1: precausative <u>get</u> + locative
Stage 2: non-causative <u>get</u> + $\begin{Bmatrix} \text{adjective} \\ \text{past participle} \end{Bmatrix}$
Stage 3: causative <u>get</u> + noun + locative
Stage 4: causative <u>get</u> + noun + $\begin{Bmatrix} \text{adjective} \\ \text{past} \\ \text{participle} \end{Bmatrix}$
Stage 5: causative <u>get</u> + noun + infinitive
Stage 6: causative <u>get</u> + noun + present participle

5.7 <u>Have</u>

DATA

Adam I
In the Adam I corpus there are seven utterances containing <u>have</u>. All are non-causatives of the form <u>have</u> + noun, and convey the meaning "possess", e.g.

2019 have pencil
2151 have one
2230 have a box

Child Nina
Nina uses <u>have</u> a total of 285 times. The overwhelming majority are simple, possessive <u>have</u> + noun constructions, e.g.

15772 doggy have a bottle
16449 elephant have a nose

Examining the context in which these constructions appear, it is obvious that many utterances constitute requests. For example, Nina says

12780 my have more bread

to which her mother replies

12781 want more bread?
12782 more bread?
12783 we'll get some bread at the store soon

Similarly, Nina's mother says

23390 let me go get some napkins

and Nina answers

> 23391   i want a napkin too
> 23392   my have a napkin

Semantically, these requests with have constitute anticipated (i.e. future) states of affairs.

Locative expressions of the form have + noun + locative occur in 19 utterances. The majority constitute simple, present declaratives, e.g.

> 6673   we have about four people in the bus
> 12083   my have more things in my box
> 25247   i have a shaving cream on me

However, there are at least three cases in which have + noun + locative constitutes a request (i.e. for a different state of affairs in the future):

> 840   have it place
> (cf. Adult Nina: 839   ok, let's put this in place)
> 16246   i have more here
> (context: Nina is requesting more toy animals to play with)
> 19139   that's have a more bobby pins over here
> (context: Nina is requesting more bobby pins from her mother)

Considering the locative expressions as a whole, it is often difficult to determine whether the intended meaning is "possession and location" or is rather some form of a resultative or causative. In a case like

> 2186   i have one in a christmas book
> (context: Erica is explaining she has a picture of a turkey (i.e. one) in a book of hers)

the meaning is possessional ("i have") and locational ("in a Christmas book") in that the location of the picture is a permanent attribute of the book (barring, of course, ripping out or adding pages). But consider now

> 16643   my have your foot on it

Nina is referring to a play bridge (it) which she wants her mother to cross. That is, Nina wishes it to be the case that she has her mother's foot on the bridge. Semantically, the sentence implies causation, futurity, and resultativeness. Because of the difficulty of correctly identifying whether a given locative phrase is being used resultatively or

causatively, I formally classify all these examples
as non-causative in both child and adult portions of
the Nina and Erica corpora. The reader should, however, bear in mind that many have + noun + locative
expressions may actually be resultative or causative.

Nina uses a present participial construction with
have in three utterances:

```
6745   nina has a ,sock missing
17377  nina has dolly sleeping
16670  have a nina crossing to maggie's house
```

This first example (6745) was uttered spontaneously.
It is possible to argue that missing functions in
Nina's grammar as a simple adjective rather than as a
verbal construction with causative or resultative
force.   The sentence

nina has a sock missing

can be paraphrased by

nina has a sock that is missing

or

nina has a missing sock

Compare a hypothetical sentence which is superficially
similar:

(a) Albert had the water running.
    (i.e. Albert was running the water)

Sentence (a) cannot be paraphrased by

(b) *Albert had the water which was running.
(c) *Albert had the running water.

While (c), and perhaps even (b) are interpretable as
possessive, they only make sense in a context such as

On my property there were a lot of stagnant
pools, but Albert had the only running water
in this whole area.

The second example of an overt present participial form (17377) occurs in a context in which the
form (sleeping) earlier appeared as a verb:

```
Adult Nina:   17373  why do we have to be quiet?
Child Nina:   17374  'cause they're sleeping
Adult:        17375  'cause they're sleeping?
Child:        17376  the dolly sleeping
              17377  nina has dolly sleeping
```

It is again possible to argue that sleeping functions
as an adjective rather than as a verbal form.   While

(17377) may be paraphrased by

> nina has a doll that is sleeping

or

> nina has a sleeping doll

there is no indication that Nina herself caused the
doll to sleep, which would be the necessary interpretation if <u>sleeping</u> is analyzed as having overt
verbal force.

The third example of a present participial form
(16670) is also part of a conversation in which the
present participle earlier appears as a verb, i.e.

Child Nina:	16644	you, you cross on the street
Adult Nina:	16647	you cross maggie's street now?
Child:	16669	crossing to maggie's house
	16670	have a nina crossing to maggie's house
	16679	where's maggie?
Adult:	16680	magie's at home
	16681	we'll go see her soon

However, unlike the earlier two cases, it is not
possible to analyze <u>crossing</u> as a simple adjective, cf.

> *have a crossing-to-maggie's-house nina
> *have a nina who is crossing to maggie's house

One interpretation of (16670) is that Nina has simply
uttered a sentence which is ungrammatical with respect
to her own grammar. Like any other speaker, she may
have begun her sentence with one syntactic and
semantic structure and then switched to another mid-
stream. However, another interpretation might be that
Nina's sentence has implied causative and resultative
force. Nina may be stating that she would like it to
be the case that she crosses to Maggie's house, and
her mother states that this wish will be fulfilled in
the near future ("we'll go see her soon").

The corpus contains eight examples of <u>have</u> in the
obligation sense of "must", e.g.

| 6625 | you take, no you have to take 'em downstairs |
| 25909 | have to do that |

One citation contains a perfective use of <u>have</u>,[34] i.e.

22071   i have seen a bed on miriam's head

although this is actually a partial imitation of
Nina's mother's

22067   have you ever seen an engine with a bed
on top of it?

Table XXVII summarizes Nina's use of have. This
and subsequent tables do not, however, indicate how
many instances imply futurity.

Table XXVII.   Causative/Non-Causative Distribution of
Have in Child Nina

Σ N = 285

Causative	N	%	Non-Causative	N	%
have + N +, loc	?	?	A. possessive		
have + N + adj	0	0	1. have + N	253	89
have + N + pres. p.	1	.4	2. have + N + loc	19	6
have + N + past p.	0	0	3. have + N + adj	0	0
have + N + infinitive	0	0	4. have + N + pres. p.	2	.8
			5. have + N + past p.	0	0
			B. have + N + infinitive	0	0
			C. must	8	3
			D. perfective, past	1	.4
			E. miscellaneous	1	.4
Total	1	.4	Total	284	99.6

Child Erica
Erica uses the verb have 328 times. The majority
of constructions are possessives of the form have +
noun, e.g.

175   he doesn't have a bed
12555   do you have some alphabet sugar?

There are two possessive constructions which occur in
the progressive:

5281   let me having tinker toys
19910   he having a bowl for...

In the first instances, a progressive form does appear
in the immediately preceding context, cf.

Adult Erica: 5277 don't you have some tea?
                5278 aren't you serving tea?
                5279 what's that?
Child Erica: 5280 that
                5281 let me having tinker toys
Adult: 5282 ok
                5283 you may have tinker toys

However, no progressive form immediately precedes line
19910.[35]
    A large proportion of the <u>have</u> + noun expressions
involve implied or explicit futurity. Several of
these are predictions, e.g.

      688 he will have another one, does he?
     3074 they're gonna have some tea
    15399 i will have some of that
    19044 shall the dolly have hair?

The majority, however, are requests, e.g.
     1507 let me have another cucumber
     5783 may i have a fork?
    15149 can i have this, maybe?
    15849 lemme have a napkin
    16618 i want to have happy birthday

    Locative elements occur with 40 <u>have</u> + noun
constructions in the Nina sample. Judging from surface
structure, three-quarters of these refer to present or
past time situations, e.g.

      602 all animals have fingernails on their
           nose, don't they?
    10360 he has white on him
    17604 because i have my nightgown on

In about ten cases, futurity is implied or expressed
through a prediction or request, e.g.

    prediction: 11447 he will not have a beard on
    request: 4377 let me have my hammer there
                  5567 let me have my...let me
                        have my alphabet up right
                  5758 i want to have it up there
                 14969 let me have children on the
                        tape recorder

As in the Nina corpus, it is sometimes difficult to
determine whether constructions are possessive or
resultative/causative.
    In addition to non-causative locative examples,
there is one figurative citation of a rather different

sort which seems to be causative:

     15506   have me on a diet

The relevant conversation proceeds as follows:

Child Erica:	15501	you have diet
	15503	here
	15504	you have diet
Adult Erica:	15505	i have diet
Child:	15506	have me on diet
Adult:	15507	you are not on a diet
Child:	15508	you are on a diet
Adult:	15509	yes, i am

Admittedly, "to have one on a diet", e.g.

    My doctor had me on a salt-free diet.

is idiomatic in English. Nevertheless, the adult
interlocutor does not use the phrase herself, nor does
the word <u>diet</u> appear in the adult sample outside of
this conversation. Erica's phrase "have me on diet"
may have causative semantic implications, and, perhaps, causative intent as well.

   Erica produced one utterance with a non-causative
infinitive complement:

    14652   me have something to write

From the context, the utterance seems to be a request
for a writing implement:

Child Erica:	14650	i gonna write...first
Adult Erica:	14651	are you going to write?
Child:	14652	me have something to write
Adult:	14659	here's a pencil

   Among other non-causative constructions, there
are 18 examples of <u>have</u> in the obligation sense of
"must", e.g.

9349	i have to give a blow on it
12002	i have to stand on here
18541	we have get it all out
	(n.b. omission of <u>to</u>. From context, it is clear that this utterance is not a reduced form of "we have gotten it all out")

Two utterances contain <u>have</u> as a perfective, i.e.

5236	my dame has lost her shoe
7389	dock-a-deedle-deedle-dee my dame has lost her shoe my master lost his pick-up -stix, doesn't know what to do

but both derive from a memorized nursery rhyme, cf.

Cock-a-doodle-doo
My dame has lost her shoe;
My master lost his fiddle stick
Doesn't know what to do.

Table XXVIII summarizes Erica's use of have.

Table XXVIII. Causative/Non-Causative Distribution of Have in Child Erica

$$\Sigma N = 328$$

Causative	N	%	Non-Causative	N	%
have + N + loc	1	.3	A. possessive		
have + N + adj	0	0	1. have + N	265	81
have + N + pres. p.	0	0	2. have + N + loc	39	12
have + N + past p.	0	0	3. have + N + adj	0	0
have + N + infinitive	0	0	4. have + N + pres. p.	0	0
			5. have + N + past p.	0	0
			B. have + N + infinitive	1	.3
			C. must	18	5
			D. perfective, past	2	.6
			E. miscellaneous	2	.6
Total	1	.3	Total	327	99.5

Adult Nina

The verb have appears a total of 563 times in the adult portion of the Nina corpus. A little over half of these examples (295) are simple, possessive constructions of the form have + noun, e.g.

15835 did the hippopotamus have a big mouth or a little mouth?
18649 mommy has no more lap, because it's become a bed

One of these examples of possessive have is used in the progressive, i.e.

21290 you having nice blankets?

although the preceding context suggests that the initial deviation from standard usage occurs in Nina's inappropriate answer to her mother's question:

Adult Nina:	21288	what are you doing?
Child Nina:	21289	have a nice blanket
Adult:	21290	you having nice blankets?
Child:	21291	yup

A large number of the possessive have + noun constructions imply futurity in the form of predictions or requests. Some examples are:

Prediction:	22911	you'll have some apples later
	15633	you going to have an umbrella?
Request:	4997	can i have a taste of the carrot?
	7240	let's have a puppet show
	25820	may i have your bottle?

Locative expressions occur with have in 142 utterances. While many examples refer to present or past time, e.g.

| 9259 | nina doesn't have any clothes on |
| 19489 | oh, i think we had it inside the truck, didn't we? |

several imply futurity through the mode of prediction or request, e.g.

| Prediction: | 7273 | at whose house are we going to have a birthday party? |
| Request: | 4382 | can i have it on my head? |

Some of the utterances containing locatives are clearly non-causative, such as those in which the locative merely designates a habitual spatial position, e.g.

| 21268 | oh, you have many animals on your pajamas (i.e. printed on the material) |
| 21546 | does your daddy have a beard in that picture? |

In most instances, the locative designates a temporary position, and is not obviously causative or non-causative, e.g.

7551	you want mommy to have the chair on her hand?
8929	you have so many toys here
23241	you have two socks on now
27303	what color blanket does he have on?

Other examples, however, imply action on the part of the subject, making the have construction at least resultative if not causative as well, e.g.

> 11289   you have it upside down
> 13195   that girl has snow on the roof
> 19119   when i sleep, can i have them back
>   after I finish sleeping?

Nine adjectival and participial expressions with
have appear in the adult portion of the Nina corpus.
The one adjectival construction is resultative, and
perhaps also causative:

> 14244   oh nina has her doll house all full of
>   christmas cards

Present participles appear in four utterances:

> 8407   we have a dog walking in the sun
> 14602 what does he have hanging out of his
>   mouth?
> 20834 oh, i have a lot of things sleeping on
>   my lap, don't i?
> 21136 now you have two little boys both carry-
>   ing sticks

Judging from the context, it seems that all four constructions function as adjectival modifications of
possession rather than causatives, cf.

> we have a dog that is walking in the sun

Four examples contain the past participial form left,
e.g.

> 15671   let's see if i have a lollipop left
> 25229   i don't think this can has any left

In all four cases, left functions adjectivally.

Verbal complements (exclusive of the obligation
sense of have) appear in four instances, three of
which are non-causative:

> 6342   well we'll put them in here until we
>   have time to fix that puzzle
> 20316   which horse can i have to play with?
> 24631   did you have something else to eat at
>   ellen's house?

The fourth example, however, is causative:

> 22580   are you going to have them play ball?

Among the remaining uses of have, 88 citations
express obligation, e.g.

> 18034   it's yucky weather outside, so he has
>   to stay inside

19253   she has to be careful not to get the
         ball in the flowers, right?

Finally, 23 instances of have are used to express
aspect or tense, e.g.

6017   have we finished with the puzzle?
19814 what other animals have you been
        playing with?
20656 i think you might have brought them to
        maggie's house

Table XXIX summarizes the distribution of have in
the adult portion of the Nina corpus.

Table XXIX. Causative/Non-Causative Distribution of
             Have in Adult Nina

$$\Sigma N = 563$$

Causative	N	%	Non-Causative	N	%
have + N + loc	?	?	A. possessive		
have + N + adj	1	.2	1. have + N	295	52
have + N + pres. p.	0	0	2. have + N + loc	142	25
have + N + past p.	0	0	3. have + N + adj	0	0
have + N + infinitive	1	.2	4. have + N + pres. p.	4	.8
			5. have + N + past p.	4	.8
			B. have + N + infinitive	3	.6
			C. must	88	16
			D. perfective, past	23	4
			E. miscellaneous	2	.4
Total	2	.4	Total	561	99.6

Adult Erica
Adult use of have in the Erica corpus totals 555.
Slightly over half of these are possessive construc-
tions of the form have + noun, e.g.

3206   it hurts the tape recorder to have
        loud noises
13871 we are going to have a population
        explosion with all these kitties

While most of these utterances refer to present or
past time, a considerable number imply futurity
through prediction or request, e.g.

> Prediction: 12064 i don't know if this parade
>   will have soldiers
>   17729 going to have a picnic?
> Request: 92 may i have a taste?
>   9819 let me have the card

Locative constructions account for 91 of the
utterances with have. Several of the possessive have
+ noun + locative constructions indicate futurity,
e.g.

> Prediction: 7703 leslie is going to have a
>   baby sitter at her house
>   and you will have a baby
>   sitter at your house

Locative expressions indicating habitual location are
clearly not causative, e.g.

>   605 do you have fingernails on your nose?
>   10972 what story do you know that has a
>   scarecrow in it?

However, in addition to a large number of ambiguous
examples, e.g.

>   2590 she had her tennis shoes on
>   11333 what do they have in their hands?

there are a few citations which are resultative or
causative, e.g.

>   3575 i can't hear you when you have your
>   finger in your mouth
>   7070 oh, you have all your animals out
>   16484 but we don't have stamps on them yet
>   19490 you have one on backwards, erica

In each case, the subject of the sentence (i.e. you
or we) is immediately responsible for the location of
the relevant object (i.e. finger, animals, stamps,
or one).

While there are no simple adjectival complements,
participial forms occur in ten examples. Six of
these are present participles. Two present
participial constructions, i.e.

>   11160 how many do you have missing?
>   12155 you have something better coming

might be analyzed as fulfilling adjectival rather than
verbal function, cf.

> how many do you have that are missing?
> you have something that is coming which is
> better

The remaining four, i.e.

> 1208   are you having difficulty making her
>   stand?
> 1266   she has a hard time standing, doesn't
>   she?
> 4286   we called him captain roo because we
>   had a hard time saying kangaroo, but his
>   name is really captain kangaroo
> 12990 she has hard time holding on to things
>   doesn't she?

all express difficulty. While I do not know how these
constructions should be analyzed, there is no evidence
that they are causative.

The four expressions with past participles are:

> 5537   no, i don't have it plugged in
> 6995   well, i had it plugged into the wall...
> 19107 you have it all colored now
> 9401   that was very expensive to have that
>   washing machine fixed

The first three indicate result: the subject, having
performed (or not performed) an action, now has (or
does not have) the object in a new state. Line 9401,
however, is causative in that someone else besides the
speaker is responsible for carrying out the action.
Because a clear dichotomy between resultative and
causative exists with past participial complements, I
classify the first three examples as non-causative and
only the last as causative.

Have occurs with infinitive complements in 13
utterances (excluding use of have in the sense of
"must"). Eleven of these are non-causative. The first,
i.e.

> 7847   and if you move the chair, think what it
>   would be like to be a tiny kitten under a
>   great big chair and have it suddenly
>   start to move

while syntactically parallel to volitional causatives,
is semantically non-causative in that the kitty (i.e.
the surface subject) is "victimized by" rather than
responsible for the moving of the chair. In another
example,

> 19353 did we have a baby visit us last night?

it is not obvious whether the visit was intentional
or happenstance. However, even if the social occasion
was planned (causative), the primary guest(s) was
(were) probably the baby's parent(s) rather than the
baby itself (i.e. happenstance). There are two
examples, i.e.

          4768   tomorrow we have the movies to see
         11177   we have some animals to put away

in which the infinitive, while not of the form "have
to", has the semantic force of obligation (in the one
case, pleasurable; in the other, drudgery). In
another seven citations, the infinitive complement has
a non-causative, possessive meaning, e.g.

          5409   yes, mommy has lots of work to do this
                 morning
          6002   i don't have any to bring you
         16531   you won't have time to read your story
                 unless you get your pajamas on

Finally, there are two causative examples:

         14267   erica, leslie would like to have you
                 come outside
         17274   what book will you have daddy read
                 tonight?

In both cases, future time is indicated.
     Have occurs 87 times in expressions indicating
obligation, e.g.

          7283   you have to be very careful with a
                 hippopotamus, too
         12864   you have to tell me louder

A total of 51 examples mark aspect or tense, e.g.

          8102   you know we have got crumbs all over
                 everything
         12839   you have had a very busy day
         13293   he must have been pretty warm then

Table XXX summarizes use of have in the adult portion
of the Erica corpus.

Table XXX.　Causative/Non-Causative Distribution of
　　　　　　　Have in Adult Erica

ΣN = 555

Causative	N	%	Non-Causative	N	%
have + N + loc	?	?	A. possessive		
have + N + adj	0	0	1. have + N	296	53
have + N + pres. p.	0	0	) 2. have + N + loc	91	16
have + N + past p.	1	. 2	3. have + N + adj	0	0
have + N + infinitive	2	. 4	4. have + N + pres. p	6	1.2
			5. have + N + past p.	3	. 6
			B. have + N + infinitive	11	2
			C. must	87	16
			D. perfective, past	51	9
			E. miscellaneous	7	1.4
Total	3	. 6	Total	552	99. 2

DISCUSSION

In both child and adult corpora, causative use
of have is extremely limited, representing less than
1% of all occurrences of the verb.　Further study
(e.g. of the Brown University corpus) would confirm
whether this low percentage is characteristic of only
child/adult interchange, or of English more generally.
However, even from the available data, it is possible
to hypothesize how children come to learn causative
constructions with have.　In the following comments,
I will discuss the importance of futurity and
locativeness in the development of causative have
constructions.　In addition, I will briefly touch upon
adjectival, participial, and infinitival forms, and
then nominal and clausal complements.

Futurity

Explicit or implied futurity is present in a wide
range of constructions with have.　In both child and
adult samples, the simple possessive have + noun
construction often constitutes a prediction or
request, as do many have + noun + locative expressions.
Both Nina's causative use of

16670   have a nina crossing to maggie's house
and Erica's non-causative

14652   me have something to write

imply futurity through an understood term "want".   In
the adult corpora, several of the infinitival constructions are explicitly future, e.g.

Adult Nina: 20316   which horsie can i have to
                      play with?
Adult Erica: 16531   you won't have time to read
                      your story unless you get
                      your pajamas on

(plus both causative infinitive constructions in adult
Erica).   Finally, many uses of have in the sense of
"must" specify states of affairs which are obligatory
in the future, e.g.

Child Nina: 6625   you take, no you have to
                     take 'em downstairs (i.e.
                     'em [they] are not down-
                     stairs yet)
Child Erica: 5468   we have to fix him
                     (i.e. he is not fixed yet)
Adult Nina: 1673   we'll have to get some
                     better music than that to
                     dance to (i.e. we do not
                     have the music yet)
Adult Erica: 1656   we have to finish that tape
                     tonight (i.e. the tape is
                     not finished yet)

Non-causative examples involving futurity are not
directly related to causative have.   However, if it is
the case that causative have constructions develop
from their non-causative counterparts, and if the
majority of early causative constructions are
implicitly or explicitly future in meaning, then it is
reasonable to hypothesize that causative constructions
with have first emerge from non-causative expressions
indicating futurity.   The high proportion of non-
causative have constructions with explicit or implicit
future meaning in both child and adult samples
provides necessary supporting data for this hypothesis.

Locative
The corpora reveal a high percentage of have
constructions with locative elements.   Many of these
constructions indicate "possession plus location".
However, in each of the four samples, there are
ambiguous or clear cases in which locative construc-

tions with <u>have</u> fill a causative (or at least resultative) function. Even though it is very difficult to determine the precise or even approximate number, a tentative analysis of the samples from both children and both adults strongly suggests that <u>have</u> + noun + locative constructions constitute a larger proportion of the instances of <u>have</u> than all non-locative, causative uses of <u>have</u> combined. These data are summarized in Table XXXI.

Table XXXI.   <u>Have</u> + Noun + Locative versus Combined
                Non-Locative Causative Expressions with
                <u>Have</u>

	Nina		Erica	
	Child	Adult	Child	Adult
have + N + loc	6%	25%	12 %	16%
combined non-locative causative expressions with <u>have</u>	.4%	.4%	.3%	.6%

Given the large number of non-causative or ambiguous constructions of the form <u>have</u> + noun + locative, it would not be surprising that causative constructions with <u>have</u> emerged in the form of locatives.

Adjective, Participles
Simple adjectival constructions with <u>have</u> are rare in all samples, the only example being one resultative or causative utterance in adult Nina, i.e.

14244   oh nina has her doll house all full
        of christmas cards

Past participles are slightly more frequent, with adjectival (resultative) examples in the two adult samples, and one causative use in adult Erica. Present participles with apparently adjectival function appear non-causatively in both child and adult Nina, and in adult Erica, and there is one potentially causative example in child Nina, i.e.

16670   have a nina crossing to maggie's house

The visible use of present rather than past participles in the Nina corpus is consonant with other knowledge about child language acquisition. As we

have seen, in both child and adult samples, several
present participles can be traced to main verbs in
immediately preceding contexts. Brown (1973) has
found that the progressive -ing morpheme is the first
grammatical marker to be used productively of the 14
he studied. In normal adult English, have + noun +
present participle is common as a non-causative construction, though fairly restricted as a causative,
cf.

My host had me staying in the guest house.

However, given the close surface similarity between
present participles and progressive main verbs, along
with the early stage at which the progressive -ing
becomes productive in children, it is conceivable that
have + noun + present participle constitutes a syntactic frame which may be interpreted causatively,
much the same way as have + noun + locative. However,
this hypothesis lacks supporting evidence.

Infinitive

Non-causative and causative infinitive complements appear in both adult corpora, along with one
non-causative example in child Erica. However, there
being no causative examples in either child sample, it
is likely that causative have + noun + infinitive
emerges quite late.

Noun, Clause

No examples of nominal or clausal complements
appear with causative have in any of the four samples.
I conclude that both of these constructions are very
late ontogenetic developments.

CHRONOLOGICAL EMERGENCE OF CAUSATIVE HAVE

Because the data on have are so sparse, the only
definitive statement possible about the chronological
emergence of causative have is that it appears later
than make or get. Nevertheless, on the basis of the
foregoing analysis, I tentatively hypothesize the
following order of development. Some of these stages
necessarily overlap.

Stage 0: "Possess"
Stage 1: have + noun + locative
Stage 2: (a) have + noun + present participle
          (b) have + noun + adjective
          (c) have + noun + past participle
Stage 3: have + noun + infinitive
Stage 4: (a) have + noun + noun
          (b) have + noun + clause

CONDITION: during at least Stages 2 and 3,
             most examples are explicitly or
             implicitly future

5.8 Evaluation of Longitudinal Data

The major purpose of the longitudinal analysis
was to trace the order in which the various complements emerge with each periphrastic causative verb.
These results are summarized by stages in the sections
above on CHRONOLOGICAL EMERGENCE.

In 5.1 and 5.2, I made a number of predictions
about the longitudinal data with respect to (1) the
order and manner of emergence of the three periphrastic
causatives make, get, and have, (2) the ontogenetic
reality of a periphrastic causative paradigm, (3)
markedness relations between the three periphrastic
causatives, and (4) differences between adult registers, or individual adults. I will now examine each
of these sets of predictions in turn.

5.81 Order and Path of Emergence

(a) Make
I predicted (cf. 5.1) that children derive the
periphrastic causative use of make from the non-
periphrastic, transitive construction. None of the
longitudinal corpora argues against this hypothesis,
although I was not able to discover any salient syntactic or semantic feature in the longitudinal data
which suggested the process via which the periphrastic
causative interpretation emerged.

The general observation that clausal complements
develop fairly late was further documented by the data
on make: clausal complements with make did not appear
in the speech of any of the children.   (In fact,
clausal complements with make did not even appear in
the speech of Nina and Erica's adult interlocutors.)
However, periphrastic causative make with infinitival
complement was used productively by two-year-olds.
The significance of this datum is discussed in 7.21.

The longitudinal data also substantiated the
importance of locative constructions in child language
which I commented upon in 5.1.   Make + noun +
locative, though ungrammatical in modern standard
English, appeared in the speech of both child Nina and
child Erica, although the construction also appeared
in the adult Nina corpus as well.

(b) Get
    I predicted that children develop a causative use
of get from non-causative (though precausative) get +
locative. The longitudinal data on Nina and Erica
strongly support this hypothesis. I also predicted
that get + locative would develop before any causative
expressions with get, and that get + noun + locative
would be the first overt get causative to appear.
Both of these predictions were borne out.
    The general observation that infinitival comple-
ments are not yet highly productive in the speech of
two-year-olds was substantiated by the longitudinal
data on get. Among the children, only Nina produced
examples of the get + noun + infinitive construction.

(c) Have
    On the basis of previous knowledge about child
language acquisition, I had no particular predictions
about the path via which causative use of have emerges
ontogenetically from non-causative, possessive have.
However, the longitudinal data suggest that the
implicit or explicit expression of futurity which was
important historically may also be important ontogenetically. The general observations that (i)
locative complements emerge early and (ii) clausal
complements emerge quite late, were both substantiated
by the longitudinal data.

5.82 Periphrastic Causative Paradigm

    In 5.11, I enumerated seven possible overgenerali-
zations of periphrastic causative constructions whose
appearance would constitute evidence that children
structure their acquisition of periphrastic causatives
on the basis of an underlying paradigm matching each
verb with each complement type. These overgeneralizations were grouped with respect to (a) infinitival,
(b) nominal, (c) adjectival, and (d) locative complements.

(a) Infinitive
    Possible overgeneralizations:
    i. no use of to in get + noun + infinitive
       caveat: the child must already use to-
                complementizer with other verbs
   ii. use of to in $\left\{ \begin{array}{c} \text{make} \\ \text{have} \end{array} \right\}$ + noun + infinitive
    The discussion of Nina's use of infinitival
complements with get revealed that Nina did in fact
not use the to-complementizer with get. However, it

was also pointed out that she did not regularly use
the to-complementizer with other verb + noun +
infinitive constructions. No child used to in $\left(\frac{\text{make}}{\text{have}}\right)$
+ noun + infinitive constructions.

(b) Noun
    Possible Overgeneralizations:
    iii.   use of get + noun + noun
    iv.   use of have + noun + noun without temporal
        modifier

No examples of nominal complements with
periphrastic causative verbs appeared in any of the
child samples. Therefore, there was no model in the
children's grammar on the basis of which to generalize
to get + noun + noun, and there were no get + noun +
noun constructions appearing either with or without
temporal modifier.

(c) Adjective
    Possible Overgeneralizations:
    v. use of have + noun + adjective with inad-
      missible adjective
    vi. use of have + noun + adjective without
      temporal modifier

Since none of the three children used have +
noun + adjective constructions, there are no relevant
examples of overgeneralizations.

(d) Locative
    Possible Overgeneralizations:
    vii. use of make + noun + locative

Both Nina and Erica, and the adult interlocutor
in the Nina sample, produced examples of make + noun
+ locative.
The only overgeneralization to appear which
supports the hypothesis of an ontogenetic periphrastic
causative paradigm is the use of make + noun +
locative. However, the lack of the other six possible
overgeneralizations does not necessarily refute the
hypothesized underlying ontogenetic paradigm. In all
six cases, the child samples may represent too early a
period of development to provide the relevant data on
overgeneralization. In Chapter 6 I will examine
experimental correlates of these spontaneous overgeneralizations by looking at the language of older
children (cf. 6.3).

5.83 Markedness Hierarchy

In 5.12, I made four predictions about the

acquisition of periphrastic causative make, get, and
have, on the basis of the syntactic theory of markedness presented in 3.3. These four predictions were:

> (1) make will appear as the first periphrastic
>   causative
> (2) make will appear more frequently than get
>   or have (frequency)
> (3) make will develop a wide range of comple-
>   ment types earlier than get or have
>   (defectivation)
> (with the inverse predictions for have)
> (4) children may use make where get or have
>   is appropriate, or get where have is
>   appropriate (neutralization)

Given the three longitudinal corpora of child
speech which I examined, it is not possible to prove
that make is the first periphrastic causative to
develop ontogenetically. Adam, who was the least
linguistically developed of the children, did use one
example of periphrastic causative make (with an
infinitive complement) and no examples of causative
have, although he also used eight examples with
precausative get + locative, and one with get + noun
+ adjective (cf. Table XIII). While the Adam I data
do indicate that periphrastic causative have appears
after make and get, and is therefore most marked, it
will be necessary to examine more samples of early
development to determine whether periphrastic
causative make becomes a productive part of children's
systems before periphrastic causative get.

Table XXXII compares the frequency of periphrastic causative make, get, and have in the three
child samples. The figures for get do not include
precausative get + locative, and those for have do not
include cases of have + noun + locative which are not
clearly causative.

Table XXXII. Frequency of Periphrastic Causative Make,
              Get, and Have in Adam I, Child Nina,
              and Child Erica

	Adam I	Child Nina	Child Erica
make	1	16	13
get	1	21	42
have	0	1	1

Comparing the rank order of frequency within each
subject, we see that the frequency prediction with
respect to make versus have, and get versus have is
upheld. For all three children, use of periphrastic
causative make and get is more frequent than that of
periphrastic causative have. However, the data do not
support the frequency prediction with respect to make
and get. While the rank order with make and get is
identical in Adam I, both Nina and Erica use periphrastic caustave get more frequently than periphrastic causative make.
    Table XXXIII compares the range of complement
types with make, get and have appearing in the three
child samples. Excluded from the comparison are
precausative get + locative and have + noun + locative
(when not clearly causative).

Table XXXIII. Range of Complement Types with
               Periphrastic Causative Make, Get, and
               Have in Adam I, Child Nina, and Child
               Erica

	Adam I	Child Nina	Child Erica
make	(1) infinitive	(3) infinitive locative adjective	(3) infinitive locative adjective
get	(1) adjective	(3) locative past participle infinitive	(3) locative adjective past participle
have	(0)	(1) present participle	(1) locative

The rank order of frequency of complement types within
each subject supports the markedness prediction that
both make and get take a wider range of complement
types at an early period of language acquisition than
periphrastic causative have. The comparative ranks on
make and get are identical for each subject, and
therefore neither support nor argue against the
markedness hypothesis as manifested in defectivation.
    Evidence for the fourth measure of markedness,
i.e. neutralization, would be the appearance of make

+ noun + locative, in that get and have, but not make
appear in this construction in standard adult English.
As I have already pointed out in discussing ontogenetic evidence for the periphrastic causative
paradigm, examples of make + noun + locative appear in
both child Nina and child Erica.

In conclusion, there is evidence from (1) order
of acquisition, (2) frequency and (3) defectivation
that periphrastic causative make and get are less
marked than have. Furthermore, the neutralization
data suggest that make does behave like an unmarked
category. However, the total frequency data on make,
have, and get (Table XXXII) argue against the hypothesis that make is less marked than get. In the next
chapter, I will reexamine the markedness hypothesis by
considering experimental data (cf. 6.3).

5.84 Registers and Individual Differences
In 5.2, I made three predictions about adult
speech registers, and individual differences in child
speech. The first was:

> 1. adult use of periphrastic causatives is
>   different when speaking to adults than when
>   speaking to children

The data on get provide some evidence for
prediction (1). First, comparison of frequency of use
of get with the meaning "acquire" or "fetch" (cf.
Table XX) showed that the adult-to-child (i.e. P - C)
corpora contained a higher percentage of use of get
with this basic meaning than did either of the adult-
to-adult (A - A) samples, i.e.

	P - C		A - A	
	Adult Nina	Adult Erica	Ten Plays	Brown University
"acquire", "fetch"	53%	39%	22 %	32%

Second, analysis of inchoative and causative get
with adjectival and past participial complements (cf.
Table XXV) very tentatively suggested that while adult-
to-child (P - C) conversation tends to use adjectival
complements more frequently than past participial complements, the reverse is true of adult-to-adult (A - A)
conversation, i.e.

	P - C		A - A	
	Adult Nina	Adult Erica	Ten Plays	Brown University
inchoative	adj < PP	adj > PP	adj < PP	adj < PP
	8% 10%	12% 8%	4% 7%	5% 8%
causative	adj = PP	adj < PP	adj < PP	adj < PP
	.5% .5%	2% 3%	.5% 2%	.5% 3%

However, in light of the fact that the generalization is violated by adult Nina's inchoative use, and adult Erica's causative scores, and that it is often very difficult to determine whether surface past participial forms are being used with adjectival or verbal force, the hypothesis about adjectival and past participial use needs to be tested more extensively.

Third, the data on infinitives (cf. Table XXVI) suggest that adult-to-child (P - C) speech employs fewer infinitives with periphrastic causative get than adult-to-adult (A - A) interchange, i.e.

	P - C		A - A	
	Adult Nina	Adult Erica	Ten Plays	Brown University
get + N + inf	1 (.5%)	0 (0%)	11 (.5%)	6 (1%)

However, given the small raw scores and frequencies, it will be necessary to examine this hypothesis with larger samples.

The second and third predictions I made with respect to adult speech were:

2. adult frequency in addressing children is an accurate predictor of order of acquisition of periphrastic causative constructions (although the correlations may only reflect parallels in markedness hierarchies in adult and child speech)
3. idiosyncracies in adult use of periphrastic causative constructions addressed to children will predict some idiosyncrasies in child speech

Table XXXIV compares the rank order (with respect to frequencies) of complements with make, get, and have,

for child Nina - adult Nina, and child Erica - adult
Erica.   I will restrict the discussion to causative
constructions, plus the basic, non-causative meanings
of make and get.

Table XXXIV.   Rank Order of Complements in Child Nina
              - Adult Nina and Child Erica - Adult
              Erica

| | Nina | | Erica | |
	Child	Adult	Child	Adult
make	non-c. 88 % inf 9 % loc 2 % adj 1 %	non-c. 73.5 % inf 21 % adj 4 % loc 1 % noun .5 %	non-c. 90 % inf 5 % adj 3 % loc 2 %	non-c. 79.5 % adj 14 % inf 6 % noun .5 %
get	non-c. 59 % loc 8 % inf 1.5 % PP .5 %	non-c. 53 % loc 9 % adj .5 % inf .5 %	non-c. 49 % loc 13 % adj 1.5 % PP 1 %	non-c. 39 % loc 14 % PP 3 % adj 2 %
have	Prs. P .4 %	adj .2 % inf .2 %	loc .3 %	inf .4 % PP .4 %

(a) Make
     The data on child and adult Nina show non-causa-
tive make to be the most frequent construction (88%,
73.5%), and the infinitival complement with causative
make next most frequent (9%, 21%).   While the rank
order of locative and adjectival complements is
reversed for child and adult Nina, the sample is too
small for the difference to be statistically
significant.
     In the Erica corpus, non-causative make is most
frequent in both child and adult samples (90%, 79.5%).
Child Nina's next most frequent construction is the
infinitival complement with causative make (5%),
followed by the adjectival complement (3%), while
infinitival and adjectival ranks are reversed in the
adult sample (adj: 14%, inf: 6%).   In 5.5, I argued
that the adult Nina ratio is more representative of
Erica's use of adjectival and infinitival complements
than is Erica's raw score. While five out of seven of

Erica's infinitives were identical (i.e. make her
stand), all four of her adjectival constructions were
unique. Child Nina only used one adjectival complement, but her 12 infinitival complements showed considerable lexical variety. These comparative data
suggest that differences between infinitival and
adjectival constructions by child Nina (C_1) and child
Erica (C_2) might be a function of the children's
immediate adult input (P_1 and P_2).

     (b) Get
     In both child and adult portions of the Nina and
Erica corpora, non-causative get with the meaning
"acquire" or "fetch" is the most frequent construction
type, and get + noun + locative the next most frequent.
There is considerable variation both within and
between corpora in the use of infinitival, adjectival,
and past participial complements. However, in all
cases, the frequencies are so low that there is no
need to attempt to explain the variation.
     There are, however, two differences between the
corpora which suggest that idiosyncrasies in the
child's use of get are a function of immediate adult
input. The first concerns use of non-causative get:
while non-causative uses account for 59% of child
Nina's examples with get (and 53% of adult Nina's),
they account for only 49% of child Erica's (and only
39% of adult Erica's). There are several possible
explanations for these differences. The two children
may, indeed, be mirroring the idiosyncratic usage of
their adult interlocutors. However, it is also
possible that (i) child Nina's score is higher than
child Erica's because Nina is younger and less developed linguistically than Erica, and that (ii) adult
Nina's higher degree of non-causative use reflects
adult Nina's interpretation of what language is
appropriate for her to address to a child of Nina's
level of development. The fact that Adam I, who
is least linguistically developed of the three subjects, has the highest frequency of non-causative get
(76%) supports at least hypothesis (i).
     Another idiosyncratic difference between the
entire Nina corpus on the one hand, and the Erica
corpus on the other involves use of locatives in
precausative and causative expressions. In Table XXI,
I listed all locatives used with get by both children
and both adults. While up, on, in, and out were most
frequent overall, there were some exceptions which
perhaps may be traced to idiosyncratic differences
between adults. On does not appear in precausative

function in child Erica, but it is also missing in precausative use in adult Erica. Similarly, child Nina does not use up in causative get constructions, but the sample of her mother's speech only includes a single example of causative get + noun + up.

(c) Have
The frequency of complements with causative have is too low in all four samples to warrant comparison of complements.

In conclusion, the frequency data do generally support the hypothesis that adult frequency is a reasonable predictor of order of acquisition of periphrastic causatives, although in many cases, the frequency of complement types appearing in the data is too low to allow statistical comparison. There is some evidence that idiosyncratic differences in periphrastic causative usage in children are a function of immediate adult input, although the three examples presented here do not offer conclusive evidence for this point of view.

Footnotes

[1]Cf. Ch. 3 for caveats about variability with respect to grammaticality judgments.

[2]Cf. Farwell (1973) for a review of the relevant literature.

[3]Brown measured adult frequency by counting absolute number of occurrences, while order of acquisition was measured by the frequency with which children used the morpheme in obligatory contexts (criterion: presence of morpheme in 90 percent of all obligatory contexts for three successive two-hour samples).

[4]Idiosyncrasies within children themselves, however, are obviously responsible for many individual differences between children.

[5]For convenience, I use the term P for parent. However, an adult addressing a child obviously need not be one of the child's parents.

[6]The following discussion is restricted to studies of morphological and periphrastic causatives. For comments on the causative conjunction because, cf. Forman (1971).

[7]"ə" is an unstressed particle which sometimes serves
as a pro-form for demonstratives, auxiliaries,
prepositions, and nouns.

[8]Here "ə" seems to have a nominal function.

[9]Linguistic and extralinguistic context is enclosed
in parentheses.

[10]Bloom's (1970:146) underlying analysis of (25)-(28)
is also phrased in terms of the non-reduced structure:

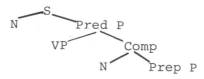

[11]The first meaningful example for Adam occurs at age
4;6. Up through age 5;5 there are no examples from
Sarah (Cromer 1968:118). Cromer hypothesizes (1968:
122) that the late development of the perfective is
not a function of morphological or syntactic
complexity, but "rests on a late-developing ability to
consider the relevance of another time to the time of
the utterance".

[12]The complete corpus is slightly larger since
partially unintelligible utterances are also numbered.

[13]The complete corpus is slightly larger since
partially unintelligible utterances are also numbered.

[14]In addition to the 20 hours which I have analyzed,
an additional 40 hours have since been recorded.

[15]While I do not have Brown's original data, the
formating of the data on the PDP-10 system was
intended to maintain Brown's original segmentation.

[16]In Adam I, almost all the morphemes constitute
distinct words (cf. Brown 1973).

[17]The ten plays are:
Barry, "The Philadelphia Story," 1947; Behrman,
"Biography," 1941; Booth, "The Women," 1939; Gibbs,
"Season in the Sun," 1951; Hart and Kaufmann, "You
Can't Take It with You," 1938; Heggen and Logan,
"Mister Roberts," 1952; Kesselring, "Arsenic and Old
Lace," 1947; Rice, "Dream Girl," 1947; Spewack and

Spewack, "Boy Meets Girl," 1939; Thurber and Nugent, "The Male Animal," 1947.

[18]Because of the large size of the Brown University corpus, I decided to examine only a sample of the relevant entries.

[19]Numbers preceding citations refer to the place of the utterance in the complete numbered listing.

[20]All sentences with make are semantically causative. However, for simplicity of exposition, I will use the term "causative" to refer only to those constructions having sentential complements as defined in 3.2.

[21]In this and subsequent tables, percentages are rounded to the nearest whole number with the exception that decimals under 2.0 are usually rounded to the nearest half. Percentages in all tables in 5.5-5.8 refer to how many examples of a particular construction type occur with respect to all citations of the periphrastic causative verb under discussion in a given corpus.

[22]I will comment upon the presence of the copula in the discussion section below.

[23]The proportion in child and adult Erica is much smaller.

[24]It is possible to argue that some of the get + locative constructions, either with or without intervening noun, function as idioms (cf. 3.2). I discuss this problem in the discussion section·below.

[25]I do not know why get back has been analyzed as two words while all other cases of get + locative are analyzed as compounds.

[26]The get + past participle category includes both inchoatives and passives. I will take up this distinction in the discussion section.

[27]I will discuss this inversion of word order below.

[28]I am considering this modifier plus nominal to be functioning as an adjective (cf. 4.5).

[29]Erica does use a number of other adjectives and adverbs which are comparative in surface form (e.g.

taller, higher, closer), but I have no evidence that
she is using the comparative morpheme productively.

[30]Only used in spontaneous imitation.

[31]In the two examples cited from Adam, however, the
underlying construction is not causative get + noun +
locative: kitty seems to be functioning as a
vocative, and ball is the object of over, not get.

[32]An alternative explanation is that the sentence
constitutes an imperative, and the block (i.e. this)
is temporarily granted animate powers. However, I do
not think this interpretation is likely to be correct
here. While I have seen many examples in the
literature in which children command inanimate objects
by name (e.g. Go away, rain!), I have not encountered
any examples in which inanimates are referred to by
pronouns.

[33]Partial exceptions are inchoative use in the adult
Nina sample and causative use in adult Erica.

[34]There is one other example, i.e.
        16923   she have hug a lady
which I am unable to interpret. While it is
conceivable that have is being used as a perfective,
i.e.
            she has hugged a lady
it is just as likely to be expressing possession or
obligation, i.e.
                she has a hug for a lady
                she has to hug a lady

[35]Brown (1973) reports that the children he studied
made almost no errors in incorrectly using progressive
forms with stative verbs. However, as Brown also
points out, there do seem to be dialectal variations
even in adult models as to what verbs can or cannot be
used in the progressive. While none of Brown's subjects used verbs such as want, like, need, know, see,
or hear in the progressive, Traugott (personal
communication) has noted that her daughter at ages two
and three did use such forms as wanting (e.g. Are you
wanting egg?) and having (e.g. Adult: What is the
little boy doing? Child: Having a whistle (i.e. he
has a whistle)).

Chapter 6

ONTOGENETIC DEVELOPMENT OF PERIPHRASTIC CAUSATIVES
IN (AMERICAN) ENGLISH: EXPERIMENTAL STUDIES

Chapter 6 discusses my experimental research on
the acquisition of periphrastic causative make, get,
and have. The purposes of the experimental studies
are outlined in section 6.1. Section 6.2 describes
the subject population and general testing conditions.
The experiments themselves are presented in 6.3
(Elicited Imitation), 6.4 (Non-Causative/Causative
Comprehension), and 6.5 (Subject/Agent Comprehension).

6.1 Purposes of Experimental Studies

6.11 Periphrastic Causative Paradigm

In 3.2, I suggested analyzing periphrastic
causatives in terms of a periphrastic causative paradigm, and I made a number of predictions about how the
paradigm might be reflected ontogenetically. Seven
explicit predictions were examined with respect to the
longitudinal data (cf. 5.11, 5.82). In only one
instance (i.e. the overgeneralization of locative complements from periphrastic causative get and have to
make) were there sufficient data for testing these
predictions. Therefore, the first purpose of the
experimental studies was to provide appropriate linguistic contexts for additional testing of these
predictions.
Out of the original seven predictions, I chose
to consider experimentally some overgeneralizations
with infinitival, adjectival, and locative complements. Nominal complements and temporal restrictions
with adjectives were excluded to reduce the length of
the experimental task. The four overgeneralizations
considered were:

Infinitive

i. no use of to in get + noun + infinitive
ii. use of to in (make) + noun + infinitive
            (have)

Adjective

iii. use of have + noun + adjective with
     inadmissible adjectives

Locative

iv. use of make + noun + locative

In the longitudinal analysis, I used the appearance of overgeneralizations of grammatical constructions as evidence for an underlying ontogenetic periphrastic causative paradigm. Experimentally, it is possible to test the validity of a paradigm by examining data from elicited imitations of sentences representing grammatical and ungrammatical cells in the periphrastic causative paradigm.

Within the experimental literature on child language acquisition, several studies have found that preschool children's ability to imitate sentences under elicitation conditions appears to surpass their comprehension and production skills (cf. Fraser, Bellugi, and Brown 1963; Lovell and Dixon 1967). Therefore, we would expect that preschool children confronted with periphrastic causative constructions that are beyond their level of spontaneous production might still be able to imitate such sentences correctly. However, if a model sentence surpasses the child's short term memory capacity, he may behave in one of two ways. First, he may imitate by rote what he can remember, making omissions without regard to content or underlying syntactic structure. Alternatively, as Slobin and Welsh (1968) have shown, he may grammatically "recode" the sentence by extracting what he understands and producing a response in language at his own level of productive control.[1] In the light of this "recoding" hypothesis, it was hypothesized that the errors produced by children (and adults) in an imitation task might give some indication of how periphrastic causative constructions are interpreted.

I predicted that if children do structure their knowledge of periphrastic constructions on the basis of a periphrastic causative paradigm, then they should imitate grammatical and ungrammatical (i.e. overgeneralized) periphrastic causative constructions with equal facility.

6.12 Markedness Hierarchy

In 3.3, I offered a set of three synchronic criteria for analyzing the relative markedness of the periphrastic causatives make, get, and have (i.e. frequency, defectivation, and neutralization). I then predicted on the basis of the synchronic analysis how the three periphrastic causatives would be acquired ontogenetically. These predictions were tested with respect to the longitudinal data (cf. 5.12, 5.83). In general, the longitudinal analysis showed that make

and get are less marked ontogenetically than have.
However, there was conflicting evidence with respect
to whether make or get is the least marked of the
three verbs. The second purpose of the experimental
studies was to re-examine the original hypothesis
(3.3) that make is least marked of the three periphrastic causatives, get is more marked, and have most
marked.

It is possible to examine both (a) frequency and
(b) neutralization by using an elicited imitation task
in which subjects are asked to imitate grammatical and
ungrammatical sentences representing pairings of verbs
and complements in the hypothetical periphrastic
causative paradigm (cf. 6.11). If the prediction is
correct that the order of markedness is make (less
marked than) get (less marked than) have, then under
the frequency criterion, subjects' responses should
contain make most often, get less often, and have
least often. Under the neutralization criterion, subjects should use make where get or have is appropriate,
or get where have is appropriate. In scoring an
elicited imitation task with a limited number of
sentences, the same data which support the frequency
criterion will also support the neutralization
criterion (and vice versa).

A second experimental procedure for testing the
markedness hypothesis is to analyze the explanations
or paraphrases subjects are asked to give of
grammatical and ungrammatical sentences. If the proposed hierarchy is valid in elicited imitation, I
predict it will also be valid in elicited explanations. That is, given a model sentence containing
periphrastic causative have, subjects will tend to
explain or paraphrase the sentence with the verbs make
or get; and given a model containing get, subjects
will tend to use the periphrastic causative make in
their responses.

In addition to examining imitation data simply in
terms of frequency (or neutralization), one might also
ask whether the kinds of changes a subject makes in
imitating a model sentence alter the grammaticality of
the original sentence. One hypothesis would be that
subjects alter models by substituting less marked
periphrastic causatives for highly marked periphrastic
causative verbs, regardless of the grammatical status
of the original model or of the resulting response.
An alternative hypothesis is that grammaticality is a
better predictor of the subjects' behavior than
markedness, e.g. subjects will tend to imitate
grammatical models correctly (regardless of the

markedness value of the periphrastic causative in the
model), but will alter ungrammatical models in the
direction of grammaticality (again, regardless of the
markedness of the periphrastic causative in the model).
I have no grounds at present for deciding whether
markedness or grammaticality will be a better
predictor of subject's responses.

6.13 Non-Causative and Causative Use of Get and Have

In 5.6 and 5.7, I attempted to show that
longitudinally, children develop a causative interpretation of get out of the non-causative construction
meaning "acquire" or "fetch", and a causative interpretation of have out of the simple possessive construction. However, the longitudinal data did not
reveal whether children who have acquired partial
facility with periphrastic causative get and have ever
mistakenly interpret causative constructions non-
causatively. The third purpose of the experimental
studies was to test the hypothesis that children do,
in fact, tend to interpret some types of causative
constructions non-causatively before gaining full pro-
ficiency with the English periphrastic causative
system.
One way to test this hypothesis is with a forced
choice experiment in which two visual stimuli are
presented. One stimulus is properly described by a
causative construction, while the other is accurately
identified by a non-causative construction. The subject is read one description and asked to indicate the
correct stimulus. In the case of non-causative and
causative get and have, the non-causative/causative
distinction may be made linguistically by reversing
the word order in the complement. Consider the
following causative sentences:

(1) get + N + adj   The dog is getting the
                     rug dirty.
(2) get + N + PP   Daddy is getting the
                     meat sliced.
(3) have + N + PP   The girl is having her
                     shoes polished.

In each instance, the noun in the complement precedes
the adjective or past participle. However, by
reversing the order of noun and adjective or past
participle, the same sentences become non-causative,
i.e.

(4) get + adj + N   The dog is getting the

		dirty rug.
(5)	get + PP + N	Daddy is getting the sliced meat.
(6)	have + PP + N	The girl has her polished shoes.[2]

I predict that children who have not yet gained full
facility with periphrastic causative get and have will
tend to interpret causative sentences (e.g. (1), (2),
(3)) as non-causative (e.g. (4), (5), (6)), rather
than vice versa.

6.14 Subjects and Agents

A synchronic analysis of English periphrastic
causatives (see Baron 1974) reveals a number of
distinguishing syntactic and semantic parameters which
were not discussed in the longitudinal analysis. One
of these concerns the question of whether or not the
higher subject of a causative construction is the
immediate agent of a causative action. At some point,
the English-speaking child must learn, for example,
that while the surface subject is the immediate agent
in the construction get + noun + adjective, e.g.

(7) The dog is getting the rug dirty.

the surface subject is not the immediate agent in
have + noun + past participial constructions, e.g.

(8) The girl is having her shoes polished.

Rather, in (8), some outside agent is immediately
responsible for the polishing. However, constructions
of the form get + noun + past participle are normally
ambiguous as to whether or not the subject is the
immediate cause. For example, in the sentence

(9) Daddy is getting the meat sliced.

Daddy might or might not be doing the slicing himself.
The fourth purpose of the experimental studies was to
examine the process by which children learn whether or
not the subject is the immediate agent in periphrastic
causative constructions of the forms (a) get + noun +
adjective, (b) have + noun + past participle, and
(c) get + noun + past participle.

The question of how children interpret surface
subjects of periphrastic causative constructions
directly relates to the broader question of how
children interpret the surface subject of any action
sentence. Research in child language acquisition has
repeatedly found that children tend to identify the

surface subject of action sentences as the immediate
agent of the action. A large number of studies (e.g.
Slobin 1966b, Turner and Rommetveit 1967; Bates 1970;
Bever 1970) have reported that preschool children
tend to interpret reversible passive sentences as
actives. Given a sentence such as

(10) The girl was kissed by the boy.

subjects report that the girl was doing the kissing.
C. Chomsky (1969) demonstrated that primary school
children retain the strategy of identifying a surface
subject as immediate agent in some more complex
sentences. For example, five-year-olds interpret a
model of the type

(11) John is easy to see.

as meaning that John is able to see easily, rather
than as meaning that someone else is easily able to
see John. Only by age nine did Chomsky's subjects
recognize the invalidity of the "surface subject =
agent" strategy. In an extension of this part of
Chomsky's work, Cromer (1970) compared the behavior of
five to seven-year-old children on various types of
sentences in which the subject may or may not have
been the agent. Cromer's experimental design utilized
two puppets (a wolf and a duck) in an acting out task.
In the sentence

(12) The wolf is happy to bite.

it is the wolf who does the biting. In

(13) The wolf is tasty to bite.

the duck is the one to take a nip. However, in

(14) The wolf is bad to bite.

either animal might be biting the other. Classifying
his subjects by mental rather than chronological age,
Cromer found that the lowest group identified the
subject as agent in all three sentence types. An
intermediate group gave mixed responses on the two unambiguous forms, as well as on the ambiguous sentences. The most advanced group correctly identified
unambiguous models, and distributed their answers
between the two strategies (i.e. subject = agent,
subject ≠ agent) on the ambiguous items. Interesting-
ly, nearly all subjects, including the lowest group,
responded correctly to two passive sentences included
in the task.

On the basis of these various studies, I made the
following predictions about behavior in a forced

choice task with periphrastic causative constructions:

(a) Young children will identify all surface
    subjects as agents in the periphrastic
    causative constructions (i) get + N + adj,
    (ii) have + N + PP, and (iii) get + N + PP.
    Older children will either be inconsistent
    in their choices, or, if they have acquired
    adult competence, they (i) will identify
    the subject of get + N + adj as agent, (ii)
    will not identify the subject of have + N +
    PP as agent, and (iii) will give mixed
    responses with get + N + PP.
(b) Developing interpretations of (i) have + N
    + PP and (ii) get + N + PP will correlate
    with behavior on reversible passives.

To test the predictions enumerated in 6.11 - 6.14,
I designed three basic experimental procedures:
elicited imitation, non-causative/causative comprehension, and subject/agent comprehension. The execution
of these three procedures will be described in 6.3,
6.4, and 6.5. Each section begins with a statement of
the hypotheses the procedure is designed to test,
followed by an outline of the experimental design,
presentation of results, and summary.

6.2 Subjects

Sixty preschool children between the ages 2;6 and
5;5 were selected from Bing Nursery School at Stanford
University. All children spoke English as their
native language and heard only English in their homes,
although children of other language backgrounds
(especially Spanish and Portuguese) also attend the
school. The Ss (subjects) were divided into five age
groups of twelve children each, as shown in Table
XXXV.

Table XXXV. Age and Sex Distribution of Preschool
            Subjects

Group	Mean Age	Male	Female	Total
2;6-3;5	3;2	4	8	12
3;6-3;11	3;8	7	5	12
4;0-4;5	4;2	3	9	12
4;6-4;11	4;8	6	6	12
5;0-5;5	5;2	7	5	12
Total		27	33	60

Testing of children was carried out in a small experimental room in the nursery school. A portable Sony tape recorder (model 200B) was used to record all sessions. Because each S took part in several different experiments, it was necessary to test each child over several different sessions, generally a week apart. The number of sessions varied somewhat from child to child. Younger children normally completed the four tasks in three sessions, but many of the older Ss were able to finish in two. Order of tasks was counterbalanced across Ss, with the one exception that the imitation task always appeared in the first session.[3]

The adult population consisted of 20 undergraduate and graduate students, 10 male and 10 female, from Stanford. They were asked to perform the same tasks as the children, the only differences being that all four experiments were run in a single session and the order of tasks was fully counterbalanced. The adults were told they were serving as a control group for a series of experiments designed for nursery school children. However, they were warned that the tasks, though superficially "childish", would contain a number of subtle distinctions, and they should therefore give the experiments their full concentration.

6.3 Elicited Imitation

HYPOTHESES

The elicited imitation experiment tested three types of hypotheses:

(a) Hypothesis 1: Periphrastic Causative Paradigm
If children do structure their knowledge of periphrastic causative constructions on the basis of a periphrastic causative paradigm, then they should imitate grammatical and ungrammatical (i.e. overgeneralized) periphrastic causative constructions with equal facility. The four overgeneralizations to be examined are:
i.   no use of to in get + noun + infinitive
ii. use of to in $\left\{\begin{array}{l}\text{make}\\\text{have}\end{array}\right\}$ + noun + infinitive
iii. use of have + noun + adjective with inadmissible adjectives
iv. use of make + noun + locative

(b) Hypothesis 2: Markedness
If make is ontogenetically the least marked of the three periphrastic causatives, get more marked,

and <u>have</u> most marked, then <u>Ss</u>' responses should
contain <u>make</u> most often, <u>get</u> less often, and <u>have</u>
least often, i.e. <u>Ss</u> should tend to replace <u>have</u>
with <u>get</u> or <u>make</u>, and <u>get</u> with <u>make</u>. This hypothesis may be tested with respect to both elicited
imitation, and explanations or paraphrases.

(c) <u>Hypothesis 3: Markedness versus Grammaticality</u>
Either markedness or grammaticality might be a
better predictor of <u>Ss</u>' responses.

DESIGN
    Fourteen test sentences were constructed as
examples of the periphrastic causative paradigm, representing infinitival, past participial, adjectival,
and locative complements. In the case of infinitives,
models were used both with and without the <u>to</u>-comple-
mentizer. All cells in the paradigm were represented,
with the exception of <u>have</u> + noun + locative.[4]
    Table XXXVI lists the 14 test stimuli as well as
four control sentences designed to measure imitative
ability with non-causative infinitive complements.
Test sentences which I am considering to be ungrammatical in adult English are indicated by an
asterisk.

Table XXXVI.   Test and Control Stimuli in Elicited
               Imitation Experiment[5]

Complement	Test	Control
V	Daddy had the dog walk Mommy made the chair move *The baby got the chair fall	The lady heard the dog bark The lion watched the ball roll
to + V	*Daddy had the girl to dance *The clown made the horse to jump The boy got the stick to break	The teacher asked the girl to paint The girl wanted the bell to ring
adj	*The teacher had the girl sad[6] The clown made the boy happy Mommy got the baby quiet	
PP	Mommy had the car washed The tiger made the monkey frightened The farmer got the flowers watered	
loc	*Grandma made the sweater off Daddy got the window up	

Sentences were typed on 3" by 5" cards and
presented in one of four random orders. Children were
told they were going to play a word game in which
their job was to "say what I say". In nearly all
cases, even the youngest children grasped the task
after a few trial sentences. Adults were merely asked
to imitate each sentence I would read to them.[7]

Most of the Ss were asked to explain the meaning
of the ungrammatical sentences they imitated (i.e.
immediately following the imitation of the particular
model). In random order, I asked such questions as
"What does that mean?", "What happened?", "What did X
(i.e. the subject of the sentence) do?", "What
happened to Y (i.e. the object of the sentence)?". In
addition, at the end of the entire imitation task, I
asked the adult Ss if they had found anything unusual
about the model sentences, and if so, what.

RESULTS

I will first present a general analysis of the
imitation and explanation data from children and
adults (a). I will then analyze the imitations and
explanations in terms of markedness (b), and compare
the extents to which markedness and grammaticality
account for the responses in the imitation task (c).

(a) <u>General Analysis of Imitation and Explanation Data</u>
    <u>i. Imitations</u>
In the imitation data, it is difficult to make
a general comparison between correct and incorrect
imitations of grammatical and ungrammatical sentences,
because so many complicating factors intervened.
First, several children became restless and replied
"I can't say that one" or "I don't know" to a series
of two or three sentences, regardless of actual
difficulty. Second, various children banged their
feet or hands against the table while imitating,
creating heavy static on the tape recording and making
scoring difficult or impossible. Third, phonological
idiosyncrasies of individual stimuli produced error
patterns relevant to only those individual sentences.
Nevertheless, when the percentage of totally correct
responses is calculated for each sentence, it is the
case that as a whole, both children and adults performed better on grammatical models than ungrammatical ones. Tables XXXVII and XXXVIII summarize
these results.[8]

Table XXXVII. Percentage of Correct Imitations by
        Children

Grammatical			Ungrammatical		
Model	N	%	Model	N	%
made chair move	51/57	89	made horse to jump	43/57	75
made monkey frightened	38/55	69	made sweater off	45/55	82
made boy happy	49/56	88	had girl to dance	42/57	74
had dog walk	45/56	80	had girl sad	42/55	76
had car washed	46/56	82	got chair fall	28/55	51
got stick to break	51/57	89			
got flowers watered	35/55	64			
got baby quiet	53/56	95			
got window up	52/57	91			
Total	420/505	83	Total	200/279	72
Controls:					
heard dog bark	50/55	91			
watched ball roll	45/56	80			
asked girl to paint	42/55	76			
wanted bell to ring	47/56	84			
Total	184/222	83			

Table XXXVIII. Percentage of Correct Imitations by
        Adults

Grammatical			Ungrammatical		
Model	N	%	Model	N	%
made chair move	20/20	100	made horse to jump	20/20	100
made monkey frightened	20/20	100	made sweater off	19/20	95
made boy happy	20/20	100	had girl to dance	20/20	100
had dog walk	18/20	90	had girl sad	20/20	100
had car washed	20/20	100	got chair fall	15/20	75
got stick to break	20/20	100			
got flowers watered	20/20	100			
got baby quiet	20/20	100			
got window up	20/20	100			
Total	178/180	99	Total	94/100	94
Controls:					
heard dog bark	20/20	100			
watched ball roll	19/20	95			
asked girl to paint	20/20	100			
wanted bell to ring	20/20	100			
Total	79/80	99			

The number of correct imitations overall improved
significantly with age across the five groups of
children (p<.005, using a Pearson product moment
correlation coefficient). Although the relation with
age is not totally consistent when the models are
differentiated into grammatical, control, and ungrammatical, it is true that in each age group, the
percentage of correctly imitated grammatical models
always surpasses the ungrammatical. Table XXXIX
summarizes these results.

Table XXXIX. Percentage of Correct Imitations by
            Children with Respect to Age

	2;6-3;5	3;6-3;11	4;0-4;5	4;6-4;11	5;0-5;5
Total	75%	78%	79%	82%	85%
Grammatical	81%	80%	83%	87%	85%
Control	72%	84%	84%	82%.	92%
Ungrammatical	66%	69%	68%	75%	80%

Imitation Errors: Children
        Table XL summarizes, by sentence, all substitu-
tions or restructurings made by children. Since the
error pattern was similar across age groups, I have
not separately classified errors with respect to age.
In a great many instances, it is impossible to
determine whether the child's response is grammatical
or ungrammatical (cf. (c) below). Column 1 lists how
many sentences were imitated correctly out of the
number of models read. The number of models varies
between 55 and 57 because three children refused to
imitate at all, and two others completed only half
the task. Column 2 designates how many times an
example was excluded from further analysis because the
child refused to answer that particular item, because
his only error involved a substitution of nouns, or
because the response was uninterpretable. Column 3
records how many instances of a given model sentence
were actually analyzed. The error analysis itself is
self-explanatory: column 4 lists examples in which
the only change is that of substitution of the periphrastic with some other verb; column 5, changes only
in the complement; column 6, general restructuring of

the sentence, especially involving the replacement of a
periphrastic causative with a morphological causative;
column 7, a combination of periphrastic, complement,
or restructuring changes; and column 8, changes in the
main verbs of the control sentences.

Table XL. Error Analysis of Children's Imitations

Form	Sentence	1 Correct	2 Excluded	3 Analyzed	4 periphrastic change only	5 complement change only	6 general restructuring	7 combined change	8 control sentences
V	made chair move	51/57	3	3			2: lady move chair, 1: misc.		
to+V	*made horse to jump	43/57	4	10		10: delete "to"			
PP	made monkey frightened	38/55	9	8		5: PP→ main verb	1: lion frightened monkey	1: {made → got, misc.}, 1: made → misc.	
adj	made boy happy	49/56	7	0					
loc	*made sweater off	45/55	6	4	2: made → had, 1: made → got, 1: made → misc.				
V	had dog walk	45/56	4	7	3: had → made	2: add "to"		1: {had → misc., add "to"}, 1: {had → misc., misc.}	
to+V	*had girl to dance	42/57	2	13	1: had → made, 2: had → got, 2: had → misc.	3: delete "to", 1: misc.	2: girl had to dance	2: {had → made, delete "to"}	
PP	had car washed	46/56	3	7	3: had → got	3: PP → main verb	1: mommy washed car	1: {had → got, misc.}	
adj	*had girl sad	42/55	6	7	2: had → got, 2: had → made	1: misc.	1: misc.	1: {got → had, misc.}	
V	*got chair fall	28/55	4	23	1: got → had, 2: got → made	2: add "to", 3: V → adj, 6: misc.	8: misc.	1: {got → misc., misc.}	
to+V	got stick to break	51/57	3	3	1: got → had	1: add "to"	1: boy broke stick, 1: misc.		
PP	got flowers watered	35/55	10	10	1: got → had	1: add "to", 5: PP → noun	1: farmer watered flowers, 1: misc.	1: {got → made, misc.}	
adj	got baby quiet	53/56	0	3	1: got → made, 1: got → had		1: misc.		
loc	got window up	52/57	4	1	1: got → made				
V	heard dog bark	50/55	2	3			1: misc.		1: heard → had, 1: misc.
V	watched ball roll	45/56	4	7			4: misc.	2: misc.	1: watched → made
to+V	asked girl to paint	42/55	1	12			3: misc.	1: {asked → misc., delete "to"}	3: asked → had, 5: asked → misc.
to+V	wanted bell to ring	47/56	3	6			4: misc.	1: {add "made", misc.}	1: misc.

Imitation Errors: Adults

Among the adult subjects, errors appeared in only four models. Two errors involved miscellaneous general restructuring. One S replaced had with made in the model "Daddy had the dog walk", and one S inserted to in the ungrammatical model "The baby got the chair fall".

What kinds of errors appeared in the imitation data? A large number consisted of the substitution of one periphrastic causative verb for another. For example, if the model was

Daddy got the window up.

the response might be

*Daddy made the window up.

In some cases, the substitution of one periphrastic for another was the sole change made, though frequently it was combined with another alteration as well, e.g.

model: The tiger made the monkey frightened.
response: The tiger got daddy to be frightened.

Addition or deletion of a to-complementizer, e.g.

model: Daddy had the dog walk.
response: *Daddy had the dog to walk.

occurred both in isolation and in conjunction with other changes (cf. *Daddy had the girl to dance —→ Daddy made the girl dance). In the child data, there were also six examples in which the periphrastic causative was imitated as a morphological causative, e.g.

model: The tiger made the monkey frightened.
response: The lion frightened the monkey.
model: Mommy had the car washed.
response: Mommy washed the car.

In addition to these readily classifiable responses, there were a large number of imitations which were peculiar to a given subject or a given sentence. For example, consider the three models with past participial complements, i.e.

The tiger made the monkey frightened.
Mommy had the car washed.
The farmer got the flowers watered.

Several children omitted the final -ed, yielding

*The tiger made the monkey frighten.
*Mommy had the car wash.
The farmer got the flowers water.

Only the last of these corresponds to a grammatical
sentence, although the actual error pattern is
identical in all three examples.. In the sentence

*The baby got the chair fall.

three children clearly substituted the adjective <u>full</u>
for the verb <u>fall</u>, and at least six others produced
phonological sequences which were indistinguishable
between <u>full</u> and <u>fall</u>.

Within the categories "general restructuring" and
"combined change", both children and adults produced a
number of responses which formed main clauses out of
the complement expressions in the model. This
strategy was applied to both grammatical and ungrammatical models. The two examples produced by
adults were:

model: Daddy had the dog walk.
response: *Daddy had [the dog walked]$_S$
model: *The baby got the chair fall.
response: *The baby got [the chair falled]$_S$

Among the children this response type was fairly
frequent, some examples being

model: Mommy made the chair move.
response: *Mommy made [the chair moved]$_S$
model: *The teacher had the girl sad.
response: *The teacher had [the girl is sad]$_S$
model: The boy got the stick to break.
response: *The boy got [the stick breaked]$_S$
model: Mommy got the baby quiet.
response: *Mommy got [the baby cried]$_S$

There are two possible explanations for these kinds of
responses. The first is that subjects recognize that
complements of periphrastic causatives are actually
full sentences and reflect this realization in their
responses. However, it is possible that both children
and adults are actually operating under the constraints
of some kind of surface structure processing strategy
(cf. Bever 1970; Slobin 1971; Sinclair 1971). For
example, it has been suggested that initial noun-verb-
noun sequences may be analyzed as actor-action-object.
However, if another verb immediately follows the noun-
verb-noun sequence, and if the child (or adult) has
not comprehended the underlying syntactic/semantic
structure of the sentence, he is left with a dangling

verb at the end of the sequence. Failing to recognize
the dual function of the second noun as both object
and subject,[9] one obvious solution is to treat the
entire string as two simple intransitive sequences
(cf. Bever 1970), i.e.

[noun verb]$_S$ [noun verb]$_S$

Such a [noun verb]$_S$ [noun verb]$_S$ analysis would
account for the subjects' behavior on these sentences.

Finally, there were several examples among the
children's responses in which get and have were interpreted non-causatively. In at least one instance, get
was analyzed as meaning "acquire" or "fetch", e.g.

model: The farmer got the flowers watered.
response: The farmer got the flower to water
            it.

And one child interpreted have as meaning "must":

model: *(The doctor said) daddy had the
            girl to dance.
response: (The doctor said) the girl had to
            dance.

ii. Explanations
Types of Explanations: Children

Not all children would respond when asked to
comment upon the meaning of the sentence they had just
imitated. Table XLI summarizes how many children
offered some explanation or paraphrase for the sentences about which they were queried, and how those
explanations differed from the model. In addition to
the five ungrammatical models, I asked about two sentences which are grammatical, though somewhat awkward
in English.[10] Column 1 notes how many times an
interpretable response was given for a particular sentence. Column 2 lists how many responses involved the
change of a periphrastic; column 3, the addition or
deletion of a to-complementizer; column 4, change
involving both the periphrastic and the complementizer;
column 5, replacement of the periphrastic causative
with a morphological causative; and column 6, all
other responses.

Table XLI. Structure of Children's Explanations

Sentence	1 ana-lyzed	2 **periphrastic** change only	3 comple-mentizer change only	4 periphrastic, comple-mentizer	5 periphrastic → morphological	6 misc.
*made horse to jump	5				1	4
*made sweater off	27	1: made → got				26
*had girl to dance	24	1: had → made		7: had → made, delete "to"		16
*had girl sad	21	6: had → made				15
*got chair fall	27	4: got → made	1: add "to"		1	21
had dog walk	4	1: had → made			1	2
got stick to break	23				11	12
Total	131					

Types of Explanations: Adults

All 20 adults responded to questions about all five ungrammatical models as well as to the grammatical "The boy got the stick to break". However, only eight were questioned about "Daddy had the dog walk".

Table XLII summarizes the structure of explanations and paraphrases offered by adults.

Table XLII.   Structure of Adults' Explanations

Sentence	1 analyzed	2 periphrastic change only	3 complementizer change only	4 periphrastic, complementizer	5 periphrastic→ morphological	6 misc.
*made horse to jump	20	2: made→ got	13: delete "to"			5
*made sweater off	20	1: made→ got 1: made→ had				18
*had girl to dance	20		3: delete "to"	3: had→ made, delete "to"		14
*had girl sad	20	13: had→ made		2: had→ made, add "to be"		5
*got chair fall	20	3: got→ made 1: got→ had	3: add "to"	1: got→caused, add "to"		12
had dog walk	8	1: had→ made		1: had→caused, add "to"	2	4
got stick to break	20			2: got→ made, delete "to"	13	5
Total	128					

Both children and adults made many of the same kinds of transformations on the original models in analyzing meaning and in imitating. A large number of responses by both children and adults consisted of the substitution of one periphrastic for another, addition or deletion of the to-complementizer, or both, e.g.

         model: Daddy had the dog walk.
         response: Daddy made the dog walk.
         model: *The baby got the chair fall.
         response: The baby got the chair to fall.
         model: *Daddy had the girl to dance.
         response: Daddy made the girl dance.

Replacement of the periphrastic construction by a
morphological causative was frequent among both
children and adults, e.g.

    model: The boy got the stick to break.
    response: The boy broke the stick.
    model: Daddy had the dog walk.
    response: Daddy walked the dog.
    model: *The clown made the horse to jump.
    response: The clown jumped the horse.

In one case, a child overgeneralized the verb <u>fall</u>,
which is intransitive in the adult model, to a
transitive, i.e.

            *[He] falled the chair.
    (model: *The baby got the chair fall.)

Children and adults produced a large variety of other
paraphrases in which the general meaning of the model
was preserved. Some representative examples are:

    <u>Children</u>
    model: *Grandma made her sweater off.
    responses: She took the sweater off.
                 Pull your arms off.
                 Pull it on or hang it up.

    model: *Daddy had the girl to dance.
    responses: He danced with her.
                 [He] told her to dance.
                 He let her go to a place that she
                 really liked so that's and that's
                 where she danced.
    model: *The teacher had the girl sad.
    responses: [The teacher] gave her no cookies.
                 I think she spanked her on the
                 bottom.
                 That means something hurt her [the
                 girl] I think.
                 [The teacher] threw a rock.
    model: *The baby got the chair fall.
    responses: He knocked it down.
                 It broke.
                 I think the mother is gonna get mad.
    model: Daddy had the dog walk.
    responses: He went with him.
                 He took the dog out for a walk.
    model: The boy got the stick to break.
    responses: He pulled on the stick.
                 He bended it.
                 [The boy] sawed it.

Adults
<pre>
  model: *The clown made the horse to jump.
  response: Maybe he kicked him.
  model: *Grandma made her sweater off.
  response: Grandma took her sweater off.
  model: *Daddy had the girl to dance.
  responses: He could have asked a girl to dance.
              It looks like he was ordering her to
              dance.
  model: *The teacher had the girl sad.
  responses: The teacher upset the student.
              She did something and the girl
              became sad.
  model: *The baby got the chair fall.
  responses: The baby put the chair on a table
              and then she pushed it off the table
              and it fell.
              The baby rocked in the chair and it
              fell.
  model: Daddy had the dog walk.
  responses: Daddy kicked the dog in the rear
              end.
              Daddy took the dog for a walk.
  model: The boy got the stick to break.
  responses: The stick was broken by the boy.
              He must have applied pressure to it
              or something.
</pre>

In addition to paraphrases or explanations in
which the basic meaning of the model was retained,
there were also a number of instances in which subjects apparently did not recognize the intended meaning of the sentence. Consider the model

*The baby got the chair fall.

which some children had imitated as

The baby got the chair full.

One of the children making this substitution in imitation explained that the sentence meant that "stuff was
on it". And an adult who had imitated the sentence
correctly (although using a question intonation)
reasoned that "the baby got the chair full with candy
or something". Another interesting model was

*Grandma made her sweater off.

Although all of the children's responses were in some
way related to the act of removing a sweater, five
adults suggested that the grandma was sewing or
knitting: in two cases, they thought that "off" meant

she had made a mistake, and in three others, that she
was "binding off", e.g.

> She probably dropped a stitch or something...
> as in knitting.
> She made the sweater wrong, or the wrong size.
> Grandma finished the sweater...She was
> knitting it.

There were a number of cases in which <u>get</u> and
<u>have</u> were interpreted in their basic meanings of
"possess" or "acquire, fetch". Two children and one
adult explained that

> The boy got the stick to break.

meant

> He got the stick and he broke it.

and one adult explained

> *Daddy had the girl to dance.

by saying

> He had a girl for the purpose of dancing...
> That means that he got one from a dancing
> studio in order to dance with her.

Finally, there was a noticeable difference in the
general reactions of children and adults to ungrammatical stimuli. When presented with ungrammatical
models to imitate, children showed no visible reaction
any different from when presented with grammatical
stimuli. Adults, however, nearly all registered
visible or audible signs of consternation. Often this
took the form of a question intonation superimposed
upon their response, or a glance which seemed to say
"you must be crazy". In general, those children who
were talkative and felt comfortable with the
experimenter could provide explanations of the sentences they had imitated, both grammatical and ungrammatical. Many of the adults, however, maintained
that the sentences made no sense, and when pushed,
frequently provided paraphrases which altered the
basic meaning of the model (cf. *Grandma made her
sweater off). At the end of the imitation task, when
asked to comment upon whether some sentences had
sounded odd in any way, adults made the following
sorts of remarks:

> "They're poor grammar."
> "They're older forms of English which are
> really out of use."

"Some of those sounded sorta like baby talk."

(b) Markedness
Markedness in Imitations: Children
        Table XLIII summarizes the data on markedness of
the three periphrastic causatives make, get, and have
with respect to the children's elicited imitations.
The tabulation of substitutions includes (i) substitutions of a periphrastic causative for some other verb
(cf. "periphrastic change only", "combined change")
and (ii) substitution of a periphrastic causative for
a main verb in the control sentences ("control sentences", "combined change") (cf. Table XL).

Table XLIII.   Markedness in Children's Imitations

RESPONSE

		make	get	have	misc.	Total
	make	x[a]	2	2	2	6
MODEL	get	4	x	5	1	10
	have	8	8	x	4	20
	misc.	2	0	4	x	6
	Total	14	10	11	7	42

[a] Where the response is the same as the model, the
figures are not reported here.

Markedness in Imitations: Adults
        Only one test item contributes data to the
analysis of markedness: in one sentence, the verb had
was replaced by made.

Markedness in Explanations: Children
        Table XLIV summarizes the data on markedness in
children's explanations. The tabulation includes all
substitutions of a periphrastic causative for some
other periphrastic causative verb (cf. Table XLI).

Table XLIV. Markedness in Children's Explanations

RESPONSES

		make	get	have	Total
	make	x^a	1	0	1
MODEL	get	4	x	0	4
	have	15	0)	x	15
	Total	19	1	0	20

a Where the response is the same as the model, the figures are not reported here.

Markedness in Explanations: Adults
    Table XLV summarizes the markedness data in the adult explanations. The tabulation includes all substitutions of a periphrastic causative for some other periphrastic causative verb (cf. Table XLII).

Table XLV. Markedness in Adults' Explanations

RESPONSES

		make	get	have	cause	Total
	make	x^a	3	1	0	4
MODEL	get	5	x	1	1	7
	have	20	0	x	3	23
	cause	x	x	x	x	0
	Total	25	3	2	4	34

a Where the response is the same as the model, the figures are not reported here.

    In the children's imitations (Table XLIII), the model have was replaced by some other verb in 20 cases, get was replaced 10 times, and make replaced only six times. Considering the resulting responses, we find that the majority of substitutions used the verb make (14), while approximately an equal number of responses contained get (10) and have (11).

In the explanations from both children and adults
(Tables XLIV and XLV), the model have was replaced
most often (children: 15; adult: 23), get was replaced
less often (children: 4; adult: 7), and make was
replaced least often (children: 1; adults: 4). Both
children and adults produced make as the most frequent
periphrastic causative in their explanations (children:
19; adults: 25). One child introduced the periphrastic
causative get. Adults, in addition to several uses of
get (3) and have (2), also used the periphrastic cause
in four cases.

(c) Markedness and Grammaticality
      In considering the changes made by subjects in the
imitation process, it is often difficult to determine
whether the resulting sentence is grammatical or not.
For example, is

      ?Grandma had the sweater off.
      (model: *Grandma made the sweater off.)

grammatical without a time phrase (e.g. "in five
seconds flat")? Similarly, although

      Mommy got the baby quiet.

is perfectly acceptable,

      ?The teacher got the girl sad.
      (model: *The teacher had the girl sad.)

is odd at best. An additional problem in discussing
grammaticality with respect to children's responses is
that we do not know what sentences are grammatical or
ungrammatical from the child's point of view. In
fact, if the paradigmatic analysis for which I have
been arguing (e.g. 6.11) is correct, then all of the
models in this experiment might be considered "grammatical" in the child's grammar.
      In spite of these difficulties, it is still
possible tentatively to assume an adult model of
grammaticality (cf. Table XXXVI) and ask which Ss'
responses rendered ungrammatical models grammatical,
which retained the grammaticality value of the model,
and which replaced grammatical models with ungrammatical responses. If it is the case that Ss "recode"
the models through their own linguistic system, one
of two kinds of behavior may be dominant. If
grammaticality within the speaker's own competence is
important, Ss should tend to render ungrammatical
models grammatical and leave unaltered those
grammatical sentences they comprehend or can imitate
by rote. Alternatively, if markedness among peri-

phrastic causative verbs is more important than
general grammaticality, then Ss should sometimes
render grammatical sentences ungrammatical through
the substitution of less marked verbs for more highly
marked periphrastics.

There is considerable evidence that both children
and adults often produce grammatical responses to ungrammatical stimuli. With infinitival complements,
this frequently involves the insertion or deletion of
a to-complementizer. For example, two children and
four adults inserted the to in

    *The baby got the chair fall.

yielding

    The baby got the chair to fall.

In a number of cases, it so happened that replacement
of a marked periphrastic by a less marked verb would
also render a sentence grammatical, and this was
evidenced in a number of cases in the child data, e.g.

    model: *The teacher had the girl sad.
    response: The teacher made the girl sad.

However, there were also many instances in which
changes either left an ungrammatical model ungrammatical, or else rendered a grammatical model ungrammatical. Some of the cases have no relation to markedness among periphrastics, e.g.

    ungrammatical ⟶ ungrammatical
    model: *The baby got' the chair fall.
    response: *The baby got the chair falled.

Yet in those cases which are relevant, there are
several examples in the child data in which markedness
principles appear to outweigh traditional notions of
grammaticality. Some examples are:

    ungrammatical ⟶ ungrammatical
    model: *Daddy had the girl to dance.
    response: *Daddy made the girl to dance.
    model: *The teacher had the girl sad.
    response: ?The teacher got the girl sad.

    grammatical ⟶ ungrammatical
    model: Daddy got the window up.
    response: *Daddy made the window up.

In several instances in which a sentence was already grammatical, or simple addition or deletion of
the to-complementizer was sufficient to make an ungrammatical sentence grammatical, many Ss chose to

alter the periphrastic as well as the complementizer.
Examples from the children's imitation data are:

        model: *Daddy had the girl to dance.
        response: Daddy made the girl dance.
        model: Daddy had the dog walk.
        response: Daddy wanted the dog to walk.

Examples from the explanation and paraphrase data are:

    Children
        model: *Daddy had the girl to dance.
        response: Daddy made the girl dance.

    Adults
        model: The boy got the stick to break.
        response: The boy made the stick break.

All of the data presented thus far support the
hypothesis about markedness. From the statistical
tables on markedness (i.e. Tables XLIII, XLIV, and
XLV),however, it can be seen that less marked periphrastics were sometimes replaced by more marked
ones. Some examples are:

    Imitation: Children
        model: The boy got the stick to break.
        response: *The boy had the stick to break.

    Explanation: Adults
        model: *Grandma made the sweater off.
        response: *Grandma had the sweater off.

However, as these examples are not as frequent as the
reverse, it may be concluded that in general, markedness seems to be as important as grammaticality (if
not more so) in accounting for Ss' responses.

SUMMARY
        At the beginning of section 6.3, I made a number
of hypotheses about (a) the validity of a periphrastic
causative paradigm, (b) markedness, and (c) the
relative role of markedness and grammaticality. I
will now discuss each of these hypotheses in turn.

(a) Periphrastic Causative Paradigm
        I hypothesized that if children structure their
knowledge of periphrastic causative constructions on
the basis of a periphrastic causative paradigm, then
they should imitate grammatical and ungrammatical
periphrastic causative constructions with equal
facility. The general results showed that performance
on grammatical models surpassed performance on ungrammatical sentences (83% versus 72% -- cf. Table

XXXVII), with superior performance on   grammatical
models appearing at all age levels (cf. Table XXXIX).
However, judging from the fact that children were both
less startled by, and more willing to explain, ungrammatical models than were adults, it seems that
preschool children are not as rigid in their
acceptance of various ungrammatical complements as are
adults.
     When the imitation data are examined with respect
to specific types of overgeneralizations, we find that
some ungrammatical constructions seem to be more
acceptable than others.

     (i) no use of to in get + noun + infinitive

     Both children and adults' lowest scores in the
imitation task were on the sentence

     *The baby got the chair fall.

(children: 51%; adults: 75% -- cf. Tables XXXVII and
XXXVIII). One might wish to argue that the problem
is not with the lack of the to-complementizer, but
rather with the strangeness of a non-volitional noun
(i.e. chair) as subject of the complement -- see Baron
1974). However, both children and adults performed
quite well on the parallel grammatical model

     The boy got the stick to break.

(89% and 100%, respectively).

     (ii) use of to in $\left\{ \begin{array}{l} \text{make} \\ \text{have} \end{array} \right\}$ + noun + infinitive

     Children scored a total of 75% and 74% correct,
respectively, on the two models

     *The clown made the horse to jump.
     *Daddy had the girl to dance.

(adults scored 100% correct in each case). While these
child scores are still lower than the average percent
correct on grammatical models (i.e. 83%), they are
considerably higher than the score on the comparable
ungrammatical sentence with get (i.e. 51%). Because
only a single model sentence was used with each
periphrastic causative verb plus complement type, it
is not possible to determine how much of the variance
in the scores is a function of the particular models
used. Given the high amount of confusion with the
verb fall in

     *The baby got the chair fall.

(cf. Table XL), I suspect that a repetition of the

same general design with a large number of sentences might reveal much smaller differences between scores on ungrammatical get + noun + infinitive on the one hand, and ungrammatical make or have + noun + infinitive, on the other, than were found in the present study.

(iii) use of have + noun + adjective with
inadmissible adjectives

Children's performance on have + noun + adjective, i.e.

*The teacher had the girl sad.

was slightly lower than the average score on grammatical models (i.e. 76% versus 83%), while the adult score was 100%. It will be necessary to examine other examples of this type to determine the status of this construction in preschool children's developing grammars.

(iv) use of make + noun + locative

Children scored 82% correct on the model

*Grandma made her sweater off.

(the adult score was 95%). In fact, one child even replaced the grammatical

Daddy got the window up.

with the ungrammatical

*Daddy made the window up.

These data support the longitudinal finding that children (and adults) spontaneously use the construction make + noun + locative (cf. 5.5).

In conclusion, the experimental data provide evidence both for and against the existence of a periphrastic causative paradigm. The strongest evidence in favor of the paradigm comes from the construction make + noun + locative. However, before ruling out the possibility of a paradigm with respect to other complement types, it will be necessary to repeat this type of experiment with a larger number of sentences.

(b) Markedness

Imitation and explanation data from both children and adults support the hypothesis that make is the least marked of the three periphrastics; get, more marked; and have, most marked (cf. Tables XLIII, XLIV, and XLV). In each case, subjects most frequently replaced have with some other verb, replacing get less frequently and make least frequently of all.

Similarly, main verbs in the models were, with one
exception (cf. Table XLIII) least often replaced by
have, more often by get, and most often by make.
These rank orders remain the same even after correct-
ing for unequal numbers of have, make, and get both
among the imitation models and among the seven sentences for which explanations were requested.

In 5.83, I discussed longitudinal evidence that
periphrastic causative make and get were (ontogenetically) less marked than have, although there were
conflicting data on the relative markedness of make
and get. The experimental data from children (and
adults) strongly suggest that make is less marked than
get. I conclude that the synchronic markedness
hierarchy which I originally proposed in 3.3 is
supported by both ontogenetic and adult data.

(c) Markedness versus Grammaticality
Markedness and grammaticality have both been
considered as possible predictors of Ss' responses.
Because of problems in defining grammaticality with
respect to both synchronic and ontogenetic grammars,
it has not been possible to conclude that the one
factor is more important than the other in determining
responses. However, there is some evidence that
markedness is at least as good a predictor as
grammaticality.

6.4 Non-Causative/Causative Comprehension

HYPOTHESES
The major hypothesis tested by the non-causative/
causative comprehension task is

(a) Hypothesis 1: Non-Causative/Causative
Children who have not yet gained full facility
with periphrastic causative get and have will tend
to interpret causative sentences of the forms

    i.   get + N + adj
    ii. get + N + PP
    iii. have + N + PP

as non-causative, i.e.

    iv. get + adj + N
    v.   get + PP + N
    vi. have + PP + N

rather than vice versa.

In this task, Ss were asked to indicate which of
two pictures was accurately described by the model

they heard.   Because of the difficulty of preserving
the non-causative/causative distinction in illustrations described by the past tense, all sentence models
were phrased in the present tense.   There was, however, one complicating factor, namely verb aspect. In
normal English, the progressive is used to describe a
one-time event occurring in the present, e.g.

>   The lady is brushing the dog.
>   (cf. The lady brushes the dog every night at
>   eight o'clock.)

With causative and non-causative get, both models are
grammatical in the present progressive, since get is a
non-stative verb, e.g.

>   The dog is getting the dirty rug.
>   The dog is getting the rug dirty.

However, while causative have is also non-stative, cf.

>   The girl is having her shoes polished.

the non-causative verb is stative, and therefore cannot normally be used in the progressive,[11] cf.

>   *The girl is having her polished shoes.

If simple present tense were retained for all
instances of non-causative have, e.g.

>   The girl has her polished shoes.

and causative have were uniformly expressed in the
progressive, e.g.

>   The girl is having her shoes polished.

one could easily argue that a child's (or adult's)
correct choices could be governed by knowledge of
aspect and not of causative syntax.   I therefore
decided to present all non-causative models with have
in the present progressive and half of the causative
models in the simple present.   To counterbalance the
strangeness of using the simple present with non-
stative (i.e. causative) have, half of all get
sentences (both causative and non-causative) would
also be presented in the simple present.

While this was the design ultimately adopted,
there still remained the problem of whether the causative sentences read in the simple present actually con-
veyed the intended meaning.   In the case of get sentences, there seemed to be no problem.   However, consider the sentence

>   The girl has her shoes polished.

This model was intended to be causative, yet the
sentence can also have the resultative interpretation
in which <u>have</u> indicates possession rather than causation, cf.

> The poor girl has been working away all after-
> noon and finally she has her shoes polished.

I assumed that preschool children (and adults) would,
in fact, interpret the simple present

> The girl has her shoes polished.

as causative rather than possessive, to the same extent that they interpreted progressive

> The girl is having her shoes polished.

as causative rather than possessive, i.e.

(b) <u>Hypothesis 2: Verb Aspect (Have)</u>
Verb aspect does not influence whether <u>Ss</u> interpret <u>have</u> + N + PP constructions as non-causative
or causative.

I also expected that

(c) <u>Hypothesis 3: Verb Aspect (Get)</u>
Verb aspect does not influence whether <u>Ss</u> interpret <u>get</u> + N + adj or <u>get</u> + N + PP constructions
as non-causative or causative.

The final dimension of this experiment was to
compare behavior with adjectival and past participial
complements. Because neither the grammatical nor
causative status of <u>have</u> + noun + adjective is clear
in English (cf. Baron 1974), I restricted examples
with <u>have</u> to past participial complements. However,
in the case of <u>get</u>, both adjectival and past
participial forms freely occur, cf.

> past participle: Daddy is getting the meat
>   sliced.
> adjective: The dog is getting the rug
>   dirty.

With past participial complements, the immediate cause
may or may not be the higher subject; with adjectival
complements, however, the higher subject is always the
immediate cause. In order to standardize the task as
much as possible, I designed all of my illustrations
with causative <u>get</u> such that the higher subject was
the immediate cause.

I had no reason to believe that ability to
differentiate between non-causative and causative
interpretations of constructions with <u>get</u> would be

influenced by whether the complement was an adjective
or a past participle. I therefore assumed

(d) Hypothesis 4: Adjective versus Past Participle
    Ss' ability to distinguish between non-causative
    and causative interpretations of constructions
    with get is not affected by whether the comple-
    ment is an adjective or a past participle.

DESIGN
     Sixteen non-causative/causative sets of test
pictures were shown to each S, four each testing non-
causative have, causative have, non-causative get,
and causative get. All sentences except those with
non-causative have were counterbalanced for simple
present and present progressive. Four control sets,
also counterbalanced for aspect, were included among
the stimuli. Two different random orders of presentation were used. In addition, because the two pictures
were presented side by side, both orders were counterbalanced for right and left positioning.
     The illustrations, approximately 6" by 6" in
size, were drawn in black ink and partially colored
with water colors. They were mounted under plastic
covers and placed in a looseleaf notebook. An
identical testing procedure was used for children and
adults: the subject was instructed to look at the
two pictures, listen to what I was going to say, and
point to the picture that went with what I said.
     Table XLVI lists the 16 types of test and four
types of control sentences used in each list.

Table XLVI.   Test and Control Stimuli in Non-Causative/
              Causative Comprehension

		TEST
Non-Causative		
-s		
	have	Daddy has the fried fish
		The girl has her ironed dress
		The boy has the glued airplane
		The girl has her polished shoes
	get	Mommy gets the towels folded
		The girl gets her dirty sweater
-ing	get	The boy is getting his wet shoes
		Daddy is getting the sliced meat
Causative		
-s		
	have	Grandma has the present wrapped
		Daddy has the pot covered
	get	The dog gets the rug dirty
		The girl gets her dress mended
-ing	have	The boy is having the box painted
		Daddy is having the toast buttered
	get	Mommy is getting the carrots chopped
		Mommy is getting the pot clean
		CONTROL
-s		The girl reads the book
		The boy paints the chair
-ing		The lady is washing the dog
		The bunny is eating the carrot

Representative sets of pictures appear in Figures 1-4.

Figure 1. Non-Causative/Causative <u>Have</u> + N + PP

The girl has her polished shoes.

The girl $\left\{\begin{array}{l}\text{has}\\ \text{is having}\end{array}\right\}$ her shoes polished.

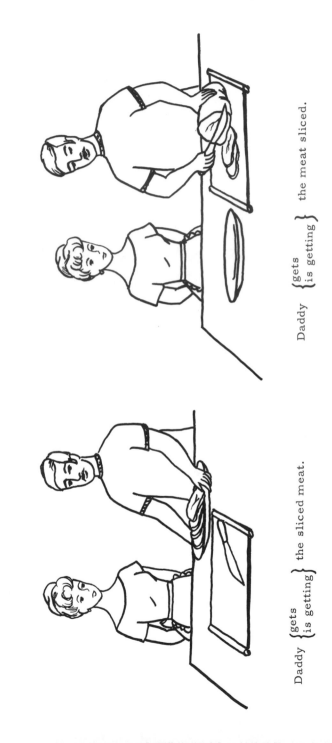

Figure 2. Non-Causative/Causative <u>Get</u> + N + PP

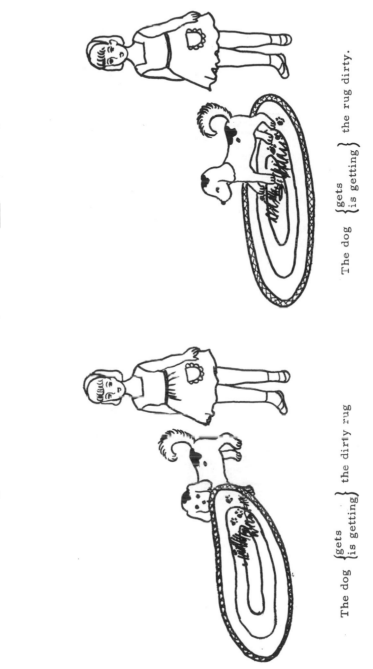

Figure 3.   Non-Causative/Causative Get + N + Adj

The dog {gets / is getting} the dirty rug

The dog {gets / is getting} the rug dirty.

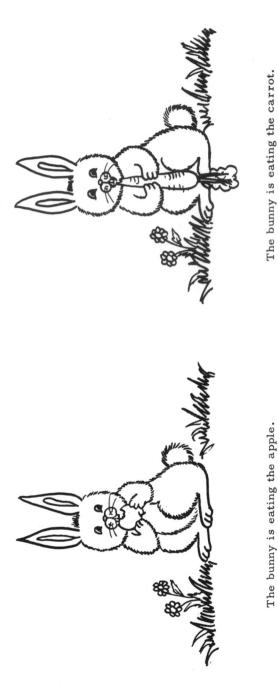

Figure 4. Control

The bunny is eating the apple.

The bunny is eating the carrot.

RESULTS
    The Pearson product moment correlation co-
efficient was used to test the significance of im-
provements in performance with age among children.
Differences between children and adults were measured
by t-tests. Sign tests were used to test differences
between performance of children or adults on any two
given syntactic factors.

General Performance
    Table XLVII summarizes overall behavior on all
20 test and control items.

Table XLVII.   Total Correct in Non-Causative/Causative
                Comprehension

Age	2;6-3;5	3;6-3;11	4;0-4;5	4;6-4;11	5;0-5;5	Total (Children)	Adults
N Correct	$146/239$	$161/238$	$157/240$	$183/240$	$182/240$	$828/1197$	$374/400$
% Correct	61	68	65	76	76	69	94

    Overall scores on this task increased slightly
with age among the children, with a fairly sharp break
occurring around the second half of the fourth year.
While the general age change was not statistically
significant when summed over both test and control
items, it was significant when only test stimuli were
considered (p < .025). Although the adult scores were
significantly higher than those of children (p < .0005),
there were enough errors in the adult data to warrant
further analysis.

Non-Causative/Causative Interpretation of Have and Get
    Tables XLVIII and XLIX summarize Ss' performance
on have and get, respectively. These data are shown
graphically in Figures 5 and 6.

Table XLVIII. Non-Causative versus Causative Have

	Age	2;6-3;5	3;6-3;11	4;0-4;5	4;6-4;11	5;0-5;5	Total (Children)	Adults
-cause	N Correct	32/49	35/48	38/48	42/48	42/48	189/241	80/80
	% Correct	65	73	79	88	88	78	100
+cause	N Correct	16/47	19/47	17/48	26/48	26/48	104/238	62/80
	% Correct	34	40	35	54	54	44	78

Figure 5.   Non-Causative versus Causative <u>Have</u>

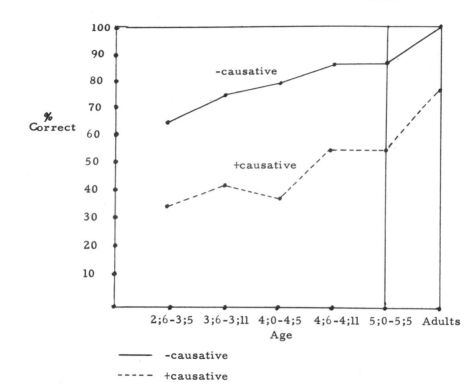

```
          -causative
    ----- +causative
```

Table XLIX.   Non-Causative versus Causative <u>Get</u>

	Age	2;6-3;5	3;6-3;11	4;0-4;5	4;6-4;11	5;0-5;5	Total (Children)	Adults
-cause	N Correct	20/48	23/48	20/47	26/47	31/48	120/238	78/80
	% Correct	42	48	43	55	65	50	98
+cause	N Correct	31/48	36/48	36/49	43/49	35/48	181/242	74/79
	% Correct	65	75	73	88	73	75	94

Figure 6.   Non-Causative versus Causative <u>Get</u>

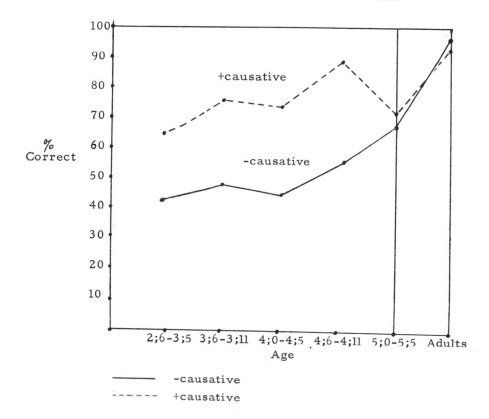

Children scored significantly higher with non-causative <u>have</u> than causative <u>have</u> (p < .001).   Conversely, children did significantly better in identifying causative <u>get</u> than non-causative <u>get</u> (p < .001).   While adults also performed better (p < .001) on non-causative <u>have</u> than causative <u>have</u>, there was no difference between their performances on causative and non-causative <u>get</u>.   Children's performances became significantly better with age on non-causative and causative <u>have</u> (p < .005; p < .05), and on non-causative <u>get</u> (p < .025), but not on causative <u>get</u>.

Simple and Progressive Aspect
        Tables L, LI, and LII summarize Ss' performance with respect to verb aspect.   These data are shown graphically in Figures 7, 8, and 9.

Table L. Have: Simple versus Progressive Aspect
                (Causative Only)

	Age	2;6-3;5	3;6-3;11	4;0-4;5	4;6-4;11	5;0-5;5	Total (Children)	Adults
simple (has)	N Correct	5/23	7/23	5/24	8/24	6/24	31/118	22/40
	% Correct	22	30	21	33	25	26	55
progressive (having)	N Correct	11/24	12/24	12/24	18/24	20/24	73/120	40/40
	% Correct	46	50	50	75	83	61	100

Figure 7. Have: Simple versus Progressive Aspect
                  (Causative Only)

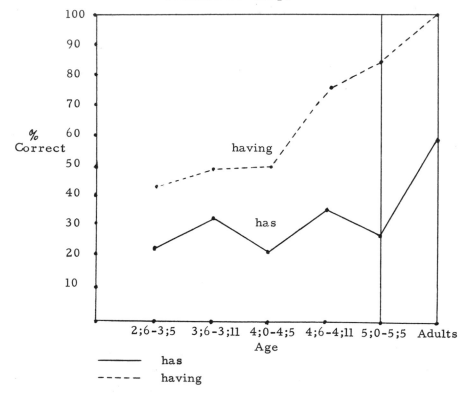

Table LI. Non-Causative <u>Get</u>:   Simple versus
          Progressive Aspect

	Age	2;6-3;5	3;6-3;11	4;0-4;5	4;6-4;11	5;0-5;5	Total (Children)	Adults
simple (gets)	N Correct	8/24	12/24	10/24	15/24	20/24	65/120	39/40
	% Correct	33	50	42	62	83	54	98
progressive (getting)	N Correct	12/24	11/24	10/23	11/23	11/24	55/118	39/40
	% Correct	50	46	43	48	46	47	98

Figure 8.   Non-Causative <u>Get</u>: Simple versus
            Progressive Aspect

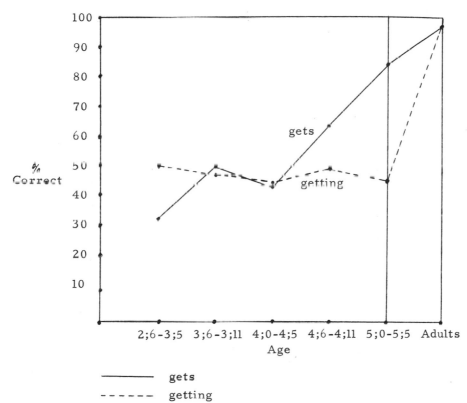

gets

getting

%
Correct

Age

——————— gets

- - - - - - getting

Table LII. Causative <u>Get</u>: Simple versus Progressive
          Aspect

		Age	2;6-3;5	3;6-3;11	4;0-4;5	4;6-4;11	5;0-5;5	Total (Children)	Adults
simple (gets)	N Correct		16/24	20/24	17/24	20/24	16/24	89/120	37/40
	% Correct		67	83	71	83	67	74	92
progressive	N Correct		15/24	16/24	19/25	23/25	19/24	92/122	37/39
	% Correct		62	67	76	92	79	75	95

Figure 9. Causative <u>Get</u>: Simple versus Progressive
          Aspect

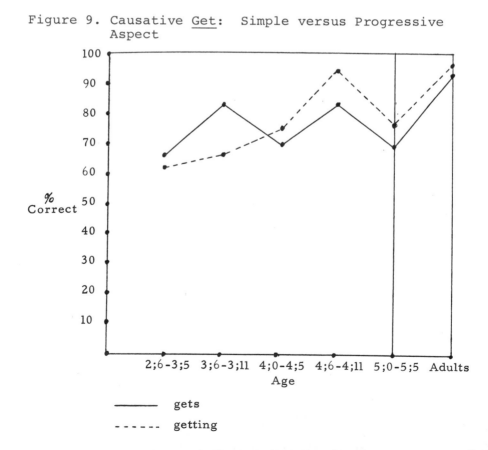

gets

getting

When the child and adult data on causative have are analyzed in terms of aspect, it becomes clear that aspectual features account for most of the incorrect interpretations. Both children and adults scored significantly better on present progressive (having) than on simple present (has) forms (p < .001). Among the children, there was a significant rise with age on progressive scores (p < .025), although change with respect to simple present tense items was non-significant.

Aspectual differences were less noticeable with get than with have. Comparison of simple (gets) and progressive (getting) forms with both non-causative and causative items revealed no significant differences with either children or adults. When children are compared across age categories, only scores on items using simple present with non-causative get show a significant increase with age (p < .025).

Adjectival and Past Participial Complements with Get

Tables LIII, LIV, and LV summarize the differences in Ss' responses to adjectival and past participial complements with non-causative and causative get. Figures 10, 11, and 12 display these data graphically.

Table LIII. Adjectival versus Past Participial Complements with Get (Non-Causative and Causative Combined)

		Age	2;6-3;5	3;6-3;11	4;0-4;5	4;6-4;11	5;0-5;5	Total (Children)	Adults
Adj	N Correct		26/48	28/48	32/48	39/48	34/48	159/240	77/80
	% Correct		54	58	67	81	71	66	96
PP	N Correct		25/48	31/48	24/48	30/48	32/48	142/240	76/80
	% Correct		52	65	50	62	67	59	95

Figure 10. Adjectival versus Past Participial
Complements with <u>Get</u> (Non-Causative and
Causative Combined)

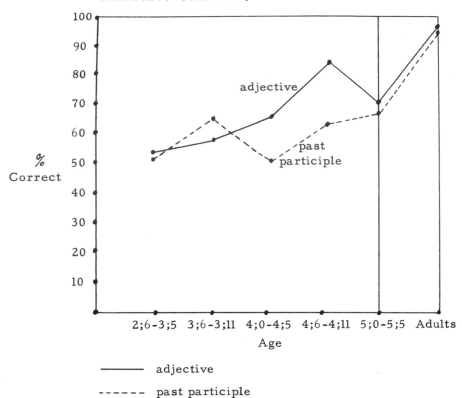

—————— adjective

- - - - - - past participle

Table LIV. Non-Causative <u>Get</u>: Adjectival versus Past
Participial Complements

	Age	2;6-3;5	3;6-3;11	4;0-4;5	4;6-4;11	5;0-5;5	Total (Children)	Adults
Adj	N Correct	13/24	10/24	13/24	18/24	19/24	73/120	39/40
	% Correct	54	42	54	75	79	61	98
PP	N Correct	7/24	13/24	7/23	8/23	12/24	47/118	39/40
	% Correct	29	54	30	35	50	40	98

Figure 11. Non-Causative Get: Adjectival versus
          Past Participial Complements

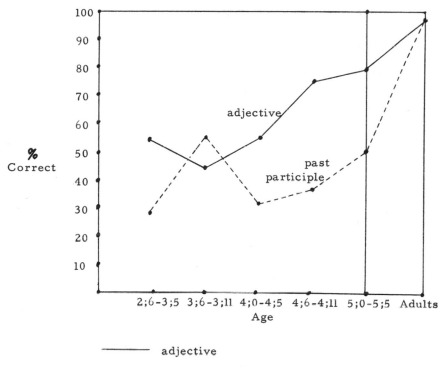

          adjective

          past
          participle

          —————— adjective

          — — — — past participle

Table LV.   Causative Get: Adjectival versus Past
          Participial Complements

	Age	2;6-3;5	3;6-3;11	4;0-4;5	4;6-4;11	5;0-5;5	Total (Children)	Adults
Adj	N Correct	13/24	18/24	19/24	21/24	15/24	86/120	38/40
	% Correct	54	75	79	88	62	72	95
PP	N Correct	18/24	18/24	17/25	22/25	20/24	95/122	37/40
	% Correct	75	75	68	88	83	78	92

Figure 12. Causative <u>Get</u>: Adjectival versus Past
Participial Complements

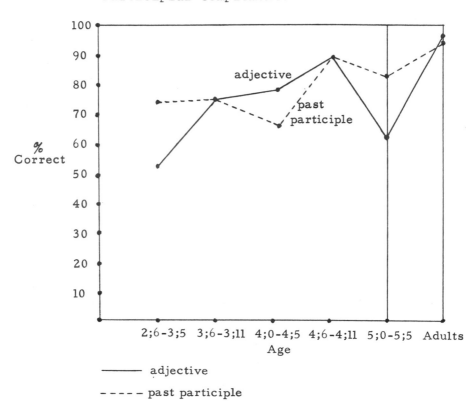

The difference between adjectival and past
participial complements may account for some of the
differences between children's performance on non-
causative and causative models with <u>get</u>. When the
data are analyzed without regard to non-causal/causal
distinction (Table LIII), it is evident that children
do slightly better on adjectival models than on past
participial ones (p < .028, two-tailed). However,
when non-causative and causative data are analyzed
separately, the distinction is even clearer. Although
there was no significant difference in performance on
causative models, children did significantly better on
adjectival forms than past participial forms on non-
causative items (p < .002, two-tailed.)

SUMMARY

I initially proposed four general hypotheses about how Ss would respond on the non-causative/causative comprehension test. I will now discuss each of these hypotheses in the light of the data.

(a) Non-Causative/Causative

I hypothesized that children who have not yet gained full facility with periphrastic causative get and have will tend to interpret causative forms with adjectival and past participial complements as non-causative. In the case of have, this hypothesis was borne out: while children interpreted non-causative have correctly 78% of the time, their correct responses to causative have reached only 44%, i.e. 56% of the time, children incorrectly identified causative have as being non-causative -- cf. Table XLVIII . However, in the case of get, children performed better on causative sentences than on non-causative ones: while 75% of the children's responses on causative models were correct, only 50% of their responses were correct on non-causative sentences.[12] These data further support the hypothesis that get is less marked ontogenetically as a periphrastic causative than is have in the sense that the causative functions of get are learned before the causative functions of have (cf. 3.3).

(b) and (c) Verb Aspect

It was assumed that aspect would be an irrelevant factor in predicting responses. However, the aspectual analyses revealed that while aspect seems to be irrelevant in determining behavior with non-causative and causative get, it is relevant in predicting both child and adult responses with causative have. How is this finding to be interpreted? One analysis focuses upon the use of -ing with causative have: children (and adults) learn that non-causative, stative have cannot be used with progressive aspect, while other verbs (e.g. get) may occur either in simple or progressive forms. Given this restriction on have, S tends to analyze all instances of having as causative. The other interpretation, which is somewhat more complicated, focuses upon the resultative value of non-progressive have: S interprets has + noun + past participle as a resultative (and, by implication, possessive) construction rather than as a causative. There is some evidence that many adults who identified has + noun + past participle as non-causative were operating under this second assumption.

Following the experimental session, I questioned all
adults who matched the non-causative illustration with
has + noun + past participle. While a few Ss said they
now realized that they had made a mistake and should
have chosen the causative picture, at least half
justified their choices by paraphrasing the original
model as a possessive, e.g.

> model: The boy has the airplane glued.
> response: See, he's already got the airplane,
>   the glued airplane... [in the
>   causative picture] he's having it
>   glued right now. It isn't finished.
>   It's not a glued airplane, it's
>   being glued. And [in the non-
>   causative picture] it's all glued,
>   it's finished, it's done with.

Intuitively, I doubt that preschool children recognize
this resultative interpretation of has + noun + past
participle. Comprehension of the resultative value
of the construction requires a simultaneous awareness
of past and present states of affairs without surface
marking of this time difference. Present data on
preschool children's linguistic knowledge of sequence
of events in time (e.g. Cromer 1968; Clark 1970, 1971)
make it somewhat unlikely that all the children in
this task were capable of this level of temporal
abstraction. Rather, I suggest that children's errors
are the function of a general strategy associating has
with possession. In the case of adults, both
strategies may have been operative, though adults'
explanations suggest that the resultative interpretation was dominant.[13]

(d) Adjective versus Past Participle

  I suggested that the difference between adjectival
and past participial complements would not affect Ss'
behavior. The hypothesis was upheld with causative
models; with get, however, children did correctly
interpret non-causative adjectival complements more
frequently than past participial forms. Why should
this be the case? With respect to the longitudinal
data (cf. 5.6), I argued that it is possible to interpret two-year-olds' spontaneous use of past participial
complements as filling adjectival function. Figure 11
shows that the responses of the youngest Ss are not
uniformly differentiated with respect to adjectives
and past participles. However, after age four, the
gap begins to widen, and subjects do consistently
better on adjectival non-causatives than on past

participial forms. It seems as though, by age four,
children have begun to recognize the potential verbal
function of past participles, and that they then
overgeneralize that knowledge to inappropriate contexts. In the next set of experiments, I will show
that other types of syntactic overgeneralizations seem
to appear at about the same age.

6.5 Subject/Agent Interpretation

HYPOTHESES
     The two basic hypotheses to be tested with
respect to the use of a subject/agent strategy in
comprehension were:

(a) Hypothesis 1: Periphrastic Causatives
    Young children will identify all surface subjects
    as agents in the periphrastic causative construc-
    tions (i) get + N + adj, (ii) have + N + PP, and
    (iii) get + N + PP. Older children will either be
    inconsistent in their choices, or, if they have
    acquired adult competence, they (i) will identify
    the subject of get + N + PP as agent, (ii) will
    not identify the subject of have + N + PP as
    agent, and (iii) will give mixed responses with
    get + N + PP.

(b) Hypothesis 2: Periphrastic Causatives versus
                  Passives
    Developing interpretations of (i) have + N + PP
    and (ii) get + N + PP will be related to behavior
    on reversible passives.

     One possible design to test these two hypotheses
consists of a forced choice picture identification
task like that in the last experiment. Ss are
presented with two illustrations which involve the
same beings (either people or animals), objects, and
actions, and which differ only in who is performing
the action. However, I also wished to investigate
whether the experimental design itself biased Ss'
responses. I therefore designed a second experiment
using a puppet acting-out task similar to Cromer's
(1970) (cf. 6.14). If Ss' performance is not influenced by design factors, then responses on comparable
constructions will be consistent across designs.

PICTURE TASK

(a) Design
    The picture experiment consisted of 20 sets of
pictures. Four pairs depicted correct and incorrect

interpretations of <u>having</u> + noun + past participle;
four, alternative correct interpretations of <u>getting</u>
+ noun + past participle; eight, active and passive
sequences; and four, controls. Two different orders
were used, each being counterbalanced for right and
left positioning. In addition, all active and passive
models were counterbalanced for both voice and
reversibility.

The causative illustrations were all based upon
the earlier experiment with non-causative versus
causative <u>have</u> and <u>get</u>. From the original set of
illustrations, I selected eight "causative" pictures,
i.e. in which the subject of the matching sentence was
not the agent of the action. With each of these
pictures I paired a complementary illustration which
could be correctly described by a sentence in which
the subject was the immediate agent. In addition,
eight sets of active/passive illustrations and four
sets of controls were drawn. The testing procedure
was identical to that of the last experiment.

Table LVI lists the 16 types of test and four
types of control sentences used in each list.

Table LVI.   Test and Control Stimuli in Picture
             Subject/Agent Comprehension

	CAUSATIVE
having	The girl is having her dress ironed The boy is having the box painted The boy is having the airplane glued The girl is having her shoes polished
getting	Daddy is getting the meat sliced Mommy is getting the towels folded The girl is getting her dress mended Mommy is getting the carrots chopped
	ACTIVE/PASSIVE
active	The boy is swinging the girl Mommy is scaring the mouse The train is bumping the car The lion is following the elephant
passive	The duck is chased by the mouse The car is pushed by the truck The boy is kicked by the cow The boy is kissed by the girl
	CONTROL
	Grandma is sewing the pants The boy is lighting the candle The girl is holding the coat The baby is kicking the balloon

Representative sets of pictures appear in Figures
13-15.

Figure 13.   Subject/Agent Interpretation of Causative
Having + N + PP

*The girl is having her shoes polished.

The girl is having her shoes polished.

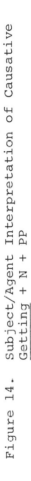

Figure 14. Subject/Agent Interpretation of Causative
Getting + N + PP

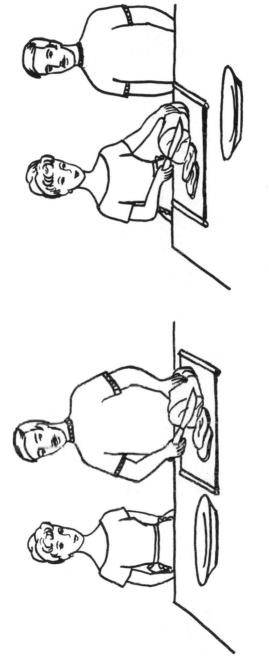

Daddy is getting the meat sliced.

Daddy is getting the meat sliced.

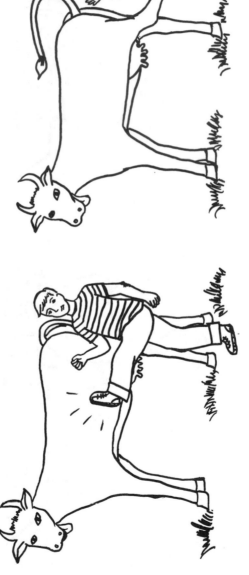

Figure 15. Active versus Passive

Active: The boy is kicking the cow.
Passive: The cow is kicked by the boy.

Active: The cow is kicking the boy.
Passive: The boy is kicked by the cow.

(b) Results
     The Pearson product moment correlation co-
efficient was used to test the significance of age
differences among children. Differences between
children and adults were measured with t-tests. Sign
tests were used to test differences between
performance of children or adults on two factors.

General Performance
     In analyzing overall performance, it is
necessary to exclude items of the form getting + N +
PP, since either response S could give is correct.
Table LVII presents the distribution of overall
correct scores on having + N + PP, active and
passive, and control models in the picture task.

Table LVII.   Total Correct in Picture Subject/Agent
              Comprehension (Excluding Getting + N +
              PP)

Age	2;6-3;5	3;6-3;11	4;0-4;5	4;6-4;11	5;0-5;5	Total (Children)	Adults
N Correct	$131/192$	$152/192$	$156/192$	$162/192$	$163/192$	$764/960$	$317/319$
% Correct	68	79	81	84	85	80	99

Summing over all models (except getting + N + PP),
we see a significant increase with age on total
percentage of items correct (p < .025). Adult
performance was perfect (100%), which was significantly better than the children's responses (p < .0005).

Active versus Passive
     Table LVIII and Figure 16 summarize the data from
the picture task on active and passive models.

Table LVIII. Picture Task: Active versus Passive

		2;6-3;5	3;6-3;11	4;0-4;5	4;6-4;11	5;0-5;5	Total (Children)	Adults
	Age							
Active	N Correct	40/47	43/48	45/48	47/48	45/48	220/239	78/79
	% Correct	85	90	94	98	94	92	99
Passive	N Correct	23/49	33/48	32/48	32/48	37/48	157/241	80/80
	% Correct	47	69	67	67	77	65	100

Figure 16. Picture Task: Active versus Passive

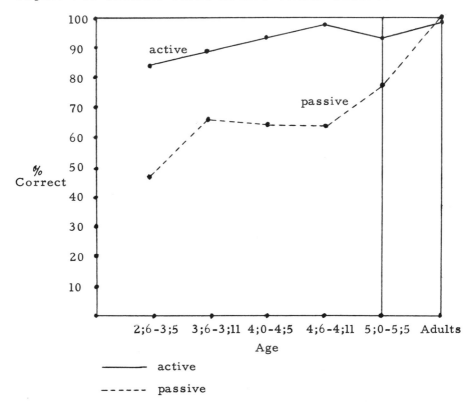

Children scored significantly better on active sentences than on passive (p $<$ .001), and performance on actives and passives significantly improved with age (p $<$ .05).

Passive versus Having versus Getting

     Table LIX and Figure 17 compare the results on passive, having + N + PP, and getting + N + PP models in the picture task. Scores on passive and having models represent percent correct. Scores on getting models indicate percent of identification of surface subject with agent.

Table LIX.   Picture Task: Passive versus Having + N + PP versus Getting + N + PP

	Age	2;6-3;5	3;6-3;11	4;0-4;5	4;6-4;11	5;0-5;5	Total (Children)	Adults
Passive	% Correct	47	69	67	67	77	65	100
Having	% Correct	46	58	67	79	69	64	99
Getting	% Subj = Ag	71	88	73	69	67	73	29

Figure 17.   Picture Task: Passive versus <u>Having</u> + N
             + PP versus <u>Getting</u> + N + PP

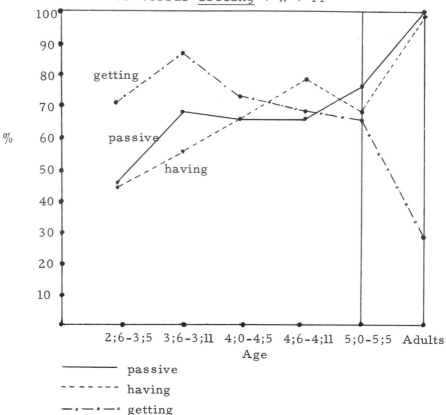

%

Age

—————————— passive

- - - - - - having

—.—.—. getting

Statistically, there is no difference between the S̲s̲
responses on (a) passives versus <u>having</u> sentences, or
(b) passive versus <u>getting</u> sentences among children.
However, the overall difference between <u>having</u> and
<u>getting</u> scores in children is significant at the .001
level.

PUPPET TASK

(a) <u>Design</u>
     In the puppet task, S̲s̲ were given two Steiff hand
puppets, a monkey and a bunny. I then produced a box
of small toys and asked S̲ to show me the monkey or the
bunny playing appropriately with one of the toys (or
with each other), depending upon what I said. For
example, if I said "The monkey is kissing the baby",
S̲ should act out the monkey kissing the toy baby.

The task consisted of 24 vignettes. Six sentences each were of the form

    i.   <u>having</u> + N + PP
    ii.   <u>getting</u> + N + PP
    iii. <u>getting</u> + N + adj

In addition, there were three active and three passive
models. No separate control sentences were used. The
sentences were arranged in two separate random orders
which were each counterbalanced for which animal was
placed on which hand. In addition, active and passive
models were completely counterbalanced for voice and
reversibility.
    Table LX lists the 24 types of stimuli.

Table LX. Stimuli in Puppet Subject/Agent
           Comprehension

	CAUSATIVE
having + N + PP	The bunny is having the baby spanked
	The bunny is having the knife dried
	The bunny is having the airplane painted
	The monkey is having the table moved
	The monkey is having the car hidden
	The monkey is having the box opened
getting + N + PP	The bunny is getting the knife sharpened
	The bunny is getting the baby fed
	The bunny is getting the airplane fixed
	The monkey is getting the box closed
	The monkey is getting the car washed
	The monkey is getting the table polished
getting + N + adj	The bunny is getting the box empty
	The bunny is getting the table clean
	The bunny is getting the table clean
	The monkey is getting the knife wet
	The monkey is getting the airplane dirty
	The monkey is getting the baby dirty
	ACTIVE/PASSIVE
active	The bunny is hitting the monkey
	The bunny is petting the monkey
	The monkey is chasing the bunny
passive	The bunny is hugged by the monkey
	The bunny is spanked by the monkey
	The monkey is followed by the bunny

(b) Results
     The same statistical procedures were used in examining data from the puppet task as were used with the picture task.

General Performance
     Table LXI summarizes the correct scores on having + N + PP, getting + N + adj, and passive models in the puppet task. Responses on getting + N + PP were excluded because either of the possible responses is correct.

Table LXI.   Total Correct in Puppet Subject/Agent Comprehension (Excluding Getting + N + PP)

Age	2;6-3;5	3;6-3;11	4;0-4;5	4;6-4;11	5;0-5;5	Total (Children)	Adults
N Correct	$128/210$	$127/210$	$127/210$	$128/210$	$148/216$	$658/1056$	$307/359$
% Correct	61	60	60	61	69	62	86

Summing over all models (except getting + N + PP), we see there is no significant increase with age in total percentage of correct items. While there is a significant difference between child and adult performance (p < .0005), adults only scored 86% correct on the puppet task.

Active versus Passive
     Table LXII and Figure 18 present the data on active and passive models in the puppet task.

Table LXII.   Puppet Task: Active versus Passive

	Age	2;6-3;5	3;6-3;11	4;0-4;5	4;6-4;11	5;0-5;5	Total (Children)	Adults
Active	N Correct	30/33	31/33	32/33	31/33	36/36	160/168	59/60
	% Correct	91	94	97	94	100	95	98
Passive	N Correct	17/33	19/33	20/33	27/33	29/36	112/168	53/60
	% Correct	52	58	61	82	81	67	88

Figure 18.   Puppet Task: Active versus Passive

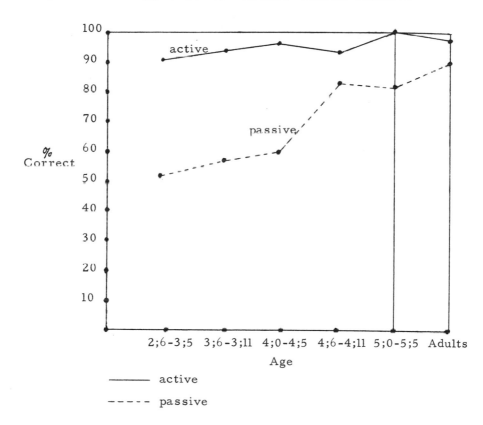

active

passive

% Correct

2;6-3;5   3;6-3;11   4;0-4;5   4;6-4;11   5;0-5;5   Adults

Age

—————— active

- - - - - passive

Children scored significantly better on active sentences than on passive (p < .001), with performance on
actives and passives significantly improving with age
(active: p < .05; passive: p < .025).

Passive versus Having versus Getting
        The data on passive, having + N + PP, and getting
+ N + PP are summarized in Table LXIII and Figure 19.
Scores on passive and having models represent percent
correct.   Scores on getting models indicate percent of
identification of surface subject with agent.

Table LXIII.   Puppet Task: Passive versus Having + N
               + PP versus Getting + N + PP

	Age	2;6-3;5	3;6-3;11	4;0-4;5	4;6-4;11	5;0-5;5	Total (Children)	Adults
Passive	% Correct	52	58	61	82	81	67	88
Having	% Correct	12	12	7	14	24	14	68
Getting	% Subj =Ag	96	89	93	82	83	89	67

Figure 19.   Puppet Task: Passive versus <u>Having</u> + N
             + PP versus <u>Getting</u> + N + PP

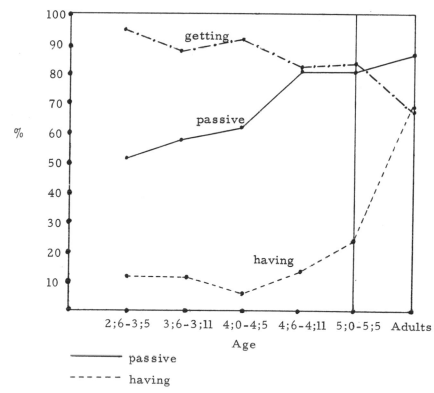

Children and adults performed better on passive sentences than on <u>having</u> items (for children, significant
at the .001 level).   The difference between <u>having</u> and
<u>getting</u> scores is also significant across children
(p < .001), as is the difference passive and <u>getting</u>
(p < .002).

Past Participle versus Adjective

     Table LXIV and Figure 20 summarize the data on
past participial and adjectival complements with
periphrastic causative <u>get</u>.   Past participial scores
represent association of subject with agent.
Adjectival scores indicate the number correct (i.e.
subject identified with agent).

Table LXIV.   Puppet Task: Getting + N + PP versus
                            Getting + N + Adj

	Age	2;6-3;5	3;6-3;11	4;0-4;5	4;6-4;11	5;0-5;5	Total (Children)	Adults
PP	N Subj= Ag	69/72	64/72	67/72	59/72	60/72	319/360	80/120
	% Subj= Ag	96	89	93	82	83	89	67
Adj	N Correct	72/72	68/72	70/72	60/72	66/72	336/360	113/119
	% Correct	100	94	97	83	92	93	95

Figure 20.   Puppet Task: Getting + N + PP versus
                          Getting + N + Adj

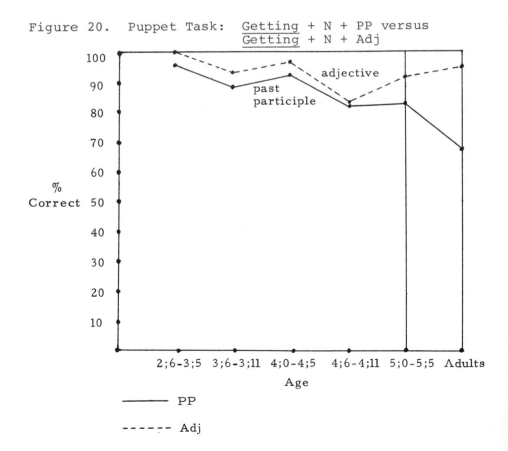

Responses to causative get with past participial and adjectival complements are highly parallel up to about age five. Two-and-a-half to four-and-a-half year olds almost all interpret the subjects of these sentences to be agents. In the second half of the fourth year, however, both scores dip slightly, with the adjectival score again rising somewhat at the final age level. With the past participial complement, the lowering score represents an increase in admissible dissociation of subject and agent. However, in the case of adjectival sentences, the chronological lowering of the score indicates that younger children are performing better than older ones. Given the very close parallels between the two sets of scores, it seems that this apparent "regression" is actually a function of applying a single interpretive strategy to both complement types.

Apparently superior performance by younger children has been observed in the literature before (cf. Bever (1970) on conservation tasks; Guillaume (1927b) on overgeneralization of originally correct irregular nouns and verbs). Cromer (1970) found that his intermediate group made errors which less linguistically developed Ss did not. In my discussion of past participial complements with non-causative get (cf. 6.4), I noted that four-year-olds incorrectly identify get + PP + noun as causative, while younger children do not. The present data on causative getting + N + adjective constitute one more bit of evidence that language learning is not merely a cumulative enterprise but rather is the output of emerging and altering strategies.

COMPARISON OF PICTURE AND PUPPET TASKS

I will compare behavior on the two tasks with respect to (i) causative having + N + PP, (ii) causative getting + N + PP, and (iii) passive versus having versus getting.

Causative Having + N + PP

Table LXV and Figure 21 compare the data on causative having + N + PP in the picture and puppet tasks.

Table LXV.   Causative <u>Having</u> + N + PP: Picture
             versus Puppet Task

		Age	2;6-3;5	3;6-3;11	4;0-4;5	4;6-4;11	5;0-5;5	Total (Children)	Adults
Picture	N Correct		22/48	28/48	32/48	38/48	33/48	153/240	79/80
	% Correct		46	58	67	79	69	64	99
Puppet	N Correct		9/72	9/72	5/72	10/72	17/72	50/360	82/120
	% Correct		12	12	7	14	24	14	68

Figure 21.   Causative <u>Having</u> + N + PP: Picture
             versus Puppet Task

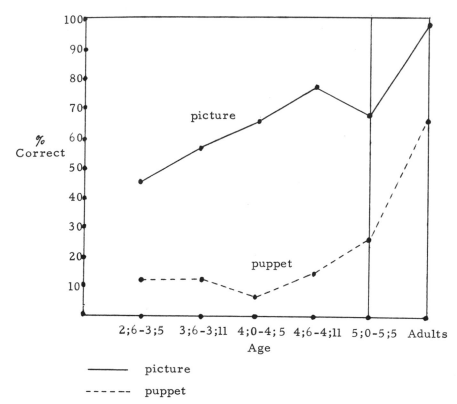

Comparison of subjects' responses to causative
having + N + PP on the two tasks reveals a sharp
discrepancy between picture and puppet experiments.
Both children and adults scored considerably higher
on the puppet task (for children, significant at the
.001 level).   In fact, the percentage correct for
adults in the puppet task was only slightly better
than chance (p < .02) in the puppet game, and
children's incorrect identification of surface subjects as agents was considerably above the level of
chance (p < .001).

Causative Getting + N + PP
    The comparative data from the picture and puppet
tasks on causative getting + N + PP are summarized in
Table LXVI and Figure 22.   Scores are based on the
association of surface subject with agent.

Table LXVI.   Causative Getting + N + PP: Picture
              versus Puppet Task

		Age	2;6-3;5	3;6-3;11	4;0-4;5	4;6-4;11	5;0-5;5	Total (Children)	Adults
Picture		N Subj = Ag	34/48	42/48	35/48	32/48	32/48	175/240	23/79
		% Subj = Ag	71	00	73	69	67	73	29
Puppet		N Subj = Ag	69/72	64/72	67/72	59/72	60/72	319/360	80/120
		% Subj = Ag	96	89	93	82	83	89	67

Figure 22.   Causative Getting + N + PP: Picture
             versus Puppet Task

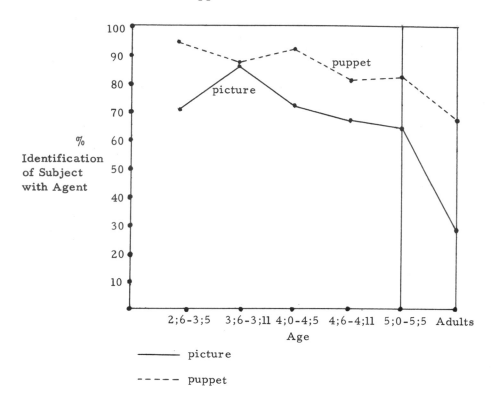

─────── picture

- - - - - puppet

Performance on the picture and puppet tasks also
differed with respect to getting + N + PP.   For
children, this difference was significant at the .001
level.   Chronologically, the percentage association of
sentence subject with agent decreased with age on both
tasks, although neither change was significant on a
two-tailed test.
     While these statistics sum over all exemplars,
there were some interesting differences in child and
adult responses to several examples in the picture
experiment.   The first such sentence was

     The girl is getting her dress mended.

for which subjects were shown illustrations with
either a girl or a grandmother doing the sewing.   Although the combined score on getting + N + PP shows
children do generally identify the subject as agent,

children dissociated subject and agent on this item
58% of the time. Similarly, adults, whose overall
mean score for dissociation of subject and agent was
71% on the picture task, chose the grandmother over
89% of the time. When I asked both children and
adults what motivated their choice, I was repeatedly
told "but little girls can't sew yet".
     Another interesting sentence was

        Daddy is getting the meat sliced.

for which either a father or mother was shown cutting
a roast. Although responses by both children and
adults were generally representative of the combined
scores, several adults who did say that the father was
doing the slicing (i.e. subject = agent) explained
that slicing of meat was a man's job rather than a
woman's. These examples are clear reminders of how
general development and socialization may affect
linguistic behavior.
     Why should older children and adults tend to
dissociate subject and agent in causative get + N + PP
models? Under questioning, a number of adults
explained that the periphrastic construction would be
superfluous if it normally meant that the subject was
actually the immediate instigator of the action. If
you wish to say that the carrots got chopped and
Mommy did it, then the simple transitive

        Mommy chopped the carrots.

will do just as well as

        Mommy got the carrots chopped.

There is, however, a semantic distinction between
these two sentences, namely, that the latter has a
resultative force which the former lacks. Often there
is a sense of "accomplishment of a difficult feat"
which is associated with this resultative interpretation. One adult subject, who said that Daddy was
doing the slicing in

        Daddy is getting the meat sliced.

but Mommy isn't chopping in

        Mommy is getting the carrots chopped.

explained the resultative meaning in terms of his own
pragmatic beliefs:

        You might say, 'Boy, it's hard to get this
        meat sliced,' but you wouldn't say, 'Boy, it's
        hard to get these carrots chopped'.

Passive versus Having versus Getting
    The data comparing passive, having + N + PP, and
getting + N + PP are given in Tables LIX and LXIII,
and Figures 17 and 19 above. Juxtaposition of the
three variables common to both experiments reveals
further differences between the two experiments. From
the picture task, it appears that the same strategy
was used in the comprehension of passives and of
causative having sentences (i.e. no statistical
difference between responses on passives and having
sentences in either children or adults). However, on
the puppet task, children and adults performed much
better on passive sentences than on having items (for
children, significant at the .001 level). It therefore seems that the apparent relation between passive
and causative having strategies is an accidental one
brought out by the design.[14]
    Another interesting difference exists between the
two causative types, having and getting. Statistically, the differences between having and getting scores
across children are significant for both tasks
(p < .001). However, the pattern of chronological
development is quite different in the two experiments.
In the picture task, children under four respond to
causative having at the chance level, though with
causative getting, they clearly associate the subject
with agentive function. These data suggest that the
youngest children have some notion of the meaning of
getting + N + PP, but have no strategy yet for coping
with having + N + PP. Four and five-year-olds
gradually learn that the subject of having cannot be
the actor, while the subject of getting need not be.
The puppet experiment presents a rather different
picture. All but the oldest children seem to apply a
single, working strategy to both constructions: subject is equivalent to agent.
    In the adult data on having and getting, the
above findings are nearly reversed. The adults seem
to have adopted a single strategy on the picture task,
i.e. subject is not equivalent to agent. On the
puppet task, however, their modus operandi is less
clear. Approximately two-thirds of the time, adults
interpret subjects of causative getting as agents, and
with the same ratio (i.e. 2/3), dissociate subjects
and agents in having models.
    There is now a fair amount of evidence that (a)
speakers often associate surface subjects with agents,
and (b) the experimental design affects the degree of
association. What is particularly interesting is that
these generalizations apply to adults as well as to

children, although to a lesser degree. We would
normally have expected that adults, who have
presumably acquired full native competence in their
language, would have scored at least 80 or 90% correct
on the having items in the puppet task (and, concomitantly, perhaps "lower" on the getting items in
the same experiment). However, these phenomena are
almost entirely explicable in terms of the order in
which all four experimental tasks were presented. In
the case of children, the four experiments were
presented in either two or three different sessions.
In nearly every instance, the puppet task appeared at
the beginning of a session. However, with adults,
all tasks were fully counterbalanced and presented in
a single session. Analyzing the adult puppet data by
orders, it becomes clear that (a) the vast majority
of errors in causative having and (b) the vast
majority of identification of subject with agent in
causative getting models occur when the puppet task is
presented first. That is, adults tested first on the
puppet task apparently used the same, monolithic
strategy of identifying subject with agent on all
causative models as did the children. Since we know
from the rest of the adult data that adults do, in
fact, tend to dissociate subjects from agents in both
causative models, it may well be the case that the
puppet task was not an accurate measure of children's
knowledge, largely because of the possibility of order
effects. These order effects seem to occur only when
S must "create" the correct answer himself (i.e.
puppet task), not when he is merely required to choose
between two alternatives which have been offered him
(i.e. picture task). To test this explanation fully,
it would be necessary to present shortened versions of
two or three tasks to children, and fully counterbalance across Ss.

SUMMARY
     I initially stated two general hypotheses about
performance on subject/agent comprehension strategies.
I will briefly summarize the foregoing data on the
picture and puppet tasks in terms of these hypotheses.

(a) Periphrastic Causatives
     I hypothesized that young children would identify
surface subjects as agents in all three periphrastic
causative constructions examined (i.e. get + N + adj,
have + N + PP, and get + N + PP), and that older
children would either give mixed answers on all three
types of constructions, or show adult competence (i.e.
identifying the subject of get + N + adj as agent, but

not identifying the subject of <u>have</u> + N + PP as agent, and giving mixed responses on <u>get</u> + N + PP). This hypothesis was, in general, upheld. In the puppet task, and, to a lesser extent, in the picture task, the youngest age groups tended to identify the subject of past participial constructions with <u>have</u> and <u>get</u> as the agent (cf. Figures 21, 22). And on the puppet task, the youngest <u>S</u>s identified the subject of <u>get</u> + N + adj as the agent 100% of the time (cf. Figure 20).

Correct scores on <u>having</u> models increased significantly with age on the picture task; there was a slight improvement of performance on the puppet task, although it was not statistically significant (cf. Figure 21). On both the picture and puppet tasks, interpretation of the subject as the agent on <u>get</u> + N + PP models decreased with age, although not significantly so. Finally, older children did show inconsistency in their responses to <u>get</u> + N + adj models by sometimes incorrectly dissociating subject from agent.

(b) <u>Periphrastic Causatives versus Passive</u>
The assumption that developing interpretations of (i) <u>have</u> + N + PP and (ii) <u>get</u> + N + PP would correlate with behavior on reversible passives was borne out by the picture experiment: there was no statistical difference between scores on (a) passive versus <u>having</u> and (b) passive versus <u>getting</u> (cf. Figure 17). However, in the puppet task, behavior on passives did not seem to be related to either <u>having</u> or <u>getting</u> models (cf. Figure 19).

Footnotes

[1]Cf. also Olson (1973).

[2]For a discussion of aspectual problems related to the verb <u>have</u>, cf. 6.4.

[3]However, some children who did not complete the imitation items in the first session were allowed to do so in the second.

[4]This last construction was originally excluded because it was not obvious whether it was causative or resultative, and, without a modifier phrase, it was not clearly grammatical or ungrammatical (see Baron 1974). Ideally, however, it should have been included to balance the design.

[5]Because of the particular facts of modern English usage (cf. Table II), it was not possible to fully balance the experimental design with respect to grammatical and ungrammatical sentences.

[6]Within this experiment, I am considering the construction have + noun + adjective to be ungrammatical (*) rather than simply marginal (?) (see Baron 1974).

[7]After testing approximately half of the children (scattered over all age groups), I found the percentage of incorrect imitations to be very low. To increase the error rate by placing the stimuli beyond the children's short term memory span, I added an initial carrier phrase "The doctor said..." to each sentence for the remaining Ss. However, this design alteration did not have the desired effect. Several of the younger children would imitate "the doctor said" and no more, rather than making errors in the test sentence itself. When I dropped the carrier phrase, however, they were able to imitate most of the model sentences correctly. Among the older children, there were a large number of substitutions between the word doctor and other nouns in the sentence, but the basic syntax of the test items did not appear to be influenced by the addition of the carrier phrase. For these reasons, I will not distinguish in my analysis between Ss given the carrier phrase and those who were not.

[8]All percentages in this chapter are rounded to the nearest whole number.

[9]There was, however, one case in which a child formed two distinct sentences, while recognizing the dual function of the second noun:

    model: The lion watched the ball roll.
    response: The lion watched the ball. It
                rolled.

[10]As informal "controls", I also asked for explanations of several typical, grammatical sentences, but these varied from subject to subject, and I will not analyze these responses formally.

[11]However, cf. 5.7.

[12] The elicited imitation experiment (cf. 6.3) also yielded several examples in which causative have and get were interpreted non-causatively.

[13] But cf. Ferreiro and Sinclair 1971.

[14] Cromer (1970), using a puppet task, found a disparity between performance on passives and adjectival models such as

> The wolf is tasty to bite.

I think that the difference might not have been as great if he had employed a picture identification task.

Chapter 7

SUMMARY AND EVALUATION

In this study, I have attempted to examine the
nature of the relationship between first language acquisition and diachrony by considering the ontogenetic and historical evolution of English periphrastic
causative constructions. I will begin this chapter
by summarizing and comparing the diachronic and ontogenetic data, with particular reference to the hypothesized periphrastic causative paradigm and markedness hierarchy (7.1). Section 7.2 evaluates the data
on make, get, and have with respect to the three
parameters of linguistic evolution which I have
proposed. Returning in 7.3 to the broader issue of
ontogenetic/diachronic comparison, I suggest possible
directions for working towards a general theory of
linguistic variation and change.

7.1 Paradigmatic and Markedness Hypotheses

In 3.2, I proposed analyzing English periphrastic
causative constructions with the verbs have, make, and
get in terms of a periphrastic causative paradigm
which matches each verb with each of seven possible
complements. I observed that diachronically, most
cells of this paradigm have been "filled in" at some
point in the history of English, and I hypothesized
that children, in the process of learning English
periphrastic causatives, might initially utilize such
a paradigm which does not place restrictions upon
which verbs may be matched with which complements.
    I also analyzed periphrastic causative verbs with
respect to markedness (cf. 3.3). Using the criteria
of textual frequency, neutralization, and defectivation, I argued that synchronically, make is the least
marked of the verbs, get is more marked, and have most
marked. I suggested that if one were justified in
literally applying this synchronic hierarchy to
diachrony, the following predictions should hold:
1. make is the earliest periphrastic causa-
    tive in the history of English (i.e. at
    least among these three verbs)
2. make appears more frequently than get or
    have
3. make might have developed a wide range of
    complement types earlier than the other
    two verbs

(with the inverse predictions about have)
However, I explained (3.3) that for theoretical reasons, attempts at the literal application of synchronic criteria for markedness to diachrony are
largely untenable, and furthermore, that limitations
of the English written record make some markedness
predictions impossible to test (cf. 4.1).

I also made a number of predictions about ontogeny on the basis of the proposed markedness
hierarchy:)

1. make will appear as the first periphrastic
    causative in child speech
2. make will appear more frequently than get
    or have
3. make will develop a wide range of comple-
    ments earlier than the other two verbs
    (with the inverse predictions about have)
4. children may use make where get or have
    is appropriate, or get where have is
    appropriate

All of these ontogenetic predictions are testable.

Bearing in mind the paradigmatic and markedness
hypotheses, I will summarize and compare the historical and ontogenetic developments of the periphrastic causatives make, get, and have.

7.11 Make

Table LXVII summarizes the historical and ontogenetic emergence of constructions with periphrastic
causative make.

Table LXVII. Diachronic and Ontogenetic Development
              of Complements with Periphrastic
              Causative Make

Date (approx.)	Diachronic	Stage	Ontogenetic
(Prim. Gmc.)	transitive "create", "build"	0	transitive "create", "build", "prepare"
1000	(a) clause (b) noun (c) adjective	1	infinitive$_{intrans}$
		2	(a) locative (b) infinitive$_{intrans}$ + locative
1175	infinitive	3	adjective
1300	past participle	4	infinitive$_{trans}$
1375	locative	5	(a) noun (b) past participle
		6	clause

Both diachronically and ontogenetically, make
emerges as the earliest periphrastic causative in
English among the three verbs under discussion,
thereby supporting the diachronic and ontogenetic
markedness predictions. Historically, clausal,
nominal, and adjectival complements developed at
least a century before infinitival complements, and
locative expressions did not appear for another 200
years. In the longitudinal data, infinitival constructions seem to precede both locative and adjectival constructions, and nominal complements do not
emerge until even later. Modern English lacks the
make + noun + locative construction. However, some
two - year-olds (and their adult interlocutors) use
this configuration in their spontaneous speech (cf.
5.5), which fact tends to support the ontogenetic
existence of a periphrastic causative paradigm with
respect to locative complements.
    Experimentally, the imitation data further sup-
port the hypothesis that make is the least marked of
the three periphrastics. Both elicited imitations
and explanations showed that get and have are more
frequently replaced by make than vice versa (cf. 6.3).
The imitation data also revealed that two to five-

year-old children have begun to learn that modern
English does not allow a to-complementizer with make:
nearly all errors children made in imitating
      *The clown made the horse to jump.
consisted of an elimination of to (cf. 6.3).

7.12 Get

Table LXVIII súmmarizes the historical and ontogenetic emergence of constructions with periphrastic
causative get.

Table LXVIII. Diachronic and Ontogenetic Development
                 of Complements with Periphrastic
                 Causative Get

Date (approx.)	Diachronic	Stage	Ontogenetic
1200	transitive "acquire", "fetch"	0	transitive "acquire", "fetch"
1300	(precausative)	1	(precausative)
1350	locative	2	locative
1400	infinitive	3	(a) adjective (b) past participle
1500	past participle	4	infinitive
1575	adjective		

As a loanword, get is not documented as a causative until approximately 1300, i.e. three centuries
after the first appearance of periphrastic causative
make (cf. Table LXVII above) but also over a century
and a half after the first citation of periphrastic
causative have (cf. Table LXIX below). Once get was
borrowed into English as a transitive verb, it
developed fairly rapidly as a causative, thereby indicating a relatively unmarked status as a causative
(cf. 3.3). Ontogenetically, periphrastic causative

get appears earlier than have, although its position
with respect to make is not clear from the data
analyzed (cf. 5.83).

Once get emerges in both diachronic and ontogenetic systems, its development has some close
parallels. Both historically and ontogenetically,
precausative get + locative constructions appear
quite early and seem to derive from earlier transitive constructions (although this hypothesis could
not be confirmed either diachronically or ontogenetically). Both historically and in child language, get
+ noun + locative is the first causative construction
to appear. Ontogenetically, there is some evidence
that causative get + noun + locative develops directly from what I have called precausative get + locative. Passive constructions are fairly late developments both diachronically and ontogenetically, and
appear to derive from noncausative, inchoative use of
get with adjectives and then with past participles.

There are, of course, many disparities between
the development of get in children's language and in
English as a language. Most of these, however, are
predictable from what we know in general about child
acquisition and about historical processes. For
example, the infinitival complement with periphrastic
causative get appears rather early in the history of
English, but is one of the last periphrastic causative constructions to become productive in language
acquisition. As a construction type, the infinitive
had a very different status in Middle English, for
example, than it does in the language of a two-year-
old. While Middle English was a full-blown language
containing many infinitive constructions (some with
periphrastic causatives), two-year-olds are just
beginning to expand their syntax to include infinitival forms (cf. Limber 1973). Furthermore, judging
from the adult samples in the longitudinal corpora,
young children hear almost no exemplars of get +
noun + infinitive (cf. 5.84).

Another predictable difference concerns the
rapidity of emergence of locative, adjectival, and
past participial complements with both causative and
non-causative uses of get. Historically, the emergence of new complements is spread over several
centuries. Children, however, rather rapidly add new
complements (especially with adjectives and past
participles) to the basic get + noun + _____
construction first established with locative complements. The difference lies in the fact that children

hear all of these constructions at once (which their
linguistic forebears only developed piecemeal), and
there is no reason to assume that children should be
aware of the original chronology of these items. However, this is not to deny that the kinds of overgeneralizations we find in children today may have
been the historical source of new complements entering the language (cf. 7.22 below).

The experimental data support the hypothesis that
get is more marked than make, but less marked than
have. In the imitation experiment, use of get substitutions ranks between make and have in both imitation and paraphrase responses (cf. 6.3). Furthermore, both picture tasks suggest that children offer
systematic interpretations of causative get + noun +
past participle before they are able to cope with
have + noun + past participle, thereby supporting the
ontogenetic hypothesis that causative get is learned
before causative have. Historically, however, have
appears with a past participial complement much
earlier than does get (i.e. have: end of 12th century; get: beginning of 16th century).

The subject/agent picture task provides evidence
for the syntactic/semantic analysis of get + noun +
past participle as a resultative construction.
Several adults used resultative paraphrases to explain violations of their basic strategy that surface
subject does not equal agent in sentences of the form
get + noun + past participle. Finally, the imitation
experiment revealed a divergence between historical
flexibility with the to-complementizer (particularly
during Late Middle and Early Modern English), and
behavior of modern English speakers. Both children
and adults made a large number of errors in
imitating
          *The baby got the chair fall.
and many adults had considerable difficulty in interpreting this sentence (cf. 6.3).

7.13 Have

Table LXIX summarizes the historical and ontogenetic
order of emergence for the constructions with periphrastic causative have.

Table LXIX. Diachronic and Ontogenetic Development
            of Complements with Periphrastic
            Causative Have

Date (approx.)	Diachronic	Stage	Ontogenetic
(Prim.Gmc.)	"possess"	0	"possess"
1200	(a) clause	1	locative
	(b) past participle		
	(c) locative	2	(a) adjective
	(d) adjective		(b) past participle
1375	infinitive	3	infinitive
1475	noun	4	(a) noun
			(b) clause

While the full-blown causative construction with
have appeared in English even before get is documented as a simple transitive verb (cf. Table
LXVIII), children do not make productive use of causative have until quite late (cf. 5.7). Nevertheless,
there are several clear developmental parallels.
Historically, locative complements appear relatively
early (documented almost immediately after the first
causative examples with clausal and past participial
complements). The longitudinal data, while scanty,
suggest that causative have may emerge ontogenetically through this same locative mode. Much more
striking, however, is the implicit or explicit notion
of futurity which is almost invariably associated
with all early examples of each complement type.
Both historically and in children's speech, causative
have seems to emerge from an underlying possessive
construction which is expressed as a prediction or
request for a future state of affairs.
     The experimental data strongly support the
hypothesis that have is the most marked of the three
periphrastics. In the imitation task, have was rarely provided as a substitute for other causatives in
either imitation or paraphrase (cf. 6.3), and both
picture tasks showed a chance level of response to
causative have among the youngest children (cf. 6.4,

6.5). In the puppet task, children's responses were
consistent, but consistently wrong, i.e. causative
constructions with have were nearly always interpreted non-causatively (cf. 6.5).
     The non-causative/causative picture task re-
vealed an awareness of aspectual properties of have
among both children and adults (cf. 6.4). The
children's responses may reflect strategies about
stative and non-stative values of have. Several of
the adults' explanations suggested a possessive,
resultative interpretation of the model has + noun +
past participle. These responses, if accurate, would
seem to support the traditional hypothesis that
causative have developed in English through reinterpretation of possessive have + noun + past participle,
in which the past participle originally functioned as
an adjective modifying the object (cf. 4.4). There
is, however, no experimental evidence that children
employ such a strategy in interpreting have + noun +
past participle. Finally, with respect to the to-
complementizer, the imitation data on have show the
same kind of rigidity among children and adults as is
found with make and get (cf. 6.3).

7.2   Three Parameters of Linguistic Evolution

     In 1.2 I proposed three general parameters of
linguistic evolution or linguistic change. These
three parameters were:
     (a)   child/adult
     (b)   initiation/promulgation
     (c)   comparative description/path of
           actuation
     In Chapter 2, I used these parameters in review-
ing previous discussions appearing over the past
century which have compared ontogenetic and diachronic data. The major findings of these analyses
(with respect to the three parameters) were summarized in Table I (at the end of the second chapter).
I will now use these same parameters to evaluate
the ontogenetic and diachronic research on English
periphrastic causatives.

7.21 Child/Adult

     It is possible to argue from the longitudinal
and experimental data that children, in the natural
process of learning to speak, may have helped
historically to initiate the development of some

periphrastic causative constructions. This initiation constitutes an elaboration of the earlier existing model. In particular, I wish to argue that
children may have provided the models for causative
interpretations of the (non-causative) verbs get and
have. In the case of get, precausative and causative
get plus locative constructions pervade the longitudinal data (cf. 5.6). With have, children often
associate futurity with the basic possessive construction. This use of the future with have often
seems to render the construction causative (cf. 5.7).
Admittedly, the same surface patterns with get and
have exist (though less strongly) in the adult
speech which children hear (cf. 5.6, 5.7), and it is
almost certain that children acquiring modern
English are directly influenced by their parents'
models of get + locative, get + noun + locative, and
possessive have used with a future interpretation.
However, given (a) the pervasiveness of these constructions in modern child language, and (b) the
absence of precausative and causative get, and of
causative have in older forms of English, it is conceivable that children living in these earlier periods may have actually initiated the causative interpretations of get and have.

  Children use periphrastic causative make with an
infinitival complement as young as age two (cf. 5.5).
However, is there reason to believe that use of make
with infinitival constructions by children centuries
ago initiated the construction in the history of
English? I think it is possible to argue strongly
against such a hypothesis.

  As Bloom (1970) observed (cf. 5.3 above), children productively use infinitival complements with the
verb make before using infinitives with other verbs
(cf. also Limber 1973). That is, the infinitive complement per se is not productive when make + noun +
infinitive constructions first appear in child
speech. Compare now the case of get and have, in
which the overt complements appearing in the earliest
causative constructions do appear in other parts of
the child's language at the time. Locative expressions are very frequent in child speech, both with
and without overt verbs (cf. 5.1 and the references
cited in that section), and the modalities of request
and permission are not tied to the lexical verb have.
Therefore, while it is possible that children draw
upon already existing complements and modalities in

developing causative constructions with get and
have, there is no evidence of such prior complement
types in the case of causative make. Since there is
no reason to believe that English-speaking children
living a thousand years ago learned to use infinitive complements any earlier than their modern
counterparts, I suggest that causative make + noun
+ infinitive is the type of construction which adults
are likely to have initiated, very possibly on
analogy with other periphrastic causative verb + noun
+ infinitive constructions already in the language at
the time (cf. 4.2).

Given the existence of some periphrastic causative functions of get, have, and make, how might the
range of possible complement types have expanded
historically? One possibility, of course, is adult
analogizing with other periphrastic causative constructions. For example, development of the infinitival complement with causative have may have been
initiated by adults (cf. immediately above) on direct
analogy with make + noun + infinitive (cf. 4.4).
However, in addition to adult analogy, children may
be the source of some new complement types with
English periphrastic causatives. This point is most
clearly illustrated with the case of periphrastic
causative get.

As I argued in my introduction of the periphrastic causative paradigm (cf. 3.2), children
frequently generalize (and overgeneralize) construction types which they already know. In modern
English, the generalization of complement structures
in the construction get + noun + _____ from locatives
to adjectives and past participles yields grammatical
constructions (cf. 5.6), while the generalization of
periphrastic causative in the configuration _____ +
noun + locative from get to make does not (cf. 5.5).
However, until the 16th century, generalization of
the complement slot with get would have been ungrammatical (in the adult model) (cf. Table LXVIII).

Children learn which generalizations are acceptable and which are not only after they have produced
the particular constructions in question. For example, a child may learn from his mother the singular
forms stone, book, and foot, and may then produce
plurals by adding -s in all three cases, i.e. stones,
books, foots. If the child is learning modern
English, then the first two plurals are accepted as
correct by adult interlocutors, and the third is
judged to be an (incorrect) overgeneralization.

However, if the child in question were living in the
year 800, only the first form would be considered
grammatical, since in Old English, only <u>stan</u>
("stone") is pluralized with an -<u>s</u>, i.e.

Old English
<u>singular</u>   <u>plural</u>

stan	stanes	(> stones)
boc	bec	(> *beek)
fot	fet	(> feet)

Historically, the form <u>books</u> may well have been introduced as an overgeneralization by children (cf.
discussion of Müller (1890) in 2.1 above), and only
later adopted as part of the adult standard. I suggest that precisely the same kind of overgeneralization by children may be the historical source of
modern English <u>get</u> + noun + adjective, and <u>get</u> +
noun + past participle. Children born 700 years ago
may have overgeneralized <u>get</u> + noun + locative constructions to include adjectives and past participles
as complements, but only within the past 400 years
have these configurations been adopted into the
adult standard.

Having emphasized the possible role of children
in generalizing grammatical constructions, we must
not forget that adults also generalize as well (cf.
Traugott 1972c). It is therefore always an empirical
issue whether a particular generalization (either in
initiation or promulgation) is due to children,
adults, or both groups.

7.22 Initiation/Promulgation

The above section (7.21) has discussed some of
the ways in which children and adults may have
initiated variations in the history of English which
led to the development of periphrastic causative constructions with the verbs <u>have</u>, <u>make</u>, and <u>get</u>. However, until now, I have not raised the question of
how these variations spread to other members of the
linguistic community. Because my longitudinal data
were restricted to three similar sets of child-to-
adult and adult-to-child conversations, I have no
direct way of finding out how these periphrastic
causative constructions vary when used with interlocutors of different ages or of different social
status. These factors will eventually need to be
considered in determining how variation spreads and

is incorporated into the standard language.

7.23 Comparative Description/Path of Actuation

There are several perspectives from which to view the periphrastic causative data with respect to the evolutionary parameters comparative description/path of actuation. First, we may ask what reevaluation of diachronic hypotheses is warranted in light of onto-genetic evidence. Second, we may evaluate the over-all diachronic effect of the change with respect to the metatheoretical descriptions simplification and elaboration. And finally, we may inquire whether the actuation process illustrated by the development of periphrastic causative constructions contributes to a fuller understanding of such notions as natural processes and hierarchization.

(a)   Reevaluation of Diachronic Hypotheses

In traditional historical accounts, the verbs have and get are said to develop causative interpre-tations from earlier non-causatives. The ontogene-tic data I have analyzed support this general hypothesis for both verbs. However, the acquisition data argue that the usual descriptions given for how the causative interpretations arose may not accurate-ly reflect history.

In 4.4, I sketched the traditional hypothesis that causative have developed historically through reinterpretation of possessive, resultative have + noun + [past participle]adj. The experimental data seemed to suggest that some adult speakers of modern English do interpret have + noun + past participle possessively rather than causatively, although this finding may be partially explained by an order effect (cf. 6.5). However, in the diachronic and longitudi-nal data, there is no evidence that the standard historical description has any relation to the actual manner in which have developed causative function. Rather, both historical and ontogenetic data suggest that the causative meaning initially developed through surface realization of the underlying semantic notion of futurity and perhaps also that of location. Once have is recognized in surface structure as being causative, surface expression of futurity (and loca-tion) becomes optional (both historically and in child language).

While grammarians have, in general, been less

explicit about the origins of causative get, it has
generally been assumed that the causative either
developed on analogy with causative have constructions, or emerged through causative reinterpretation
of (non-causative) transitive get + noun + [past
participle] adj (cf. 4.5). Again, the diachronic and
ontogenetic data force us to reject these hypotheses.
Instead, the locative complement, first directly
following the verb and later in get + noun + locative
constructions, seems to have provided the initial
syntactic frame from which further get causative
constructions later developed. This overt locative
complement is still common in modern adult constructions with get (cf. 5.6).

(b) Simplification and Elaboration

    I argued throughout Chapter 2 that one shortcom-
ing of most ontogenetic/diachronic comparative studies
has been the failure to realize that children may
initiate changes which, when incorporated as part of
the standard language, may constitute elaborations
rather than only simplifications of the earlier model.
The present study offers some evidence of child
elaboration.
    In 7.21 I argued that English-speaking children,
in the process of acquiring their native language, may
have initiated causative interpretations of have (via
a possessive plus future construction) and get (via
an intransitive verb plus locative complement).
Further, children may have been the source of additional complement types such as adjectives and past
participles with periphrastic causative get. How are
these conclusions to be evaluated in terms of simplification and elaboration?
    Ontogenetically, children elaborate their own
grammars when they add constructions which did not
appear in earlier stages of acquisition (i.e. get +
locative, get + noun + locative, have (future) + noun,
get + noun + adjective, get + noun + past participle).
However, in the case of adjectival and past participial
complements with periphrastic causative get, one might
argue that the child is simplifying his own system by
allowing a broader range of complements to appear in
the same basic construction type than were possible
at an earlier stage. Diachronically, the same type of
elaboration and generalization appears. The English

language was elaborated to the degree that it added
new periphrastic causative verbs, but was later
simplified in that these verbs gained generality with
respect to possible complement types. Furthermore,
both ontogenetically and diachronically, English became simpler when periphrastic causative have was no
longer restricted to future modality.

(c)   Natural Processes and Hierarchization

Stampe (1969) is responsible for introducing the
term natural process into recent comparative studies
of ontogeny and diachrony. However, since his examples are all from phonology, where naturalness may
be physiologically determined, it is difficult to
know precisely what range of phenomena constitute
natural processes in syntax. As an informal criterion, I will consider as "natural" those syntactic
modes which seem continually to reassert themselves
in child language and (perhaps derivationally) in the
history of language.

From this point of view, there are at least two
natural processes identifiable in the evolution of
English periphrastic causatives. The first of these
is that locative expressions will be given surface
structure realization. Having noted in 5.1 that many
observers of child language have commented upon the
frequency of certain surface locative expressions in
early child lanauge, I proceeded to show (5.5, 5.6,
5.7) that overt locatives frequently appear with make,
get, and have in both their causative and non-
causative functions. This ontogenetic tendency to
express location has the diachronic ramification of
providing the syntactic source for at least one (and
possibly two) periphrastic causatives in the history
of English (i.e. get, and possibly have, cf. 5.7).

The second process I would identify as natural
is the use of word order to distinguish between meanings. Slobin (1966a) has observed, for example, that
children learning Russian as a native language use
word order as a surface marker of underlying noun -
verb relationships before learning overt morphological indicators. In the history of English, word order
has largely taken over the function of surface case
markers. However, order has also given distinct
surface realization to new syntactic constructions.
In the case of both get and have, causative and non-
causative interpretations of these verbs with

adjectival and past participial complements are differentiated in terms of the order of the noun and
adjective and past participle (cf. 6.13). Ontogenetically, children must eventually learn this
function of word order (cf. 6.4). While I have no
evidence at the moment that the ontogenetic natural
process regarding word order was the direct source of
the historical developments in Late Middle and Early
Modern English (i.e. using order to distinguish between causative and non-causative constructions--cf.
4.4, 4.5), this is a plausible hypothesis and should
be investigated further.

In addition to discussing naturalness with
respect to particular processes, it is also possible
to speak of the naturalness of a particular order of
two or more diachronic or ontogenetic processes
(natural or otherwise). As in the case of single
syntactic processes, I consider a hierarchy as
natural if it keeps recurring diachronically and/or
ontogenetically.

The data on English periphrastic causatives suggest several sets of hierarchies which might be explored in future research. The most obvious of these
is that verbs appear in non-causative function before
appearing as periphrastic causatives. Historically,
this generalization holds true not only for get and
have but also for the verbs do and let (cf. 4.2). It
might be interesting to see, for example, if children
ever interpret verbs like do causatively, and, if so,
how they relate the causative to the non-causative.
Future ontogenetic/diachronic research might also
test whether the non-causative/causative hierarchy
applies to lexical and suppletive causatives as well
as to periphrastics (cf. Baron 1974).

A second kind of hierarchization exists both
ontogenetically and diachronically between locative
and temporal relations in that temporal expressions
are dependent upon the prior appearance of locative
forms (cf. Traugott 1972c). While the present study
is not decisive, the longitudinal data on have (cf.
5.7) clearly suggest that overt locative markers appear before overt expression of futurity (cf.
Benveniste (1968) for historical parallels in Latin).

Third, there is some indication that overt
expression of causation may involve prior surface
realization of inchoative. In both ontogenetic and
diachronic data, possessive have appears with a
future marker (which, I have argued, has inchoative

function) before it appears as a full-blown causative.
In addition, the non-causative, transitive verb get,
which is essentially inchoative in meaning (cf. Baron
1974), appears before causative constructions with
get, and ontogenetically, children learn surface inchoative expressions with get (e.g. get dirty) before learning causative forms with adjectival and
past participial complements (cf. 5.6).

Finally, the longitudinal data suggest an ontogenetic hierarchy with respect to complement types.
I have already proposed that the surface realization
of locative expressions constitutes a natural process.
From the longitudinal data on get (cf. 5.6), one may
argue that the appearance of adjectival complements
implies the prior emergence of locative complements,
that the development of past participial complements
implies the existence of locative and adjectival
complements, and that the infinitival usage implies
the prior development of locative, adjectival and
past participial complements, i.e.

   locative < adjective < past participle <
        infinitive

While this hierarchy obviously does not apply to all
verbs (e.g. infinitival complements appear with make
before past participial complements--cf. 5.5), it
will be interesting to explore how generally this
hierarchy applies to the developing verbal system as
a whole.

7.3   Directions for a General Theory of Linguistic
      Variation and Change

One of the world's keenest observers of biological structure, Aristotle, maintained that women have
fewer teeth than men.[1] The philosopher also hypothesized that in females, the jejunum may occupy any
part whatsoever of the upper intestine, but in males
it comes just before the caecum and the lower stom-
ach.[2] Medically, there is no basis for either of
these claims. Most modern linguistic diachronists
have tended to behave like Aristotle in his weakest
moments. The current theoretical vogue has been to
explain historical change largely in terms of child
language acquisition, yet almost no one has actually
examined ontogenetic data to test the empirical
plausibility of their hypotheses.

In this examination I have attempted to show
empirically how ontogenetic data can be incorporated

into diachronic analysis.   In 1.4 I proposed a possible methodology for studying linguistic evolution. The present study has, in effect, tested the methodology through an examination of the ontogenetic and diachronic evolution of English periphrastic causative constructions.   The methodology has been useful to the degree that (a) it has suggested that the traditional diachronic accounts of the rise of periphrastic causative <u>have</u> and <u>get</u> may not accurately reflect the actual path by which these constructions arose, (b) it has established the plausibility of the hypothesis that children, in the natural course of learning their native language, may have helped initiate or spread various new periphrastic causative constructions in the history of English (i.e. an elaboration of the structure of English), and (c) more generally, it has shown the value of child language acquisition as an evaluation metric for diachronic hypotheses.

This methodology must now be tested on a broader range of linguistic phenomena.   In addition to examining other syntactic constructions besides English periphrastic causatives, it is necessary to look at the phonological and semantic levels of the grammar as well.   Moreover, besides studying acquisition and diachronic change in established languages, it should also be possible to apply the methodology to (a) the development of a pidgin into a creole through its acquisition of native speakers (cf. Kay and Sankoff 1972), and (b) the acquisition or development of a second language, including trade jargons or pidgins. By examining various levels of grammar in terms of native and non-native acquisition and use, it should be possible to extend the discussion in this book of how children and adults initiate and promulgate change, and how these changes may be analyzed in terms of comparative descriptions and paths of actuation (cf. Table I).

Many diachronists have implied that it is not possible to observe the process by which language change occurs, but that it is only possible to observe its results.   In the present work I have attempted to show that we may, in fact, be able to study the origins of some linguistic changes <u>in vivo</u> by analyzing how children learn to speak, or, <u>more</u> generally, how children or adults acquire native or non-native languages.   However, with the exception

of my discussion of adult speecn registers (cf. 5.84),
I have said very little about the sociolinguistic
factors which condition the use of particular speech
styles with specific interlocutors and which determine
who provides the primary model for children learning
language. In working towards a single framework in
which to define linguistic variation and change in
general, it will be imperative to study in detail the
sociological milieu which regulates linguistic
behavior.

Having presented the outlines of a unified
approach to linguistic variation and change, it is
now possible to ask how such an approach relates to
synchronic accounts of language. At the beginning of
2.2, I pointed out that with the exception of Stockwell (1964), generative studies in the early and mid-
1960's tended to discount the role of diachrony in
determining the shape of synchronic analysis. However, within the past few years, a small but growing
number of linguists (e.g. Kiparsky 1968; Labov 1969,
1971; Bailey 1970; Traugott 1972c) have begun to work
towards the integration of synchrony, diachrony, and
acquisition within a single general framework. While
the establishment of such an all-encompassing model
is still in the distant future, it is clear that the
kind of partial integration which I have proposed in
the present study should be able to contribute to
such a model.

Footnotes

[1]Historia Animalium Book II_3:501b

[2]De Partibus Animalia Book III_{14}:675b.

Bibliography

A.   GENERAL BIBLIOGRAPHY

Abbott, Edwin A. (1870; 1966 reprinting).   A Shake-
    spearian Grammar. New York: Dover.

Andersen, Henning (1969), "A Study in Diachronic Mor-
    phophonemics: The Ukrainian Prefixes," Language
    45: 807-830.

Andersen, Henning (1973), "Abductive and Deductive
    Change," Language 49:765-793.

Anderson, John (1968), "Ergative and Nominative in
    English," Journal of Linguistics 4:1-32.

Anderson, John (1969), "The Case for Cause: A Pre-
    liminary Enquiry," Journal of Linguistics 6:99-
    104.

Anderson, John (1971). The Grammar of Case.
    Cambridge: Cambridge University Press.

Anonymous (1904), "The Making of 'Make'," Living Age,
    243: 571-573.

Appleby, Mary Jane (1967), "The Infinitive: Form and
    Syntax from Old English to Modern English,"
    Unpublished Ph.D. Dissertation, University of
    Wisconsin, Madison.

Aristotle. Works, ed. and trans. J. A. Smith and W.
    D. Ross. Oxford: Clarendon Press, 1908-1931.

Babcock, Sandra (1972), "Paraphrastic Causatives,"
    Foundations of Language 8: 30-43.

Bailey, Charles-James (1970), "The Integration of
    Linguistic Theory: Internal Reconstruction and
    the Comparative Method in Descriptive Analysis,"
    Working Papers in Linguistics, Department of
    Linguistics, University of Hawaii, vol. 2, no. 4,
    93-102.

Baron, Naomi (1971), "A Reanalysis of English Gram-
    matical Gender," Lingua 27: 113-140.

Baron, Naomi (1974), "The Structure of English Causa-
    tives," Lingua 33: 299-342.

Bates, Roberta Reed (1970), "A Study in the Acquisi-
    tion of Language," Unpublished Ph.D. disserta-
    tion, University of Texas, Austin.

Benveniste, Émile (1968), "Mutations of Linguistic
    Categories," In W. P. Lehmann and Y. Malkiel
    (eds.), Directions for Historical Linguistics.
    Austin: University of Texas Press, 83-94.

Bever, Thomas G. (1970), "The Cognitive Basis for
    Linguistic Structures," In J. R. Hayes (ed.),
    Cognition and the Development of Language.
    New York: John Wiley, 279-362.

Bever, Thomas G. and D. Terence Langendoen (1971),
    "A Dynamic Model of the Evolution of Language,"
    Linguistic Inquiry 2: 433-463.

Bloom, Lois (1970). Language Development: Form and
    Function in Emerging Grammars. Cambridge
    (Mass.): M.I.T. Press.

Bloom, Lois (1971), "Why Not Pivot Grammar?" Journal
    of Speech and Hearing Disorders 36: 40-50.

Bloomfield, Leonard (1933). Language. New York:
    Holt, Rinehart, and Winston.

Bloomfield, Leonard (1939), "Linguistic Aspects of
    Science," International Encyclopedia of Unified
    Science 1: 4, Chicago.

Blount, Ben G. (1972), "Parental Speech and Language
    Acquisition: Some Luo and Samoan Examples,"
    Anthropological Linguistics 14: 119-130.

Bøgholm, N. (1939). English Speech from an Historical
    Point of View. London: George Allen and Unwin.

Braine, M.D.S. (1963), "The Ontogeny of English
    Phrase Structure: The First Phase," Language
    39: 1-13.

Braine, M.D.S. (1971), "Two Models of the Internaliza-
    tion of Grammars," In D.I. Slobin (ed.), The
    Ontogenesis of Grammar. New York: Academic Press,
    153-186.

Brown, Roger (1958), "How Shall a Thing be Called?"
    Psychological Review 65: 14-21.

Brown, Roger (1973). A First Language. Cambridge
    (Mass.): Harvard University Press.

Brown, Roger and Colin Fraser (1964), "The Acquisi-
    tion of Syntax," In U. Bellugi and R. Brown (eds.),
    The Acquisition of Language. Monographs of the
    Society for Research in Child Development 29 (No.
    92), 43-78.

Brunner, Karl (1962). Die englische Sprache: ihre
    geschichtliche Entwicklung, vol. 2. Tübingen:
    Max Niemeyer.

Calloway, Morgan (1913). The Infinitive in Anglo-
    Saxon. Washington, D.C.: Carnegie Institution
    of Washington.

Chamberlain, Alexander F. (1906), "Preterite-Forms,
    Etc., in the Language of English-Speaking
    Children," Modern Language Notes 21: 42-44.

Chamberlain, Alexander F. (1907). The Child: A Study
    in the Evolution of Man. London: Walter Scott.

Chomsky, Carol (1969). The Acquisition of Syntax in
    Children from 5 to 10. Cambridge (Mass.): M.I.T.
    Press.

Chomsky, Noam (1965). Aspects of the Theory of
    Syntax. Cambridge (Mass.): M.I.T. Press.

Chomsky, Noam and Morris Halle (1968). The Sound
    Pattern of English. New York: Harper and Row.

Clark, Eve V. (1970), "How Young Children Describe
    Events in Time," In G.B. Flores d'Arcais and W.J.
    M. Levelt (eds.), Advances in Psycholinguistics.
    Amsterdam: North-Holland, 275-284.

Clark, Eve V. (1971), "On the Acquisition of the Meaning of Before and After," Journal of Verbal Learning and Verbal Behavior 10: 266-275.

Cohen, Marcel (1925), "Sur les langages successifs de l'enfant," In Mélanges linguistiques offerts à M. J. Vendryès. Paris, 109-127.

Cohen, Marcel (1927), "A propos de la troisième personne du féminin au pluriel en français," Bulletin de la Société de Linguistique de Paris 27.

Cohen, Marcel (1933), "Observation sur les dernières persistances du langage enfantin," Journal de Psychologie Normale et Pathologique 30: 390-399.

Cromer, Richard (1968), "The Development of Temporal Reference During the Acquisition of Language," Unpublished Ph.D. dissertation, Harvard University.

Cromer, Richard (1970), "'Children are Nice to Understand': Surface Structure Clues for the Recovery of a Deep Structure," British Journal of Psychology 61: 397-408.

Crowell, Thomas Lee (1955), "A Study of the Verb Get," Unpublished Ph.D. dissertation, Columbia University (Cf. Crowell's bibliography for references to get).

Curme, George O. (1905). A Grammar of the German Language. New York: Macmillan.

Curme, George O. (1931). Syntax. Boston: D.C.Heath.

Curme, George O. (1935). Parts of Speech and Accidence. Boston: D.C. Heath.

Dahl, Torsten (1956). The Auxiliary Do. Copenhagen: Ejnar Munksgaard.

Dam, Johannes Van (1957). The Causal Clause and Causal Prepositions in Early Old English Prose. Groningen: J. B. Wolters, Academisch Proefschrift, Amsterdam.

Darden, Bill J. (1970), "The Fronting of Vowels after Palatals in Slavic," In Papers from the 6th Regional Meeting, Chicago Linguistic Society, April 16-18, 459-470.

Darden, Bill J. (1971), "Diachronic Evidence for Phonemics," In Papers from the 7th Regional Meeting, Chicago Linguistic Society, April 16-18, 323-331.

Darwin, Charles (1877), "A Biographical Sketch of an Infant," Mind 2: 285-294.

Dekker, Arie (1932). Some Facts Concerning the Syntax of Malory's Morte Darthur. Amsterdam: M. J. Portielje.

Dowty, David R. (1972), "On the Syntax and Semantics of the Atomic Predicate CAUSE," In Papers from the 8th Regional Meeting, Chicago Linguistic Society, April 14-16, 62-74.

Drach, Kerry M. (1969), "The Language of the Parent: A Pilot Study," In Drach et al., "The Structure of Linguistic Input to Children," Language-Behavior Research Laboratory Working Paper No. 14, University of California, Berkeley.

Earle, John (1887). The Philology of the English Tongue. Oxford: Clarendon Press.

Ellegård, Alvar (1953). The Auxiliary Do. Stockholm: Almqvist and Wiksell.

Engblom, Victor (1938), "On the Origin and Early Development of the Auxiliary Do," Lund Studies in English 6.

Ervin [-Tripp], Susan (1964), "Imitation and Structural Change in Children's Language," In E. H. Lenneberg (ed.), New Directions in the Study of Language. Cambridge (Mass.): M.I.T.Press, 163-189.

Farwell, Carol (1973), "The Language Spoken to Children," Stanford Papers and Reports on Child Language Development, vol. 5, 31-62.

Ferreiro, Emilia and Hermine Sinclair [-de Zwart]
    (1971), "Temporal Relations in Language," In-
    ternational Journal of Psychology 6: 39-47.

Fillmore, Charles J. (1968), "The Case for Case," In
    E. Bach and R. T. Harms (eds.), Universals in
    Linguistic Theory. New York: Holt, Rinehart,
    and Winston, 1-88.

Fillmore, Charles J. (1971), "Some Problems for Case
    Grammar," In R. J. O'Brien, S.J. (ed.), Mono-
    graph Series on Languages and Linguistics.
    22nd Annual Round Table. Washington, D.C.:
    Georgetown University Press, 35-56.

Forman, Michael L. (1971), "Questions on CAUSE and
    Transposition in the Development of Pre-School
    Children's Speech," Working Papers in Linguis-
    tics, Department of Linguistics, University of
    Hawaii, vol. 3, 119-128.

Franz, Wilhelm W. (1900). Shakespeare Grammatik.
    Halle: Max Niemeyer.

Fraser, C., U. Bellugi, and R. Brown (1963), "Con-
    trol of Grammar in Imitation, Comprehension,
    and Production," Journal of Verbal Learning and
    Verbal Behavior 2: 121-135; reprinted in R.C.
    Oldfield and J.C. Marshall (eds.), Language.
    Baltimore: Penguin, 1968, 48-69.

Fridén, Georg (1948). Studies on the Tenses of the
    English Verb from Chaucer to Shakespeare.
    Upsala: Almqvist and Wiksell.

Fridén, Georg (1959), "On the Use of Auxiliaries to
    Form the Perfect and the Pluperfect in Late
    Middle English and Early Modern English," Archiv
    für das Studium der Neueren Sprachen und
    Literaturen 196: 152-153.

Gehlen, Arnold (1938), "Das Problem des Sprachur-
    sprungs," Forschungen und Fortschritte 14:291-
    293.

Givón, Talmy (1971), "Historical Syntax and Synchron-
    ic Morphology: An Archaeologist's Field Trip,"
    In Papers from the 7th Regional Meeting, Chicago
    Linguistic Society, April 16-18, 394-415.

Gleason, Jean Berko (1973), "Code Switching in
    Children's Language," In T. E. Moore (ed.),
    Cognitive Development and the Acquisition of
    Language. New York: Academic Press, 159-167.

Grammont, Maurice (1902), "Observations sur le
    langage des enfants," In Mélanges linguistiques
    offerts à M. Antoine Meillet. Paris:
    Klincksieck, 61-82.

Greenberg, Joseph (1966), "Language Universals," In
    T. A. Sebeok (ed.), Current Trends in Linguis-
    tics, vol. 3. Mouton: The Hague, 61-112.

Greenberg, Joseph (1969), "Some Methods of Dynamic
    Comparison in Linguistics," In J. Puhvel (ed.),
    Substance and Structure of Language. Berkeley:
    University of California Press, 147-203.

Guillaume, P. (1927a), "Les débuts de la phrase dans
    le langage de l'enfant," Journal de Psychologie
    Normale et Pathologique 24: 1-25; English trans-
    lation (E.V. Clark, trans.), "The First Stages
    of Sentence-Formation in Children's Speech,"
    In C.A. Ferguson and D. I. Slobin (eds.),
    Studies of Child Language Development. New
    York: Holt, Rinehart, and Winston, 1973, 322-
    541.

Guillaume, P. (1927b), "Le développement des éléments
    formels dans le langage de l'enfant," Journal
    de Psychologie Normale et Pathologique 24: 203-
    229; English translation (E.V. Clark, trans.),
    "The Development of Formal Elements in the
    Child's Speech," In C. A. Ferguson and D. I.
    Slobin (eds.), Studies of Child Language Devel-
    opment. New York: Holt, Rinehart, and Winston,
    1973, 240-251.

Gzhanyants, E.M. (1958), "Development of the Means
    of Expressing Causation in English," Leningrad,
    Gosudarstvennyĭ pedagogichenskiĭ institut imeni
    A. I. Gertsena, Uchenye Zapiski 181: 131-156.

Haeckel, Ernst (1866). Generelle Morphologie der
    Organismen. Berlin.

Haeckel, Ernst (1879). The Evolution of Man: A
   Popular Exposition of the Principal Points of
   Human Ontogeny and Phylogeny. 2 vols. New York:
   D. Appleton; 2nd edition, 1897.

Halle, Morris (1962), "Phonology in Generative Grammar," Word 18: 54-72; reprinted in J. A. Fodor
   and J. J. Katz (eds.), The Structure of Language.
   Englewood Cliffs (New Jersey): Prentice-Hall,
   1964, 334-352.

Halliday, M.A.K. (1967), "Notes on Transitivity and
   Theme in English: Part One," Journal of
   Linguistics 3: 37-81.

Halliday, M.A.K. (1968), "Notes on Transitivity and
   Theme in English: Part Three," Journal of
   Linguistics 4: 179-215.

Harwood, F. W. (1959), "Quantitative Study of the
   Speech of Australian Children," Language and
   Speech 2: 236-271.

Hatcher, Anna Granville (1949), "To Get/Be Invited,"
   Modern Language Notes 64: 433-446.

Herzog, Eugen (1904). Streitfragen der romanischen
   Philologie I.

Hirtle, W.H. (1969), "-Ed Adjectives like 'Verandahed'
   and 'Blue-Eyed'," Journal of Linguistics 6:
   19-36.

Hockett, Charles F. (1950), "Age-Grading and Linguistic Continuity," Language 26: 449-457.

Hymes, Dell (ed.) (1971). Pidginization and Creolization of Languages. Cambridge: Cambridge
   University Press.

Jakobson, Roman (1941). Kindersprache, Aphasie, und
   allgemeine Lautgesetze. Upsala: Almqvist and
   Wiksell; English translation (A. Keiler, trans.),
   Child Language, Aphasia, and General Sound Laws.
   The Hague: Mouton, 1968.

Jespersen, Otto (1909-1949, 1961 reprinting). A
   Modern English Grammar, vols. 3, 5. London:
   George Allen and Unwin.

Johnston, Charles (1896), "The World's Baby-Talk,"
    Fortnightly Review 60 (N.S.): 494-505.

Kay, Paul and Gillian Sankoff (1972), "A Language-
    Universals Approach to Pidgins and Creoles,"
    Paper presented at the 23rd Georgetown Round
    Table on Languages and Linguistics.

Kellner, Leon (1905). Historical Outlines of English
    Syntax. London: Macmillan.

Kennedy, Arthur (1920). The Modern English Verb-
    Adverb Combination. Stanford: Stanford
    University.

Kessel, F.S. (1970). The Role of Syntax in Children's
    Comprehension from Ages Six to Twelve. Mono-
    graphs of the Society for Research in Child
    Development 36 (No. 139).

Keyser, Samuel Jay (1963), "Review of Hans Kurath and
    Raven I. McDavid, Jr., The Pronunciation of
    English in the Atlantic States," Language 39:
    303-316.

King, Robert D. (1969). Historical Linguistics and
    Generative Grammar. Englewood Cliffs (New
    Jersey): Prentice-Hall.

Kiparsky, Paul (1965), "Phonological Change," Unpub-
    lished Ph.D. dissertation, M.I.T.

Kiparsky, Paul (1968), "Linguistic Universals and
    Linguistic Change," In E. Bach and R. T. Harms
    (eds.), Universals in Linguistic Theory. New
    York: Holt, Rinehart, and Winston.

Kiparsky, Paul (1971), "Historical Linguistics," In
    W. Dingwall (ed.), A Survey of Linguistic
    Science, University of Maryland, 576-642.

Klima, Edward (1964), "Studies in Diachronic Trans-
    formational Syntax," Unpublished Ph.D. disserta-
    tion, Harvard University.

Kruisinga, E. (1925). A Handbook of Present-Day
    English; Part II: English Accidence and Syntax.
    Utrecht: Kemink en Zoon.

Kruisinga, E. (1940), "Beginselen van Beschrijvende Syntaxis," _Taalen Leven_ 4: 1-11.

Kučera, Henry and W. Nelson Francis (1967). _Computational Analysis of Present-Day American English._ Providence: Brown University Press.

Labov, William (1966). _The Social Stratification of English in New York City._ Washington: Center for Applied Linguistics.

Labov, William (1969), "Contraction, Deletion, and Inherent Variability of the English Copula," _Language_ 45: 715-762.

Labov, William (1971), "Methodology," In W. Dingwall (ed.), _A Survey of Linguistic Science_, University of Maryland, 412-491.

Lakoff, George (1965), "On the Nature of Syntactic Irregularity," NSF 16, Computation Laboratory, Harvard University; also appears as _Irregularity in Syntax._ New York: Holt, Rinehart, and Winston, 1970.

Lakoff, George (1968), "Some Verbs of Change and Causation," In NSF 20, Computation Laboratory, Harvard University, III-1--III-27.

Lakoff, Robin (1971), "Passive Resistance," In _Papers from the 7th Regional Meeting_, Chicago Linguistic Society, April 16-18, 149-162.

Langenfelt, Gösta (1933). _Select Studies in Colloquial English of the Late Middle Ages._ Lund: Håkan Ohlsson.

Leopold, Werner (1939-1949). _Speech Development of a Bilingual Child._ Evanston: Northwestern University Press.

Lévy-Bruhl, Lucien (1926). _How Natives Think_ (L. Clare, trans.). London: George Allen and Unwin.

Limber, John (1973), "The Genesis of Complex Sentences," In T.E. Moore (ed.), _Cognitive Development and the Acquisition of Language._ New York: Academic Press, 169-185.

Lindemann, J.W. Richard (1970). Old English Pre-
    verbal Ge-: Its Meaning. Charlottesville:
    University Press of Virginia.

Lockwood, W.B. (1968). Historical German Syntax.
    Oxford: Clarendon Press.

Lovell, K. and E.M. Dixon (1967), "The Growth of the
    Control of Grammar in Imitation, Comprehension
    and Production," Journal of Child Psychology and
    Psychiatry 8: 31-39.

McCawley, James D. (1968), "Lexical Insertion in a
    Transformational Grammar without Deep Struc-
    ture," In Papers from the 4th Regional Meeting,
    Chicago Linguistic Society, April 19-20, 71-80.

McCawley, James D. (1970), "Syntactic and Logical
    Arguments for Semantic Structures," to appear
    in Proceedings of the Fifth International
    Seminar on Theoretical Linguistics. Tokyo:
    The TEC Corp.

McCawley, James D. (1971), "Prelexical Syntax," In
    R.J. O'Brien, S.J. (ed.), Monograph Series on
    Languages and Linguistics. 22nd Annual Round
    Table. Washington, D.C.: Georgetown University
    Press, 19-33.

McNeill, David (1966), "Developmental Psycholinguis-
    tics," In F. Smith and G. A. Miller (eds.), The
    Genesis of Language. Cambridge (Mass.): M.I.T.
    Press, 15-84.

Macháček, Jaroslav (1969), "Historical Aspects of
    the Accusative with Infinitive and the Content
    Clause in English," In J. Firbas and J. Hladký
    (eds.), Brno Studies in English 8: 123-131.

Manly, J.M. (1930), "From Generation to Generation,"
    In N. Bøgholm, A. Brusendorff, and C. A. Bodel-
    sen (eds.), A Grammatical Miscellany Offered to
    Otto Jespersen, 287-289.

Meillet, A. (1921), "Quelques remarques sur des mots
    français," Bulletin de la Société de
    Linguistique de Paris 21: 166-168.

Meillet, A. (1926). Linguistique historique et
    linguistique générale, vol. 1. Paris: Champion.

Meillet, A. (1951). Linguistique historique et
    linguistique générale, vol. 2. Paris: Klincksieck.

Mencken, H. L. (1938) The American Language . New
    York: A. Knopf.
)
Menyuk, Paula (1964), "Alternation of Rules in
    Children's Grammar," Journal of Verbal Learning
    and Verbal Behavior 3: 480-488.

Miller, Wick and Susan Ervin [-Tripp] (1964), "The
    Development of Grammar in Child Language," In.
    U. Bellugi and R. Brown (eds.), The Acquisition
    of Language. Monographs of the Society for
    Research in Child Development 29 (No. 92), 9-34.

Moore, Samuel (1918), "Robert Mannyng's Use of Do as
    Auxiliary," Modern Language Notes 33: 385-393.

Mossé, Fernand (1952). A Handbook of Middle English
    (J.A. Walker, trans.). Baltimore: Johns
    Hopkins University Press.

Müller, Max (1890). The Science of Language. New
    York: Charles Scribner.

Mustanoja, Tauno (1960). A Middle English Syntax.
    Helsinki: Société Neophilologique.

Ohlander, Urban (1942), "A Study on the Use of the
    Infinitive Sign in Middle English," Studia
    Neophilologica 14: 58-66.

Olson, Gary M. (1973), "Developmental Changes in
    Memory and the Acquisition of Language," In
    T.E. Moore (ed.), Cognitive Development and the
    Acquisition of Language. New York: Academic
    Press, 145-157.

Passy, Paul (1890). Étude sur les changements
    phonétiques. Paris: Firmin-Didot.

Paul, Hermann (1880). Prinzipien der Sprachgeschichte.
    Halle: Max Niemeyer; 6th edition, Tübingen, 1960.

Paul, Hermann (1888). Principles of the History of
    Language (H. A. Strong, trans., based on 2nd
    edition, Prinzipien der Sprachgeschichte).
    London: Swan, Sonnenschein, Lawrey.

Pfuderer, C. (1969), "Some Suggestions for a Syntac-
    tic Characterization of Baby-Talk Style," In
    Drach et al., "The Structure of Linguistic In-
    put to Children," Language-Behavior Research
    Laboratory Working Paper No. 14, University of
    California, Berkeley.

Poldauf, Ivan (1967), "The Have Construction," Prague,
    Acta Universitatis Carolinae, Philologica 5:
    Prague Studies in English 12: 23-40.

Postal, Paul (1968). Aspects of Phonological Theory.
    New York: Harper and Row.

Poutsma, H. (1904-1928). A Grammar of Late Modern
    English. Groningen: D. Noordhoff.

Preussler, W. (1938), "Keltischer Einfluss im
    Englischen," Indogermanische Forschungen 56:
    178-191.

Preussler, W. (1939), "Keltischer Einfluss im
    Englischen," Indogermanische Forschungen 57:
    140-141,

Reighard, John (1971), "Some Observations on
    Syntactic Change in Verbs," in Papers from the
    7th Regional Meeting, Chicago Linguistic
    Society, April 16-18, 511-518.

Révész, G. (1956). The Origins and Prehistory of
    Language. New York: Philosophical Library.

Royster, James Finch (1915), "The Do Auxiliary-1400
    to 1450," Modern Philology 12: 449-456.

Royster, James Finch (1916), "A Note on Lydgate's Use
    of the Do Auxiliary," Studies in Philology 13:
    69-71.

Royster, James Finch (1918), "The Causative Use of
    Hātan," Journal of English and Germanic
    Philology 17: 82-93.

Royster, James Finch (1922), "Old English Causative
    Verbs," Studies in Philology 19: 328-356.

Salmon, Vivian (1965), "Sentence Structures in
    Colloquial Shakespearian English," Transactions
    of the Philological Society, 105-140.

Sankoff, Gillian (1972), "A Quantitative Paradigm for
    the Study of Communicative Competence," Paper
    presented at the Conference on the Ethnography of
    Speaking, April 20-22, University of Texas.

Sankoff, Gillian and Suzanne Laberge (1971), "On the
    Acquisition of Native Speakers by a Language,"
    Paper presented at the Northeastern Linguistic
    Society, October 23-24.

Saporta, Sol (1965), "Ordered Rules, Dialect Differ-
    ences, and Historical Processes," Language 41:
    218-224.

Schank, Roger C. (1971), "Conceptual Dependency: A
    Theory of Natural Language Understanding,"
    Computer Science Department and Committee on
    Linguistics, Stanford University, Mimeo.

Schlauch, Margaret (1952), "Chaucer's Colloquial
    English: Its Structural Traits," PMLA 67: 1103-
    1116.

Sechehaye, Albert (1926). Essai sur la structure
    logique de la phrase. Paris: Champion.

Sinclair [-de Zwart], Hermine (1971), "Acquisition of
    Language, Linguistic Theory, and Epistemology,"
    Paper presented at CNRS, Colloque International:
    Problèmes actuels en psycholinguistiques, Paris.

Slobin, Dan I. (1966a), "The Acquisition of Russian as
    a Native Language," In F. Smith and G. A. Miller
    (eds.), The Genesis of Language. Cambridge
    (Mass.): M.I.T. Press, 129-148.

Slobin, Dan I. (1966b), "Grammatical Transformations
    and Sentence Comprehension in Childhood and
    Adulthood," Journal of Verbal Learning and Verbal
    Behavior 5: 219-227.

Slobin, Dan I. (1971), "Cognitive Prerequisites for
     the Development of Grammar,"   In W. Dingwall
     (ed.), A Survey of Linguistic Science, Univer-
     sity of Maryland, 298-400.

Slobin, Dan I. (1972). Leopold's Bibliography of
     Child Language: Revised and Updated. Blooming-
     ton: Indiana University Press.

Slobin, Dan I. and Charles A. Welsh (1968), "Elicited
     Imitation as a Research Tool in Developmental
     Psycholinguistics," Language-Behavior Research
     Laboratory Working Paper No. 10, University of
     California, Berkeley; also in C. Lavatelli (ed.),
     Language Training in Early Childhood Education,
     ERIC Clearinghouse on Early Childhood Education,
     1971; reprinted in C.A. Ferguson and D.I. Slobin,
     (eds.), Studies of Child Language Development.
     New York: Holt, Rinehart, and Winston, 485-497.

Smith, Robert (1972), "The Syntax and Semantics of
     Erica," Unpublished Ph.D. dissertation,
     Stanford University.

Smyser, H. M. (1967), "Chaucer's Use of Gin and Do,"
     Speculum 42: 68-83.

Snow, Catherine E. (1972), "Mothers' Speech to
     Children Learning Language," Child Development
     43: 549-565.

Stampe, David (1969), "The Acquisition of Phonetic
     Representation," In Papers from the 5th Regional
     Meeting, Chicago Linguistic Society, April 18-
     19, 443-454.

Stein, Leopold (1949). The Infancy of Speech and the
     Speech of Infancy. London: Methuen.

Stern, Clara and William Stern (1907). Die
     Kindersprache. Leipzig: Barth.

Stockwell, Robert (1964), "Realism in Historical
     Phonology," Paper presented at the annual winter
     meeting of the LSA.

Sully, James (1896). Studies of Childhood. New
     York: D. Appleton.

Suppes, Patrick and Robert Smith (forthcoming),
    (untitled), Unpublished ms., Stanford Univer-
    sity.

Sweet, Henry (1888). A History of English Sounds.
    Oxford: Clarendon Press.

Taine, Hippolyte (1876),,"De l'acquisition du langage
    chez les enfants et les peuples primitifs,"
    Revue Philosophique 1: 5-23; English transla-
    tion of first section, "M. Taine on the Acquisi-
    tion of Language by Children," Mind 2: 252-259,
    1877.

Tobler, Adolf (1921). Vermischte Beiträge ·zur
    französischen Grammatik. Leipzig.

Traugott, Elizabeth Closs (1969), "Toward a Grammar
    of Syntactic Change," Lingua 23: 1-27.

Traugott, Elizabeth Closs (1972a). A History of
    English Syntax. New York: Holt, Rinehart,
    and Winston.

Traugott, Elizabeth Closs (1972b), "On the Notion
    'Restructuring' in Historical Syntax," Paper
    presented at the 2nd Annual California
    Linguistics Conference, May 6-7, UCLA.

Traugott, Elizabeth Closs (1972c), "Historical
    Linguistics and Its Relation to Studies of
    Language Acquisition and of Pidgins and Creoles,"
    Lectures given at UC Santa Cruz, August.

Trnka, Bohumil (1924), "Příspěvky k Syntaktickému a
    Fraseologickému Vývoji Slovesa To Have (Studies
    in the Syntactical and Phraseological History of
    the Verb To Have)," Prague, Facultas Philosophi-
    ca Universitatis Carolinae, Studies in English
    by Members of the English Seminar of the Charles
    University 1: 1-38 (English Summary).

Trnka, Bohumil (1930). On the Syntax of the English
    Verb from Caxton to Dryden. Prague: Travaux
    du Cercle Linguistique de Prague 3.

Turner, Elizabeth A. and R. Rommetveit (1967), "The
    Acquisition of Sentence Voice and Reversibil-
    ity," Child Development 38: 649-660.

Van der Gaaf, W. (1931), "Beon and Habban Connected
    with an Inflected Infinitive," English Studies
    13: 176-188.

Van Draat, P. Fijn (1897), "Chips II: The Accusative
    + the Infinitive After to Make,"
    Tijdschrift «De Drie Talen» 14: 43-44.

Velten, H.V. (1943), "The Growth of Phonemic and
    Lexical Pattern in Infant Language," Language
    19: 281-292.

Visser, F. Th. (1963-1969). An Historical Syntax of
    the English Language. 3 vols. Leiden: E. J.
    Brill.

Watt, William C. (1970), "On Two Hypotheses Concern-
    ing Psycholinguistics," In J.R. Hayes (ed.),
    Cognition and the Development of Language. New
    York: John Wiley, 137-220.

Weinreich, Uriel, William Labov, and Marvin I.
    Herzog (1968), "Empirical Foundations for a
    Theory of Language Change," In W.P. Lehmann and
    Y. Malkiel (eds.), Directions for Historical
    Linguistics. Austin: University of Texas Press,
    95-195.

Whitney, William Dwight (1889). Language and the
    Study of Language. New York: Charles Scribner.

Whitney, William Dwight (1895). The Life and Growth
    of Language. New York: D. Appleton.

Yamakawa, Kikuo (1958), "On the Construction 'Have
    (or Get) + Object + Past Participle'," Anglica
    3: 164-196.

Yoshioka, Gen-Ichiro (1908). A Semantic Study of the
    Verbs of Doing and Making in the Indo-European
    Languages. Tokyo: Tokyo Tsukiji.

Zilling (1918). Das Hilfsverb Do im Mittel-
    Englischen. Halle Inaugural Dissertation.

Zipf, George (1949). Human Behavior and the Principle of Least Effort. Cambridge (Mass.): Addison-Wesley.

B.   PRIMARY TEXTS

Ælfric. Genesis. In The Old English Version of the Heptateuch, ed. W. Skeat. London: E.E.T.S. O.S., No. 160, 1922.

Ælfric. The Homilies of Ælfric. In Homilies of the Anglo-Saxon Church, ed. B. Thorpe. London: Ælfric Society, 1844-1846, 2 vols.

Chronicle. Two of the Saxon Chronicles Parallel, ed. C. Plummer and J. Earle. Oxford: Clarendon Press, 1892-1899, 2 vols.

La3amons Brut, ed. F. Madden. London: Society of Antiquaries, 1847, 4 vols.

Malory. Morte d'Arthur, ed. O. Sommer. London: D. Nutt, 1889.

Wulfstan. Sammlung der ihm zugeschriebenen Homilien, ed. A. Napier. Berlin: Weidmannsche, 1883.

Author Index

Subject Index